¡VIVA CALIFORNIA!

Seven Accounts of
Life in Early California

Edited by

Michael Burgess

and

Mary Wickizer Burgess

The Borgo Press
An Imprint of Wildside Press

MMVI

West Coast Studies
ISSN 0748-0784
Number One

Library of Congress Cataloging in Publication Data:

Viva California! : seven accounts of life in early California / edited by
Michael Burgess and Mary Wickizer Burgess.
    p. cm. — (West Coast studies, ISSN 0748-0784 ; no. 1)
    Includes bibliographical references and index.
    Contents: Introduction — Life of a ranchero / by José del Carmen
Lugo — My life in early California / by Benjamin Davis Wilson —
California's Gold Rush days / by Alexandre Holinski — The
autobiography of Mark Lafayette Landrum / by Mark L. Landrum —
The statement of Alexander H. Todd — The adventures of William T.
Ballou — The letter of Amos Carpenter Rogers.
    ISBN 0-8095-2800-2. — ISBN 0-8095-3800-8 (pbk.)
    1. Frontier and pioneer life—California. 2. California—History—
To 1846—Biography. 3. California—History—1846-1850—Biography.
I. Burgess, Michael, 1948- . II. Burgess, Mary Wickizer, 1938- . III.
Series.
F864.V77 2006   96-44354
979.4/0099 [B]—DC21   CIP

FIRST EDITION

CONTENTS

DEDICATION

For Our Dear Sister,
BETTY WICKIZER CARLSON

And to the Memory of
JOSEPH WARD CARLSON
JOSÉ DEL CARMEN LUGO
BENJAMIN DAVIS WILSON
ALEXANDRE J. J. HOLINSKI
MARK LAFAYETTE LANDRUM
ALEXANDER H. TODD
WILLIAM T. BALLOU
AMOS CARPENTER ROGERS

¡Viva California!

INTRODUCTION

Compiling these diaries and journals has been a joy. When we first discovered the materials reproduced here we anticipated publishing them as separate pieces. Upon reflection, we became convinced that these fascinating recollections of some of California's earliest residents took on new meaning when studied and compared with like documents.

B. D. Wilson's account of the various skirmishes which took place during the struggle between native-born Californians and colonists from the United States is interesting in itself. When read in conjunction with José Lugo's remembrances of the same events, however, Wilson's account of a territory at war with itself becomes compelling. Lugo and Wilson were neighbors and had always had a friendly relationship until forced into conflict with each other.

Lugo tells us even more poignantly of a standoff with his dead sister's husband, Julián Williams, where he is forced to burn the family out of their home. He makes every effort to save the lives of his young nephew and nieces, and to protect their property as best he can, but they turn their backs on him, and he seems bitter at the memory. Both of these gentlemen were peace-loving farmers and family men who were drawn into conflict during the former Mexican territory's painful rebirth as one of the United States.

European Alexandre Holinski's essay touting the virtues of frontier California as an experimental proving ground for a new classless society contrasts vividly with Mark Landrum's more mundane perspective as a native-born Georgian. After great difficulties, Landrum came with his family to the new state just prior to America's Civil War. A self-educated man, he settled in the small community of Peach Tree, in Monterey County, where he became a respected member of the community, serving on the school board, and as postmaster and justice of the peace. Eventually, his interest in things political would see him nominated as a People's Party candidate from the Sixth District. His essays range from the most personal home and family details, to his considered opinions on local, state and national politics, and government in general.

Special thanks are due to Erin B. Rogers, who did the rough keyboarding on several of the pieces included herein while working as an intern for the old Borgo Press lo these many years ago; and also to our dear friend and fellow bookman, Allan Adrian, who supplied copies of the originals of many of these documents. Dr. William Aguilar was kind enough to review a few of the more obscure passages in the first two essays at the very last moment. However, it should be noted that we have reproduced the Spanish-language phrases and songs exactly as given in the original manuscripts, except where an obvious typographical error has occurred, even when it is clear that some word or words are missing or misconstrued.

These pieces are published in the hope that they may stand as a lasting tribute to the memory of the early pioneers and patriots who toiled so diligently in California's fertile soil.

—Mary Wickizer Burgess
Prof. Michael Burgess
San Bernardino, California
21 August 2004

I.

LIFE OF A RANCHERO

BY DON JOSÉ DEL CARMEN LUGO

ACKNOWLEDGMENTS

Dictada por **DON JOSÉ DEL CARMEN LUGO**, natural de la Alta California, donde nació el año de 1813 en al pueblo de Los Ángeles. Se incluye una narración de la Batalla llamada del "Rancho del Chino," acción de guerra en que tuvo parte el autor. Escrito por D. Tomás Savage para la Bancroft Library, año de 1877.

NOTE

The following translation of José del Carmen Lugo's *Vida de un ranchero* has been made in the belief that the original narrative in the Bancroft Library in Berkeley in its one hundred and thirty foolscap pages of longhand, will be of greater use to students of early California history if rendered into English. For the sake of greater clarity, there has been a departure at times from a literal translation, but it is believed that the real meaning has never been sacrificed thereby.

—Helen Pruitt Beattie
East Highlands, California
January, 1950

INTRODUCTION

Don José del Carmen Lugo was a native and for many years past a resident of the City of Los Ángeles. I (the writer) was introduced to him by an uncle of Judge Ignacio Sepúlveda named Dolores Sepúlveda, who led me to believe that I should find in Señor Lugo a man who could furnish much valuable information on the past history of his country and on other matters—and to secure such material for Mr. H. H. Bancroft in consideration of Lugo's extreme poverty, I had to offer him a gratuity for his time. But I was quite disappointed—having soon discovered his ignorance on history and on most other things, the result of living nearly all of his best years on his ranch in San Bernardino, away from all associations that could keep him informed upon past and current events. Indeed, he assured me that from the time he went to work on his father's ranch at the age of about sixteen, he never read a book or wrote a line, until his election to the position of *Regidor* for 1839 brought those early acquisitions into some use for awhile.

Owing to that ignorance and to his feebleness both in body and mind, I had much difficulty in obtaining the annexed one hundred and thirty pages. However, the events therein related are important, and Lugo was the best source to get them from, as he was the chief actor in them.

Lugo bears the reputation of an honorable, truthful man, and is connected by blood with the oldest and most prominent families of California: Vallejo, Alvarado, Carrillo, de la Guerra, Cota, Sánchez, etc.

—Thos. Savage
Los Ángeles, California
October, 1877

LA NARRACIÓN

I, José del Carmen Lugo, was born March 19, 1813, in the Pueblo of Los Ángeles. My parents were Antonio María Lugo, the head, who was of the Compañía de Santa Bárbara, and María Dolores Ruiz—both born in California.

My paternal grandfather, Francisco Lugo, came from *la otra banda* (Sinaloa, México) with four children: Salvador, who was killed while a boy by a fall from a horse; José Antonio, a soldier at Santa Bárbara, who married and left two children; María Tomasa, who married Don Raymundo Carrillo and left a family; and Rosa, who married the *Alférez* Cota and also left a family. One daughter, María de los Ángeles Cota, married Don José Joaquín de la Torre and was the mother of many children, among whom the best known were Don Joaquín, Don Gabriel, Don Raymundo, and Don Estevan de la Torre.

After coming to California Francisco Lugo had three sons and two daughters: José Ignacio, Antonio María, Juan, María Antonia, and María Ignacia. The three men became soldiers, married, and left many descendants. María Antonia married Don Ignacio Vallejo and was the mother of Don Mariano Guadalupe Vallejo and all his brothers and sisters. María Ignacia married José Ruiz, and left a large family in Santa Bárbara. My paternal grandmother was named Juana Vianazul.

My aunt, María Antonia, and various other members of my family told me that when she was born Ignacio Vallejo happened to be in her parents' home when her father, my grandfather, was in the garrison at the mission of San Luis Obispo. Vallejo rocked the little girl in a hammock, and arranged that when she reached an age for marriage they should give her to him in matrimony, promising to wait for her. He was serious in this, and when she reached fourteen or fifteen years, Vallejo came and claimed his sweetheart and was married to her.

I passed the first years of my life in Los Ángeles with my parents, who then enjoyed considerable means.

I learned my first letters in a little school with Luciano Valdez as teacher. There were no books at that time other than the spelling book, the reading charts, and *Ripalda* Catechism.

During the time that I was in this school we had three different teachers: after Valdez came Francisco Morales, and after him José María Herrera.

Herrera was my last teacher. I left the school, because there was in Los Ángeles a gentleman named Don Tomás Yorba who gave me a little book entitled *Eucarístico*, charging me carefully to read it but not to loan it to anyone else. I began to follow the first lines of this work (it must have been but a few pages long). The teacher wished to take it from me to give it to another, as I had memorized the entire contents. The teacher wished it to pass from hand to hand so that all the pupils could learn it, since it was very interesting and treated of religion. Furthermore, the school had no other book [of this sort]. I protested and refused, remembering the instructions of Sr. Yorba. This happened in September, 1826. I took my hat and the book and went home. My mother reproved me, asking me why I had left the school so early. I told her what had occurred and afterward went in search of Don Antonio Carrillo (who was my first cousin), who was occupying himself in giving lessons to some children. I gave him to understand why I had left the school so early and begged him to instruct me, and we would return the favor suitably. He agreed and began to give me lessons. With him I learned in two years all that he could teach me, to write, to count, and some other trifles.

This Sr. Carrillo went to México in 1828 as a delegate to the Congress and wished to take me with him, but my parents would not permit it. This same year I began regular work on my father's Rancho San Antonio.

I remember that in the latter part of the year 1818, I being then about six years old, word came that two insurgent frigates had invaded Monterey, and that the men on them

10

disembarked and sacked and burned the *presidio*. From there they went to the Ortegas Rancho at Refugio, sacking it also, setting fire to the buildings and doing as much damage as they could. After that they proceeded to Santa Bárbara. At this, the citizens of Los Ángeles capable of bearing arms left for Santa Bárbara to lend their aid. The same day that these citizens set out, the rest of us, including women and children, started in *carretas* for Misión San Fernando, fearing that the enemy would attack Los Ángeles. But it did not disembark at Santa Bárbara, going instead to San Juan Capistrano; there it committed many like depredations, sacking and burning. The citizenry of Los Ángeles who had gone to aid Santa Bárbara followed the insurgents, some by sea and some by land, but all in vain. When they reached San Juan the enemy had left, although a few remained in hiding and afterwards offered battle to our people.

The insurgent vessels did not show themselves again on our coasts, and we never knew where they went.

At this time aid was requested from the viceroy and other authorities in México, and a year later there arrived a squadron of dragoons calling themselves the squadron of active militia from Mazatlán. Their captain was Don Pablo de la Portilla. After I reached manhood I knew all the individuals of this squadron who were living in California.

I do not remember having witnessed the ceremonies accompanying the change of flag when it passed from under the Empire of México. It is probable that I was then on my father's ranch.

In the year 1824, there was an uprising of Indians at the Misiones of La Purísima, Santa Inez, and Santa Bárbara. At the first one some men from Los Ángeles who were returning from a trip to Monterey were killed. The mutinous Indians killed them. I remember the names of only three of them—Dolores Sepúlveda, Don [Ramón] Sotelo, and Simón Sánchez.

As soon as the Indians learned that troops were coming from San Diego, Los Ángeles, and Monterey to aid those at Santa Bárbara, they retired to the *tulares* to join forces with the pagan Indians who were numerous in that region.

11

The troops and the citizens from Los Ángeles followed them until they located them in the *tulares*. Sergeant Don Carlos Antonio Carrillo was commanding a detachment of soldiers and citizens.

A Los Ángeles citizen, or rather a soldier from San Diego named Guillermo Zúñiga, composed a song. It began thus:

> *El Sargento Carlos*
> *Por la Trinidad*
> *Se vistio de guerra*
> *Con mucho crueldad*
> *En fin, como padre de Compañía*
> *Rompimos el fuego al venir el dia*
>   *etc. etc. etc.*

He continued from that point naming each of the chiefs and soldiers.

There was an active attack upon the Indians, killing some of them, but they fled to hiding places in the *tulares* where they could not be dislodged.

Some time later peace was established thanks to the influence of the Father Prefect, Fr. Narciso Durán (Sarria), and they (the Misión Indians) returned to their missions.

I remember that the citizens from Los Ángeles and the detachment from Santa Bárbara came through the Cajón de las Uvas, in which a citizen and a soldier, brothers, were wounded. The citizen was named Demesio Domínguez, and the soldier Francisco Domínguez.

In this fight with the Indians, in the region near Castaic, the Indians went up into the hills and the troops and the citizens followed them as far as possible. It was here that the two brothers were wounded. Francisco died of his injuries. From there the troops returned to Santa Bárbara via Camulos, and the citizens returned to Los Ángeles.

Into the hands of this detachment of our troops fell some leaders of the rebelling Indians who had so treacherously slain the travelers from Monterey as already described. A council was held, and these leaders were shot.

12

In April or May, 1825, I then being twelve years old, there was a general flood of all the rivers in California. I saw that of the Los Ángeles River. At twelve o'clock in night, my father heard a great noise. He was sleeping at the time in a house here in the *Pueblo*. He spoke to me—I was sleeping outside—and asked what that dreadful noise was. I responded that I did not know. He then said we should investigate.

The river ran about one hundred yards from our house. I went to the bank, and discovered that it was a sea of water which was overflowing vegetable gardens, fences, trees, and whatever was before it. The water was running with great violence, making enormous waves. I warned my father immediately of the terrible danger in which we were. He remained there watching and sent me without a moment's delay to inform the Commissioner of the *Pueblo*, Sergeant Don Anastacio Carrillo, who was my first cousin. This gentleman was asleep when I reached his home, as was the entire *Pueblo*.

Don Anastacio directed me to waken the *Alcalde* Anastacio Ávila and all the people along the road. My brothers and some of my father's servants were already running through the town warning the people. There was a moon almost as bright as the light of day. The sky was perfectly clear.

Orders were given speedily for all the inhabitants of the town to move to a place of safety on the high land to the east. They did so, everyone loading family and belongings into *carretas* drawn by oxen which all had in the corrals near their homes along with their cows and other animals.

At daybreak I saw that the water in the old channel of the river was subsiding, and was running toward the other side of the narrow valley—which is where that river has its bed today. The channel changed.

Before, the river ran through the underbrush bordering the fields of home gardens and corn cultivated by the citizens until it reached the hill of Iajonte [*sic*], where it spread out into flats, marshes, and hilly country. It turned back to the Domínguez *rancho* at the point known as Suanga

13

[*sic*]. Here it formed a large lake—the overflow stretching onward. Finally, the river emptied into the sea at San Pedro.

To prove this change of direction of the river in 1825, it went through the middle of my father's *rancho* San Antonio, destroyed a vineyard, the corral and the cornfields, a house, and quarters occupied by servants. The fields destroyed were excellent in every way. The vines remained buried in the mud, and I had to dig them out later, with great difficulty.

Two days before the flood it had rained with force, but on that morning the rain ceased. By afternoon the river began carrying a large amount of waters but it caused no alarm, everyone believing that it was merely the runoff from the hills. It was after this that the mustard was noted for the first time. Before, mustard was unknown in the San Gabriel Valley and in the *ranchos* about Los Ángeles. After this, the entire country was covered with mustard and also with mallows. The stems of all the plants were very coarse.

Immense numbers of cattle and horses perished in this flood.

In this same year of 1825, there came to California with the title of *Jefe Político y Comandante General* the Lieutenant Colonel of Engineers, Don José María de Echeandía, with some officials, among whom were the Lieutenant Agustín V. Zamorano and the *Alférez* Romualdo Pacheco, both engineers also; the *Alférez* José María Ramírez of cavalry; and a graduate *Alférez* of artillery named [Juan José] Rocha.

I do not recall any event worthy of mention in the years 1826, 1827, and 1828. I do know of a military mutiny in Monterey because the troops had not been given necessary supplies; but I believe that they returned to service without the shedding of blood.

In the year 1829 the soldiers of the cavalry and artillery at Monterey rebelled, and later those from San Francisco joined them. United they came almost to Santa Bárbara, to the Arroyo del Burro, under the command of Joaquín Solís—but they soon disbanded. Solís and some followers returned to Monterey. Before arriving there they learned that the garrison they had left in Monterey had gone over to the existing government (that of Echeandía). Solís betook himself to his ranch, and the others scattered. In time they (the government) took Solís and the other ringleaders in the revolt, and sent them to México. Among these ringleaders was my second cousin, Raymond de Torre. Years afterward three of these prisoners returned to California: Raymundo de Torre, Pablo Véjar, and Victorino Altamirano.

In 1831, at the end of November or the beginning of December, there was an uprising in San Diego against the *Jefe Político and Comandante General*, Don Manuel Victoria, who had been in power since the first of the year. They accused Señor Victoria of being an absolute despot who was not willing to recognize any authority in the committee. It was alleged that he had not been appointed by the legitimate government of México, and was therefore a usurper who had inaugurated a régime of absolute power and cruel executions; and even if these executions had been of criminals, they were not justified by the crimes committed against the victims of his wrath. These and many other things which I do not remember were said of Victoria.

Since I was on the ranch, I could not secure accurate news of these affairs. But I do know that a group of the disaffected in San Diego came to Los Ángeles, where various persons united with them. On the hill where today are the properties of Mons. Beaudry, on the road to Santa Bárbara, this group met the forces of Señor Victoria. Each side fired a volley at the other, but no injuries resulted. Later there was a clash, which I shall call personal, between the Commander General and the insurgents.

Captain Romualdo Pacheco was killed by a pistol shot fired by José María Ávila, and he in turn died at the hand of Señor Victoria, after he had been wounded by a Victoria follower. The latter was badly wounded by a lance Ávila had hurled at him after his pistol failed to discharge.

The forces disbanded, Captain de la Portilla, who commanded the *insurrectos*, leaving the field to his opponents; and these retired to San Gabriel where Victoria surrendered. His followers embarked for San Diego, *en route* for México.

I do not know enough about the events of this period to give an accurate account of them. In the first place, I had no part in any of the revolutionary movements, since my father did not permit his sons to do so. The only one who had any part was my brother Felipe, who was married, and consequently lived in his own home and managed his own affairs.

In the year 1836, a revolution broke out in the North with the object of disowning the authority of the *Jefe Político y Comandante General*, Don Nicolás Gutiérrez. After the insurgents took possession of the *plaza* of Monterey, they put Gutiérrez and other officials on shipboard. The *Diputación* (Provincial Legislature) or a part of it reformed, naming Juan Bautista Alvarado as Governor, and declaring California a free and sovereign state, while the federal government was being restored in México. The measures taken by the people in Monterey were not adopted either in Los Ángeles or San Diego.

Alvarado and José Castro came South with a considerable force expecting to bring pressure to bear on the people of the South. In time an arrangement was reached, and the force from Monterey retired to Santa Bárbara, while those of the South, who had been concentrated at San Fernando, came back to Los Ángeles. These arrangements did not satisfy the people in the North, but the people in Los Ángeles demanded that they be carried out.

Things continued in this unsatisfactory state; and from time to time reports were heard that the Government in México was proposing to send troops in numbers sufficient to subdue the rebel Californians. Then Don Carlos Antonio Carrillo received his appointment as temporary Governor of California, an appointment which was obtained for him by his brother, Don José Antonio Carrillo, who had just become deputy to the National Congress representing California.

Don Juan Bautista Alvarado and his partisans of Monterey and other parts of the North refused to recognize Carrillo as governor, and took a considerable force with them to force people in the South (who had already accepted Carrillo) to disavow this act and adhere to the arrangement reached in the revolution.

Don Mariano Guadalupe Vallejo had been elevated by the people of the North to the rank of General Commander, but those in Los Ángeles and San Diego had not accepted him as such.

In the year 1838, when Don Carlos Antonio Carrillo was in Los Ángeles, learning that a force from the North was coming down with hostile intentions, he organized a force to go to meet the northerners and fight them. Captain Don Juan Castañeda went as commander of the expedition. In his company was one of the justices of peace in Los Ángeles, Don Luis Arenas.

The force from the South encamped first at San Buenaventura, and from there proceeded to the salt flats near Santa Bárbara, in the place called "the lone hill." Representatives came from Santa Bárbara to persuade the force from the South not to enter that town, promising that whatever those from the North should propose, they (in Santa Bárbara) would make the greatest possible efforts to arrive at a friendly settlement of all the differences. They asked Castañeda to return to San Buenaventura with his force, where they would forward the terms which they could arrange with the opposing leader, Señor Castro.

The Southerners came to San Buenaventura, and in good faith left their horses and proceeded to rest without taking the precaution to establish outposts or to take other measures customary in such cases. When they least expected it, Castro descended upon them, delivering a lively fire which obliged them to seek cover in the Misión church.

Exchanges of shots between the opposing forces followed, lasting through the entire night. It continued the next morning, and lasted through the day. In this exchange an artilleryman named Juan Cordero was killed. He was my first cousin, and was serving in the Castro forces. We did not know of any casualty among those from the South.

When night came, Castro's men laid siege to the Misión, and promptly at daybreak its inmates let Castro in, leaving an opening through which those who had been interned could escape. Castañeda's force left, although a few remained in the Misión and were made prisoners. The same fortune befell those who had left, for as soon as it was light

Castro's forces went in pursuit; and in about two or three leagues captured those who were not fortunate enough to hide themselves. The number reaching Los Ángeles was small.

I figured that the number of prisoners taken by Castro and Alvarado amounted to some ninety or more men. Among these were people from Los Ángeles, San Diego, Lower California, and even New Mexico. The most important prisoners, Captain Castañeda, Luis Arenas, Ignacio Palomares, Teodosio Yorba, and some others, were taken to Santa Bárbara, the others being set at liberty after giving their word of honor not to bear arms against the powers in the North.

Don Carlos Antonio Carrillo reunited the people from San Diego and Lower California, and retired with them to San Diego to make himself strong there.

I believe that he expected some aid from Sonora or from México, but from Sonora came merely the Mexican army captain, Juan José Tovar, with two or three Sonorans.

This force went to meet the Castro forces and encamped at Las Flores. Castro came with his troops and besieged them. Some shots were exchanged, but no one on either side was killed or even wounded. Finally they went into conference. To tell the truth, the firing Castro had done was to frighten the enemy. Many of the shots were fired into the air.

The result of the conference was that Tovar left— some said secretly, but others declared that he was allowed to go. Those made prisoners were Don Gabriel (?) Carrillo, his brother José Antonio [Carrillo], Don Ignacio Palomares, Gil Ibarra, Narciso Botello, and Don Andrés Pico. Later, Castro seized Pío Pico in San Diego.

Governor Alvarado decided to send these prisoners to Sonoma to be in charge of the Commander General. In fact, all were sent there, by way of Misión San José, where Administrator and Military Commander Don José de Jesús Vallejo then was. The two not sent were Don Carlos Antonio Carrillo and Don Pío Pico. The first, Alvarado permitted to return to his home under a promise to commit no further foolish acts; the second, was permitted to return home also, since he was ill, and the Indians had looted his ranch, leaving him without movables or anything else of value.

In this same year of 1838, in June, I went to Monterey to ask about the prisoners, and was told that they were in Sonoma, some ill with smallpox. I believe that the prisoners were detained on the Northern frontier something like a year. They told me on returning that in Sonoma the Commander General treated them very well, but that at the Misión San José, the treatment that Don José de Jesús Vallejo had given them was very bad.

Finally, there came an order from the Supreme Government to Don Carlos Antonio Carrillo removing him from office and recognizing Juan Bautista Alvarado as temporary Governor, Mariano Guadalupe Vallejo as Commander General, and José Castro as military commander of Monterey and Captain of the presidial company there.

This provisional appointment of Alvarado as Governor came accompanied by an order of the Government that the Departmental Assembly would be sent a report of what had to do with the appointment of the provisional Governor. The report came, with the name of Alvarado in the lead, and to him came the appointment in full.

Each time that Sr. Castro made one of his incursions into the South, he located his officers on the different *ranchos*; and they carried away such gentle animals as they found, in some cases without leaving the owners even a horse for their own use.

These horses were invariably taken North, and there was never a time when the animals were returned to their owners. In my case, they robbed me in this way of two mares and seventy horses on one of their visits, and I never saw the animals again. When the horsemen reached the North and needed more animals, they searched for some excuse for visiting us and carrying off our animals and whatever more they could secure.

When Sr. Alvarado obtained the full governorship, he dedicated himself to organizing the region, and divided the territory into three prefectures. The first was that of the North, with its capital in Monterey; the second was that of the South, with its headquarters in Los Ángeles; the third was that of the frontier areas. He named Don Tiburcio Castro as Prefect of the first district, and on Castro's death named his son, Captain José Castro. At the head of the prefecture of the second district he placed the *licenciado*, Cosme Peña. He named no prefect for the third district.

I was *Regidor* in 1839, when Señor Peña came to govern us as Prefect, and he found me in San Bernardino on leave. This same Peña gave me a provisional authorization from Governor Alvarado to work on this certain *rancho*, which until then had belonged to Misión San Gabriel.

For this reason I had moved there and had begun work, waiting for the Assembly to reconvene, and make me a formal grant of the ranch.

Senor Peña performed the duties of the prefecture a very short time, on account of the disapproval by the Superior Government of the appointment given him by Governor Alvarado. As a result, he delivered the *prefectura* over to the first *Alcalde*, Don Tiburcio Tapia.

In November, 1839, I returned from the *rancho* to Los Ángeles, and found myself with the...[text missing] of a dissolved *Ayuntamiento*, awaiting certain authorizations of the temporary Prefect Tapia and the second *Alcalde* Manuel Domínguez. I was told that I was free to go back to the duties of the *rancho*, because the *Ayuntamiento* was closed. I was so happy to be at liberty to return to my labors on the ranch, that I did not even ask how or why the corporation had been dissolved.

If I remember rightly, there was no *Ayuntamiento* in Los Ángeles until 1844 to 1845. The *Jefe Superior*, General Micheltorena, being here, I lived entirely at the ranch, and never, except casually, returned to Los Ángeles, and when I did go, I left...[text missing] without delaying longer than to obtain that which I was seeking.

Oftentimes I left my ranch at San Bernardino (the grant to which I had had since 1842) at one o'clock in the afternoon, reaching Los Ángeles at seven in the morning; and at nine I was on the road back to reach home at daybreak to begin work, since I never had a *mayordomo*.

During the entire time Micheltorena was in control, I remained at the ranch without engaging in political affairs.

20

For this reason I know nothing except hearsay regarding things that happened at this time. I know that the people at Monterey rebelled against Micheltorena, that the insurgent forces put themselves under the command of Don José Castro, and that he counted upon the support of Don Juan Bautista Alvarado, Don Manuel Castro, Don Francisco Rico, and my relatives Joaquín and Gabriel de la Torre, José de Jesús Pico, José María Villavicencio, los Soberanes, etc.

Micheltorena organized a considerable force, with which he set out in pursuit of Castro and his forces, then in San José. On the way a company of foreign riflemen and another of trained Indians under the command of Captain Sutter joined him. Castro, being unable to stand against him, left for the South, and Micheltorena followed him.

The Assembly had reconvened at the call of its first head, Don Pío Pico; and being aware of the determination of Micheltorena to punish those who had risen against him because of the evil behavior of his officials and the force he brought from México in 1842, resolved to consider him a person prejudicial to the country, ignoring his authority, and authorizing the older head, Pico, to take the reins of government into his hands.

In Los Ángeles forces were organized to unite with the few men José Castro led from the North. These with their chief, the said Castro, recognized as Commander General, posted themselves at San Buenaventura. He did not wait long before Micheltorena came to attack him. Castro, with a force so inferior, not exceeding one hundred fifty men, could not make a determined stand, and retired south to the rancho of Cahuenga, which belonged to Misión San Fernando. The temporary Governor, Pico, had by this time collected three hundred or more men, including some foreigners under leadership of Sr. Workman, and had hastily secured two pieces of artillery.

In a few days the enemy force appeared, commanded by General Micheltorena in person. The Californians chose their site for battle, and at nine o'clock the following day began hostilities with a lively artillery fire, but without harm to either side, owing to the great distance between them. The only casualty was a horse.

After a heavy discharge of musketry, Micheltorena, who had made several offers to suspend fire in order to parley, without being heeded, made a move as if to retire, but really with the idea of returning and attempting to gain possession of the road leading to Los Ángeles. Unable to do this, he tried to take the other road for Cahuenga. The Californians managed to reach the ranch house there much sooner than Micheltorena. He camped about two miles away, it having become dark. During the night Castro besieged him.

The following day saw a conference between the two leaders, and Micheltorena was obliged to surrender the artillery and arms of the Department, and leave the country with his officers and the regular California battalion. All this occurred in the first part of 1845, and Don Pío was the recognized Temporary Governor of the Department, with Don José Castro as Commander General.

In 1846, on receiving notice that Don José Castro was coming with a force to remove him from his position as Governor, Pico left for the North with a hundred or more men, to halt him. At a small ranch known as Santa Margarita, above San Luis Obispo, they had an interview and there was a reconciliation. Then Don Pío Pico was led to comprehend the situation in which the country was—Sonoma in the power of the Bear party, and Monterey taken by the Americans.

From there the Governor returned with his people to Los Ángeles, and Castro remained with his people at Santa Margarita with the idea of coming later. The result was as expected—the two leaders found themselves in Los Ángeles with their forces, each prepared for an attack; but neither saw nor heard of them.

I was not living in Los Ángeles, but was dedicating myself wholly to the labors of my ranch at San Bernardino—but I knew that Don José Castro had decided to leave the country since he had not the power to combat an enemy of such strength. He dissolved his force, reserving merely a small escort. He buried the few cannons he had, and some time later a Californian revealed their whereabouts to the military authority of the United States.

Castro set out for Sonora, with the intention, as was said, of begging aid from the Mexican government to enable him to return and rescue his country from the hands of the attackers. Don Pío Pico found himself under the necessity of doing the same as Castro, and retired to his _rancho_ Santa Margarita, from which he set out for the frontier of Lower California.

* * * * *

I believe that it was in September that the United States force came to this city, and remained as a garrison under command of Captain Gillespie. I knew this officer very well, as he was a good friend of my father.

A few days later the Americans began making prisoners of certain Californians and others who had given information that tended to be unfavorable to the United States. I remember that about twenty were arrested at this time, among whom were Juan Bautista Moreno, Hilario Varelas, and Pedro Romero.

As a result of this some young men of Los Ángeles and vicinity rose in revolt, with Sérvulo Varelas as leader. They made an attack upon the _cuartel_ but were unable to take it. In truth, there were only a few youths, practically unarmed, and as soon as the force in the _cuartel_ returned their fire they retired precipitately.

The following day, the American commanding the _plaza_ forbade travel by horse through the streets, and adopted other means for assuring peace.

The Californians had encamped on a little hill near the city, and were joined by a number of other men. In view of this, Gillespie and his men constructed a breastwork on the highest part of the hill facing Pico House, very near the _cuartel_ to which they returned now and then.

A few days later it was announced at San Bernardino by some youths who came from Los Ángeles that preparations were being made for an uprising of the youths of the country against the Americans. At this time Don Benito Wilson, with a small detachment of foreigners and some from this country, was occupying himself in the mountains.

23

It was said that word came from Los Ángeles summoning him to that point at the earliest possible moment.

Wilson reached his ranch, situated between Jurupa and Guapa—a tract of land belonging to the Guapa Rancho which Don Juan Bandini had sold him. Immediately upon arriving home he sent a New Mexican named Rafael Blea to advise me to enlist what force I could, because he was coming to my home to take me prisoner. Midway between his ranch and mine lived my older brother, José María Lugo, to whom Blea repeated the message he was carrying to me. Together the two proceeded to my home.

Before Blea gave me the message, my brother spoke to me in alarm, saying that he was uneasy over the threat Señor Wilson had made toward me. He asked what I had done to arouse the enmity of Wilson. I replied that I had done absolutely nothing—that I had done no harm to anyone, directly or indirectly. Blea then delivered the message he had shown my brother earlier, who could say that he was there representing our father.

I told Blea to tell Don Benito Wilson that he could come when he wished, but that it would be best for him to come alone to take me and not compromise others. I promised to meet him without calling anyone to my assistance.

I should explain here that no ill will had ever existed between us before this day.

Late in the afternoon of this day Blea returned with the same message, and said that Wilson and his men were ready to start for my house when he (Blea) left. My brother returned with Blea, and he advised me not to remain on the ranch, but to hide myself somewhere in the hills. I refused to do this, because it did not seem fitting to hide myself without cause.

I saddled my horse and went with them along the highway toward my brother's house. There I said "You take care of your affairs, and I will do the same with mine...." I told Blea to notify Don Benito that he could come with all confidence.

I returned home and prepared myself with men and arms to go to meet Wilson. The night was pretty well advanced when I left for Jurupa, a village inhabited by people from New Mexico. The rest of the night was spent in enlisting what Mexicans I could. With this force that I had collected, numbering about twenty-one men, I proceeded to the home of Wilson. I found no one there except his family and one or two men of the country. I took one of them and proceeded to question him as to the place toward or the direction in which Wilson had gone. I learned that he had left for the Rancho Chino, and I accordingly started for that point also. About three leagues before reaching Chino I met a small party of wild Indians who were going to their homes. Some of them were carrying arrows, and I took them for use of the men I had with me.

The Indians told me that Wilson was at Chino. In the meantime a scouting party of five of my men went forward, and in a short time encountered an American and two Californians. The first was acting very courageous, carrying a rifle of eighteen shots and threatening my five men. As soon as he aimed it the men were upon him, and then without firing a single shot he took to flight. My people managed to overtake him, and the head of the party struck him a blow because on attempting to discharge his pistol it failed to go off. He then struck the man on the head, and knocked him from his horse. The head of the party was Diego Sepúlveda, and the foreigner was named Callaghan.

When the man fell he was still aiming menacingly with his rifle. He got up, and ran a short distance to an enclosed cornfield, stretching almost to the Chino ranch house. He managed to climb into the field, protecting himself with his gun from being taken. In this way Callaghan managed to escape.

My scouts came back to join me, bringing the two Californians they met with Callaghan. One of them was named José María Bermúdez, and the other Morales, a son of Lower California. I made them prisoners, but they offered to serve in my force, and I accepted their services.

In this locality there was a willow thicket, and here I encamped, very near the Chino house. An officer came to me, ordering me to the Commanding General, Don José María Flores, in Los Ángeles to join him with the force I had.

Until this moment all that I had done had been the result of threats made by Señor Wilson. But now, I was taking orders from a recognized military authority.

Within an hour I sent a request to Los Ángeles for aid, since Wilson was in the Chino home strengthened by about fifty men. Evening came on and I started for Chino. (This was at the end of September or the beginning of October in 1846). A message came to me from my brother-in-law, Julián (Isaac) Williams (an American who had married my sister, María de Jesús, now dead), saying that he wished to speak to me, at a point a hundred yards in front of his house.

I sent word that I had no business to transact with him, but that if he wished to meet me he should come where I was. He was the master at Chino, which my father had given to his daughter with four thousand head of stock. He did not come to the place he had suggested, nor did he come to where he would meet me.

At about this time there arose a violent north wind, just as I was moving around the Williams house at a distance of three hundred yards or more. The wind blew the hat from one of my boys, who had become soldiers just as I had become a captain. The hat went flying toward the Chino house. The boy ran after it, and from the house there came a shot. My people responded with three or four shots—but I ordered them not to waste the little ammunition we had.

We were beside the road to Los Ángeles all afternoon, watching to see if those inside the house would come out to fight us. If this had been done, they would have finished us, since we had no more than four or five guns and a few pistols—plus one or two lances and a few Indian arrows.

All afternoon we were under fire from the house. We walked about separately, and only now and then responded with a shot. It grew dark, and I put my men on horseback about the house; that is, at places where it was possible. We remained mounted and alert during the night. Next morning the aid I had asked from Flores came. It consisted of some thirty men commanded by Sérvulo Varela[s] and Ramón Carrillo, the first being the head.

I concealed them, so that the foreigners would not suspect that this reinforcement had arrived. I united all my men. While we were debating whether it would be better to wait till they came out to attack us or whether we should move against the house, a boy sallied from the house on horseback, heading down or toward the South. Those of us in the conference numbered eight or ten. We saw the boy leave, and I directed two of my associates, Vicente Lugo and Ricardo Véjar, to go catch him. They started to ride after him. When the men who were hidden heard the shouted order to catch the boy, they were alarmed and sallied from their hiding place to come to me. I made signs to stop, but they did not understand the signals and came with even greater haste.

Seeing that I could not halt them, we approached the house and surroundings, firing shots at the four sides of the building. Before reaching the house there was a ring of palings, against which those of us who were nearest made a rush. In this rush two horses leaped over the circle. Nearer the house was another circle of palings, and within it an open moat. We knocked down the circle by driving our horses against it, Carlos Ballesteros and I leading. On jumping our horses over the moat, Ballesteros's horse did not make it, and fell, throwing the rider. On recovering his mount, Ballesteros was struck in the right temple by a bullet and fell dead.

Ten boys who were behind us reached the house, because, fearing the moat, they had left their horses before reaching it. I was beside the house, on horseback, when they arrived. Some of the ones who were unarmed, at my orders set themselves to gathering grass, and those who had arms pointed them at the doors and windows of the house. I ordered the grass thrown on the roof of the house and set on fire. They answered that they had nothing with which to start the fire. There was an Indian village near at hand, and they had a fire outside it. I went at full speed amid the bullets that were coming from all directions. I rode hugging the sides of the horse and crouching low to keep a bullet from hitting me. During this onrush of the horse, stretched alongside as I was, I reached down and seized a blazing stick, with which I returned at full speed to the house. I set fire to a corner of it, and ordered that the same be done to the others.

I then went at full gallop to make the circuit of the house and enter it by the main door. I reached it stretched along my horse, knocked at the door, and no one cared to open it.

I should say that before reaching this main entrance I had heard the cries of my brother-in-law's children, who were calling for me. I saw the children, a boy and two girls, on the wall above the place behind the corral. I called them and one of my soldiers lifted them down, telling them that I was waiting for them. I put the three children and two Indian women who were servants in the house in charge of José María Ávila and Ramón Carrillo until I could return.

While I was at the entrance of the house, the great door was opened by Don Diego Sepúlveda who had entered by the other door. At this entrance all the foreigners were gathered. They surrendered their arms and were made prisoners. I made them come out, and named a guard to look after them while I occupied myself with my men in putting out the fire and removing furniture and other effects from the house. I set a guard to watch these things, and then proceeded to inspect the house, which had escaped the fire almost entirely. I searched the hidden places, and found some individuals who had hidden themselves, and these I summoned forth.

I now called the children, my nieces and my nephew, and delivered them over to their father (my sister had died in 1842). I told him that he should thank me for saving his children, but neither he nor they gave me any sign of thanks afterward. The little boy, who then was eight years old, died soon after. The girls are still living, and care nothing about their uncle.

An hour after finishing the arrest of the prisoners, the house was left to cool, the furniture to be returned, etc. We left for Los Ángeles with our prisoners, arms, ammunitions, fighting equipment, saddle horses, and so on. We reached Don Julián Workman's Rancho de la Puente, where we all rested, although the main object was to give this benefit to the prisoners.

I changed my horse here for one loaned me by Señor Workman. He told me that Ramón Carrillo and Sérvulo Varela[s] were not willing that John Rowland should be permitted to talk there with his wife. Don Julián and I betook ourselves to where the prisoners were, and called Mr. Rowland out so that he could talk with his wife. He conversed as long as he wished, and we then continued the journey to Los Ángeles. On reaching the *Paredón Blanco* (the camp of the Californians), the Commander, General Flores came, and I said, "*Señor está ud. servido. Aquí tiene esa presa.*" In the affray they had killed one man for me (Ballesteros) and had wounded two or three men—they were people from Sonora or New Mexico, whose names I do not recall. They were not men I had known before.

It was already dark, and I informed Sr. Flores that I wished to betake myself to a small ranch near by that belonged to my brother, Felipe Lugo, since I was very tired, hungry, and sleepy. He gave me permission to go and I went.

In the affair at Chino we took forty or fifty prisoners, and a great many firearms with ammunition. One of the prisoners, who seemed to be a French-Indian *mestizo* from Canada, and who assured me almost crying that they had put him in the house by force, (this man) I set free at Chino, near where he lived. He was known by the name of Flores.

I remained for several days in the Californian camp, but without lending any aid in the taking of the *plaza*. They made their arrangements with [Archibald H.] Gillespie, and he retired with his men to San Pedro to embark. After this I returned to my ranch with eight men. I left all my arms behind for use by my compatriots.

In a few days I received a message from Commander General Flores to the effect that I should repair immediately to San Pedro, on the Rancho Domínguez. I left shortly, and men from all the ranchos and villages joined me, so that I arrived at San Pedro at daybreak with twenty-two men. This was in October, 1846. I presented myself to the Major General, Don José Antonio Carrillo, and requested permission to proceed with armed men to his encampment. This he granted. When I arrived Carrillo told me that I was to leave for Los Ángeles with prisoners and with a sufficient escort. With five men as guards, and a message for Flores, I left with three prisoners, men from his own forces. One of them was Simplicio Valdez, a Californian. I was ordered that if one of the prisoners should attempt to escape, he should be shot, in the act.

Arrived at Los Ángeles I delivered the message to Flores, and he ordered me to take the prisoners to Don Ignacio Palomares, who was in charge of the foreign prisoners. Palomares refused to receive them unless I delivered them in irons. In the guardhouse there was a forge and there was iron there. I put irons on the three prisoners, and delivered them after which I gave my account to General Flores. The General gave me leave for two days, at the end of which I presented myself again for orders. I was there a few days, and from there we went to the *rancho* of Don Antonio María Lugo, where we remained some days longer. I then set out for my own ranch, and on the way met Don Sepúlveda, who informed me that it was well known that an official named [José María] Segura had left for Sonora with a great amount of money and horses, all belonging to others. The money consisted of loans which merchants in Los Ángeles had made to Commander General Flores. Sepúlveda said that it seemed most unfair to him for Segura to take these funds out of California, since the loans had been made for the defense of the country. The belief was that Segura had fled with the money by arrangement with Flores, who was planning to overtake him on the road.

Sepúlveda asked if I was disposed to collect some men and go in pursuit of Flores. I was willing. We collected five or six men and set out in search of Segura. (This Segura, like Flores, had come to California with General Micheltorena.)

We delayed only long enough to secure food for the journey. We reached the *rancho* Temécula belonging to Misión San Luis Rey, which is on the road to Sonora. Here we learned from the Indians that the natives in San Bernardino had risen and were coming to commit outrages on the *ranchos*.

Sepúlveda urged that I go to placate the rebellious Indians while he continued the pursuit, and afterward overtake him. I did this. I reached San Bernardino that same day, did all I could to calm the Indians, and succeeded. Everything being calm, the following morning very early I collected six men who had fled Los Ángeles, and two or three more who were on leave, and retook the road to Temécula. At San Jacinto I enlisted four Indian cowboys with lances and arrows, along with the *mayordomo* of the rancho, and together we traveled to Sepúlveda. We slept in Temécula. The following day we proceeded to San José Valley in the Warm Springs region and passed the night in the valley opening. The next day we took the road to Buena Vista de San José.

There we learned that Sepúlveda had turned back, one of his men having been killed. I learned also that Segura had passed that point eight days before. There was nothing for me to do but turn back also, and I did so. When I reached the opening of San José Valley, known as Santa Isabel, I saw a number of horses and some men guarding them. I hastened toward them, and found the men to be Sonorans going in the direction of Sonora. I stopped them by right of the general order I had, as that seemed to be in the interest of the country. I told the leader, one Nazario, that he should return to Los Ángeles. It was growing late. We passed the night there, and during the night a captain of the Indians at Santa Isabel came to warn me that the Indians from Pauma and Temécula and Agua Caliente were going to attack me during the darkness.

I had known this captain for a long time as a trustworthy man. He was called Mateo, and acted as servant for white people. He offered me the aid of his people. Within three or four hours Captain José Alipáz came from the *presidio* at San Diego with eleven men and joined me. All of us, white men and Indians, guarded the horses carefully. I ordered Alipáz and his eleven men to sleep quietly that night, for the next morning they would be sent to escort the Sonorans to San Luis Rey.

31

Nothing more happened during the night, and next morning we all left together after expressing our thanks to Captain Mateo.

When we reached Pauma I took leave of Alipáz, charging him to watch the Sonorans closely. The reason for this attitude toward them was that they were conveying stolen horses, and also I had orders to allow no one to leave California.

I returned to Temécula and passed the night there. I then left for San Bernardino to satisfy myself regarding the behavior of the Indians there. I found nothing new. At sunset I had a message from the Commander General ordering me to return to Los Ángeles without delay.

The Mexicans said that we, the Californians, would not amount to anything in an emergency, because we would not trouble ourselves enough. My promptitude in carrying out the orders that the _podido_ of Flores gave me at all times gives them the lie. (I call it this because he was an intriguer and a thief who kept us out undergoing fatigues while he was in Los Ángeles with the Americans.)

At daybreak I reached the general headquarters of Flores in Los Ángeles. He told me that he had only a few men here, and for that reason it was necessary for me to be at the _cuartel_. In order to meet his demand and at the same time be satisfied regarding the safety of my family, I left for the ranch the following day. I remained there, placing guards and making rounds day and night, until the message from San Diego came saying that the Indians had killed some Californians in the San José Valley.

I was returned to go to San Diego to take charge of the force there, and before starting to call Flores. He said that such a request had reached him, and that in consequence I should proceed in pursuit of those Indians. I left for San Diego with only fifteen men, but with orders to arrest the chiefs and shoot them. In addition he gave me a separate order to send him two hundred steers from San Jacinto Ranch to feed the troops in Los Cerritos. On this same day he moved the general _cuartel_ from Los Ángeles to Los Cerritos.

I collected men along the road as I went, and reached San Bernardino with twenty-three men. There I enlisted five more. I went to San Jacinto and sent the two hundred steers in charge of six men, leaving myself twenty-two. This was in December, 1846. I gave the men in charge of the stock of one of my chicken coops.

At Santa Gertrudis I camped. I sent eight men with an officer to reconnoiter the country around Aguanga, where the Indians who had committed the murders were. As soon as they caught sight of him and he saw what a multitude of Indians were there, this officer, who was a Mexican peasant named Rojas, began running back in terror with four or five Indians chasing him on horseback. The men [who] reached my camp reported that the Indians were so numerous that it was undesirable for us to remain so near so hostile a force.

I did not take the report very seriously. But during the night I thought of sending word to Los Ángeles to see if they would lend me some aid, since the officer said that the Indians numbered no less than a thousand fighting men.

The messenger would have to take three days or more to go and return, losing more than a day uselessly. Before he came back I heard that Ramón Carrillo was in San Luis Rey with ten men. I sent word for him to come, and he came immediately with his men. I ordered him to watch the Indians, and I left that same hour for Jurupa, where I could enlist an Indian chief named Juan Antonio. We went together to Temécula, carrying two pieces of white cloth to use as a special signal to Juan Antonio's Indians. We reached Santa Gertrudis and rejoined Ramón Carrillo and his force. We notified our people that we were leaving immediately, to fight the hostile Indians at daybreak. We started at eleven o'clock at night. It was daylight when we came to the enemy. We arranged our plan of attack. There were high hills and rather deep canyons, but not extensive. In one of the canyons from which we could reach the enemy, I placed an *ambuscade* of fifty Indians and fifteen white men with strict orders to not show themselves until the last of the Indian enemies passed.

I stationed myself in the mouth of the canyon with some men, and Carrillo went to trick the enemy by calling their attention and leading them to follow him. As soon as they saw him they rose and went after him. He passed them, fired at them and retreated slowly and in an orderly manner until he came to where I was. The Indians followed him eagerly. My men, who had rifles and other good arms, whom I had placed five on ridges or high places in the canyon, were told to fire only at the fighters because they were the chiefs and came in the middle of the main body.

We lured them on about a league until they passed the *ambuscade*. Then the men rushed out from the ambush upon them from the back at the same time that we fought them from in front.

We made a great slaughter, and falling upon them from the rear killed many of them. Before reaching Aguanga in their flight, eighteen or twenty of them turned back and gave up their arms. They were made prisoners and placed in charge of chief Juan Antonio, who told me to care for my men and he would care for the prisoners.

On reaching Aguanga we amused ourselves killing some three Indians who continued fighting. After terminating the affair, in which perhaps a hundred Indians perished, we went back to Juan Antonio and found that he had killed all the prisoners. I reproached him for these acts of cruelty, and he answered me very coolly, that he had gone to hunt and fight and kill Indians who would kill him, that he was sure that if they had caught him they would not have spared his life but would have burned him alive.

The booty that was collected amounted to no more than a few *serapes*, arrows, lances, and other trifles, all of which I gave to Juan Antonio and his people.

We betook ourselves to the camp where we had to await the arrival of the aid we had asked, to a little house between Temécula and Santa Gertrudis. There I had my wounded men treated, six in number. We had no deaths. One horse perished.

I had a small beef brought to feed the men. Shortly afterward the aid arrived under command of my friend Diego Sepúlveda, and consisting of twenty-five men. He informed me that owing to bad condition of the horses he had had to make short trips, and this had delayed him.

I took some of his men to act as lookouts at the four points of the compass, for we were not sure that the hostile Indians would not return to attack us.

Daybreak came without anything occurring. The outposts were redoubled, and we decided to return to Aguanga where we had left the Indians in order to rest our animals.

On arriving there we saw only a few Indians—old ones, blind, lame, and so on, of both sexes. At the *ranchería* we found seeds, chickens, *ollas*, and so forth, which our own Indians collected. Our people occupied themselves in registering everything, cooking, eating, and so on, on the hillside. I lay down to sleep after giving my horse an allowance of barley.

I had slept for some time when the men came arguing that we should go forward. I did not agree, because I neither wished nor felt able to do so. One of the soldiers who had come with the aiding party, named Carlos Domínguez—son of the Mariano Domínguez whom the Indians had killed in the valley of San José—begged permission to advance, and that he be given an escort of twenty men, in order to avenge the murder of his father. (The Californians that were killed numbered three—men who had gone there because they did not wish to have any part in the war against the United States.)

I answered that I could not accommodate him in that manner, and he promised he would not go more than one or two miles forward. He wished to discover whether there were Indians on the road, since there was another settlement farther on known as El Negro. He promised that if he encountered any Indians he would let me know. Upon this, I put twenty men at the disposal of Carlos Domínguez, and they started out at once. About two o'clock in the afternoon that same day they returned saying that they had met none but dead Indians on the road they traveled.

I left Aguanga for Santa Gertrudis, spent the night there, and then pushed on toward San Bernardino. From there I sent the men who had been with me to await me there. The following day I joined them there, and we went on together to Los Ángeles.

When we had gone about three leagues we met five or six men and a woman who were on their way to Sonora. They were Sonorans. I had them turn back, and charged Diego Sepúlveda to keep them with him as far as the San José ranch.

I went on ahead, and in a short time met a courier who brought word that I should hasten my return, and send ahead most of the men who were with me. In San José came another message during the night, ordering me to remain there with fifteen men, and send the rest on with Sepúlveda. Also that I should take charge of the foreign prisoners who had been left under guard, and take them to the Rancho Chino, guarding them there until further orders. He cautioned me that if I noted any movement either of revolt or of flight, I should stop it by force of arms.

Among the prisoners I gathered in and whose names I remember were John Rowland, Louis Rubidoux, Michael White, three Callaghan brothers, (Joseph L.) Perdu, and my brother-in-law, Julián (Isaac) Williams.

When he had made all these foreigners prisoners at Chino, my father, shortly afterward, assumed responsibility for a part of them and these were given their liberty on their word of honor to engage in no acts unfavorable to the country while the war was in progress.

I continued in charge of the prisoners until January 8, 1847, when I was ordered to set them free and remain there with all the men of the country I could enlist, since Flores and his forces would come to Chino within a few days. I did as he ordered, and gathered in some twenty-three men in addition to the fifteen I already had, forming a force of thirty-eight or forty men.

On January 11 I heard that Flores was in Cucamonga with a goodly force, heading for Chino. I then dissolved the force I had and ordered them to their homes, since I knew that Flores and the men with him were on their way to Sonora.

I then went with one of my boys to Cucamonga to see Señor Flores. He suggested that I go with him to Sonora, because he was not in as great danger in Los Ángeles as I was. I declined to accept his advice, saying that if I had to

36

die, I should want death to overtake me in my own country. I came on to Los Ángeles to see if they were going to kill me as Flores said.

I stopped for a short time at my father's ranch near there, and was not molested by anyone, although I made repeated visits to my ranch in San Bernardino openly.

In the month of March, while I was on one of my father's *ranchos*, I learned from a countryman that Señor Frémont wished to see me at his stopping place. Believing what Flores had told me in Cucamonga, I feared that he wished to crush me, when in reality he was seeking me for an entirely different reason. In my fear I prepared to go in search of a hiding place somewhere in the mountains. I left with two boys for San Bernardino with the idea of taking to the hills there. Two days after, I received a message from my father saying that he wished to see me at his Rancho San Antonio. He told me there what Señor Frémont wanted of me, and that they had charged him to arrange for my return to Los Ángeles.

Against my wishes, I went to the city, alone but well armed and on horseback. My father and I met again there, this time in his orchard, and together we presented ourselves to Señor Frémont, my father on foot but I on horseback, because I could not give up my distrust.

After courteous greetings, Frémont told me that he wished to entrust me with a mission to all the *rancherías* of hostile Indians (since all the Indians were rebellious and uttering boasts and threats against the *rancheros*). He gave me to understand that he had consulted with the principal men in Los Ángeles, and they had recommended me as the man most fitted to induce the Indians to quiet down.

Frémont did not wish to give me more than four or five men, and I explained that without a force sufficiently large and important I could not undertake so risky an attempt, in view of the great number of Indians who were actually hostile toward the white people.

He could not bring himself to give me the force, and then charged me with another undertaking—that of going to collect the horses that Flores and his men had abandoned in the flight to Sonora. He promised to furnish me with funds to pay the expenses I would incur.

I left with ten men and on the way to San Bernardino I collected all the horses I encountered within eight leagues of that place. I returned with some sixty horses, and at Frémont's order delivered them to the *Juez del Campo*, Felipe Lugo, my brother.

Frémont invited me to come to see him in his home, because as he said, he wished that we should be friends. I was there with him some four or five hours, talking about many things. Afterwards he said that he wished that I, with my friends many or few, would take him with us on a visit through Los Ángeles and vicinity. That day we went to San Gabriel, and I introduced him to many friends there, men and women, as a friend of my own.

A few days later he gave me another invitation to go about the region and certain friends accompanied us. On a second visit to San Gabriel we gave a ball in his honor. The young women danced and talked with him, and he returned to Los Ángeles pleased and happy.

The next day I said farewell to Frémont as I was returning to my ranch, but I told him that I would not cease to call upon him whenever it was possible for me to do so.

I attended to my own affairs entirely apart from politics until the year 1849, when I was elected to the post of First *Alcalde* of Los Ángeles; and on the first of April Estevan C. Foster delivered the office to me. I discharged the duties of this office during this year, and on the first of the ensuing January I turned it over to Don Abel Stearns.

While I was *Alcalde* the Second *Alcalde* was Don Juan Sepúlveda. We had a municipal government composed of four *Regidores* (aldermen); namely, Tomás Sánchez, Francisco Ocampo, Francisco Ruiz, y José López; Recorder, Don Juan Temple; Secretary, Jesús Guirado.

Señor Foster continued as Mayor, or *Corregidor*, the year that I was *Alcalde*. In the middle of this year, about August, I was appointed Justice of the Peace; and when I ceased to be it, on January 1, I was notified that I should send to San Francisco for the salary I had been allotted as Justice, some $500. This sum they sent me from that place.

* * * * * * *

In May, 1851, I received word at my ranch at San Bernardino that some Texans were coming up along the river from Jurupa, heading for my place. According to the report, they were murderers and thieves who had come from the placer mines, robbing and killing people along the way.

I learned that they had been at the home of Don Luis Rubidoux, and he had begged them to spare him because he was a poor man; but that farther on they would find me, a rich man, who had received $13,000 at my home. They left and proceeded toward my ranch. On this day I was conducting a stock roundup when the word came. I went to a military camp that was on my ranch in search of the captain to have him aid me in withstanding these evildoers. I found no one but his lieutenant.

This troop was stationed on my ranch to guard against the Indian Chaguanosos and other thieves who were entering the valley by the Cajón. All I could get from the lieutenant was that if I wished to remain in his camp I might do so, but that he was not authorized to take the troops away from there. As I needed help for the protection of my home and belongings, as well as my gentle horses and so on, his offer was of no value to me, so I set out to hunt assistance elsewhere.

I then ordered the Indian Captain, Juan Antonio, with his men and four servants of my own to guard my house, while I and three boys went to hide the horses. I hid them in a thicket and returned home. On arriving there my people were already fighting the highwaymen who had entered the house, having broken down the doors, and were looking for chests and so on. Everything that could be carried away was stolen, that is my riding saddles and such things, my ropes and so on—to the value of $1500 or $2000.

The evildoers had arrived and committed their outrages before Juan Antonio and his people had reached the place. These latter went in chase of the robbers, but they succeeded in escaping with their booty. However, they were overtaken and surrounded on a logging road near Yucaipa which they mistook for the real road. There was a skirmish there in which Juan Antonio's lieutenant was killed. The Indians climbed the slopes of the canyon and from there killed with their arrows the thieves, who numbered twelve or thirteen.

Shortly after they came to my house. I was there then, and they reported what had happened to those villains. Of my effects, I recovered only a pair of pantaloons I found tossed down on the hillside. Everything else had been taken by the Indians who had come at the call of Juan Antonio from the three villages, to the number of a hundred or more.

Next day, Señor Estevan C. Foster arrived with a great number of Californians who were pursuing the thieves. With Sr. Foster came the commander of the troop, angry with me because I had incited the Indians against the evildoers. He even wished to arrest me, but did not dare to do so in view of the people there who were on my side. They gave him to understand that before taking matters into my own hands I had gone to his camp to seek aid and had been refused.

That same day I left for Los Ángeles to give a formal account of what had occurred. A committee was named to go to the scene of the events to make a full investigation. This was done, and when it was ended I went to Los Ángeles with the committee.

During my stay in the city I received word that members of the troop and other foreigners went at night to insult both the Indians and my servants for having killed those bandits. I hastened back to the ranch, and within two or three days, for this reason, the troops were withdrawn from that place.

My branding-place for cattle was near their camp. I went there with my people to work, carrying all my arms and artillery. I continued working there through May, June, and July on account of the inconveniences the troopers caused me. That same year [1851] I decided to sell the ranch and end the constant danger to my life. I sold it to a company of Mormons who came, and retired to Los Ángeles. Since that time I have continued to live here.

* * * * * * *

The Californian way of living in my early years was as follows: at eight o'clock in the evening the entire family was occupied in its prayers. In commending themselves to God, they recited the rosary, and other spiritual prayers which each one addressed to the male or female saint of his or her name or devotion. Husband and wife slept in the same room and nearly always the same bed. The children—if there were any, and the dwelling had conveniences and separate apartments—slept, the men in the galleries outside the house in the open air, and the women in an enclosed quarter of which the parents kept the key, if there was a key, a thing that was not very common.

At three o'clock in the morning the entire family was summoned to their prayers. After this, the women betook themselves to the kitchen and other domestic tasks, such as sweeping, cleaning, dusting, and so on. The men went to their labor in the field—some to herd cattle, others to look after the horses.

The milking of the cows was done by the men or the Indian servants. Ordinarily some woman of the family had charge of the milking, to see that the milk was clean and strained. The women and the Indian servants under them made the small hard, flat cheeses, the cheese proper, butter, curds, and a mixture made to use with beans.

The women's labors lasted till seven or eight in the morning. After that they were busy cooking, sewing, or washing.

The men passed the day in labor in the fields according to their location, some preparing the ground for sowing seed, bringing in wood, sowing the seed, reaping, and so on. Some planted cotton, some hemp, some planted both. This was done by those who had facilities for it; they planted and harvested the things they needed most for the benefit of their families, such as rice, corn, beans, barley, and other grains, squash, watermelons, and cantaloupes.

The lands in the immediate vicinity of the town of Los Ángeles were set to fruit trees such as grapes, pears, apples, pomegranates, here and there an olive, cactus fruit in some places, peaches, nectarines, and other minor fruits. The owners of fields could not obtain seeds of oranges, lemons, cider-producing fruits, or others that were found at the missions, because the *padres* selfishly refused to allow these fruits to be raised elsewhere than at their missions.

Fruit trees were not cultivated on the *ranchos*, because very few persons were able to own *ranchos* until very recently; that is, by 1836 or 1837 and on.

During the time Spain was in power here, a few *ranchos* were granted, those of the Nietos, Verdugos, Domínguez, and el Maligo de Bartolo Tapia, I am not positive, but I have heard it said that the Rancho de la Bayona was also granted in the time of the King, to the family of Zúñiga. These are the only *ranchos* that I know of as having been granted during the Spanish régime.

Many people occupied *ranchos* provisionally with their stock, and this was allowed because there was not room enough for them in the town or the community corral. In 1822, an order came that the *Alcalde* or the Judge should destroy corrals on the *ranchos*, and the owners of stock should place them in a community corral. At this time my father was in Monterey, and he secured permission to maintain a corral on the little ranch where he lived, the one that the river destroyed in 1825, as I described earlier.

Returning to the way of living of the Californians, the type of ordinary life that I have described was more or less that followed by people living on *ranchos* as well as by those residing in the town.

The house on a little ranch was of rough timber roofed with *tules*. It rarely had more than two rooms. One served as the entry and living room, the other as a sleeping room. If the family was large, the two rooms were divided. Many of these houses had a door of *vasita* faced with sheepskin, cowhide, or horsehide. No door had a lock or key, neither was it necessary to close it on the outside when the whole family left, because there was none who would enter to steal, and nothing which would be worth taking. If the family was to be absent for several days, they would take with them their one thing of value; namely the little chest of clothes, and some bedding and a cot.

Some ranchers or other people of the town had beds of cottonwood or poplar, lined with leather on which they slept. On this bed there were sheets, blankets, coverlets, pillows, and so on, according to the resources of the owner.

Some slept in a great framework resembling a hammock with cross-bars on which was thrown a cowhide. The person who had nothing else slept on a cowhide or horsehide.

I am speaking, of course, of the first years that I knew. Later some conveniences were introduced when trade with the outside began. The families who were able usually had furniture of the sort most needed, such as a table, a long bench, and a few little stools. Some had seats of whale bones, others little stools often of reeds, narrow slats, or some other splints. These stools were the most common. Outside the house on each side of the door there were benches of adobe on which people could sit; they were less than a *vara* in height. Some were plastered and whitewashed like the wall of the house. Others, like some of the houses, were not whitewashed because lime was scarce and hard to obtain without bringing it from a distance.

The kitchen in some places was supplied with a small adobe stove-like arrangement on which were placed the cooking pots. In other places there were only stones, upon which the pots were placed, the fire being underneath them.

The hour for breakfast was very early for the men who had to go to their labors. Others breakfasted later. For this breakfast the wealthy had good Spanish chocolate made with milk or water according to taste, with bread, *tortillas*, and wheat or corn porridge with butter, and so on. The poor people had for their early meal milk with *pinole* or *esquito*, or perhaps parched corn. Others breakfasted on beans, while some had a solid meal of roasted or dried meat with chili, onions, tomatoes, and beans, since there would not be another meal until four or five in the afternoon, according to the time of the year.

During Lent, when fasting was observed, people did not have their first meal until twelve o'clock at noon, and the second at eight in the evening. These two meals, at midday and at night, generally consisted of fish, abalone, *colachi* (which was merely squash chopped fine and boiled), *quelites* (which were native herbs well boiled, and mixed with beans half and half). There was no coffee or tea.

Another dish was *lechetole*, which was wheat cooked in milk with plenty of *panocha* (a sort of candy made of brown sugar), or squash cooked with milk and *panocha*, curds, cheese, cottage cheese, and clabber. The supper during Lent was of *colachi*, *quelites*, and beans, with corn meal *tortillas*.

There was another *tortilla* which the old women made of corn. It was of corn meal, the last that was made, and they called it *niscayote*. They add butter, and to sweeten it sugar, *panocha*, or honey is used. The only difference between the Lenten season and the rest of the year was that in Lent no meat was eaten except by the individual who had permission from the Church, because of sickness or other exemption.

Those who had plates, who were few in number, ate on them. Those who did not have them used flat clay bowls, which had the same shape as the ordinary plates. Knives, forks, and spoons such as are used today on the table, were possessed by only a few people. With the poorer class, which was the greater part of the population, the general thing was to use forks and spoons of horn. Those who did not have even this, made a spoon for every mouthful, loading the meat, or beans, or whatever they had, on a piece of *tortilla*, and all went together to the stomach. Their knives were the ones they used for all work.

The food was generally eaten in the kitchen beside the fire. Those who had the conveniences, of course, with tables, ate as is done today, with table, cloths, and so on. But the number of these was very limited.

The mode of living was the same in town as in the country. The government exacted compliance with the precepts of the Church from all. All, excepting the sick or crippled, had to attend Mass every Sunday and on other days at the call of the Church. If it was found that anyone failed continuously in this duty, without satisfactory reason, the authorities were ordered to hunt him out and reprimand him.

At Easter time, all without exception had to confess and receive the Holy Sacrament, and take part in the catechism; and the *padre* gave each one a paper saying that he had complied with the precepts of the Church in that year. Nevertheless, when I reached the age for confession, this requisite was not in use, or at least not enforced. We confessed and did Penance and took part in the catechism because our parents obliged us to comply with the orders of the Church, but the government did not mix in these things. I am speaking of the years 1826 or 1827 and on.

There was a very poor old man named Sotelo. When he went, without hat or shoes, and covered only with a blanket, to where the *padre* was, to be examined in the Christian doctrine, so that they would give him the paper to present for confession, the *padre*, as a joke, asked him two or three questions, although the old man could hardly see or speak.

"Tell me, Sr. Sotelo, why did our Lord choose death on the cross?"

"Because my soul needed it."

"Why did God make man?"

"For the woman."

This was the doctrine of old Sotelo. After a short dialogue of this sort the *padre* gave him the paper, and the old man went contentedly to his confession.

As to the way the Californians dressed in my early years: men did not cut their hair, especially if in military occupations. It was combed back and parted in the middle. It was tied behind, and then made into a braid of three strands. This braid, or tail, hung over the shoulder as the Chinamen hung their hair. The women let their hair fall over the ears—parted in the middle and braided behind like the men.

The beard was shaved leaving only the whiskers from the temple to the edge of the jaw. The common way was to shave every four or five days, although this did not keep one from shaving Saturday afternoon or Sunday morning, in order to go clean-shaven to Mass to hear the Word of God.

Most men bound the head with a cloth or handkerchief of black silk, some making a knot behind, and others crossing the points over the forehead in front, and forming the knot there. Over this the hat was worn as we wear it to-day, but always secured with a guard-cord, of leather, or per-haps with a ribbon or a tape of silk. This latter was used by persons with sufficient means. Those who wished to appear dashing wore the hat on one side or the other, or far back on the head.

The hats in most general use were called *poblanos* because they came from the city of Pueblo in México. Some were of *vicuña* (something like the wool of the South Ameri-can *alpaca*), and these were bought by officials or people of means. Others were of tanned cow-hide, and some were of palm-tree leaves—these latter worn by the Indians. The *po-blanos* were "slouching," with brims of a moderate width.

The shirts in use were of cloth, either linen or cotton; with the very poor of *jerga*. Above was a waistcoat which went only to the edge of the belt, and had a lapel or turn back collar. The material of the waistcoat varied, according to the wealth of the wearer, as it could be of Indian *nankeen*, cor-duroy, velvet, satin, wool, and so on. Over this waistcoat was the short jacket like it and made of the same material. The colors used were always blue and black.

Short pants of some woven cloth were worn, of vel-vet, velveteen, satin, *nanquín* (*nankeen*), blue or black, and reached to the knees, around which was a sort of garter of gold or silver lace called a *galón*, if the owner of the pants could buy such adornment. The width of this varied from one to three fingers' breadth, according to individual taste and ability to buy. If he could not afford the *galón* he wore a band of the same material as the pants, some two or more fingers wide. Underneath the pants under drawers were worn.

The pants had a short stretch on the outside of each thigh three or four fingers in breadth according to the size of the man that was stitched to form the seam. From the upper part of this seam the pants were open to the waist. The same was the case from the lower part of the stitching to the knee. In the lower part that was open, there was inserted a piece of colored woolen cloth with an edging or border on each side. On the upper edge of this were five or six buttonholes worked in blue silk, and on the under side opposite were the

46

buttons. Some men buttoned all of these, but most men buttoned only one or two of them.

The pants had a flap on one side at the top, and this had a single button and buttonhole to close it. In the waist were two or three buttonholes with corresponding buttons. In the open stretch above the seam along the thigh there was one button and buttonhole. The pocket, or what corresponded to our pocket today, had a buttonhole and button.

The leggings were of *gemuza* (a sort of *chamois* made from deer, sheep, or calfskin), each of an entire skin minus the leg. The foot of the legging was the sides of the neck sewed together. Most men stretched the skin before making them. Others doubled it into two folds, while still others made three folds. The legging was closed by a strap, a ribbon, or even a silk garter trimmed with sequins and lace, these last being added to give a glittering effect. Of course, the leggings were already fringed and embroidered in the ways favored by well-to-do persons. Poor men used a strip of leather or ribbon; in fact, whatever they could afford.

The shoes were of calfskin embroidered with white thread of the *maguey* plant. They reached only to the ankle. They were open on the outside to admit the foot, and were trimmed with open-work and edgings of different colors. There were eyelets for narrow laces for fastening the shoes. These laces were usually black. Some used silk cords.

The man of means wore a large handkerchief of pure silk around the neck. The soldiers used the same clothes as other men, except that they wore devices on the jacket to show their rank; and when on a campaign they wore the *cuera*, which was a sort of leather jacket of several layers of deerskin. The seams of this were trimmed on the outside with green ribbon. This was the uniform of the *cavalry de cuera*, as they were called. Other troops dressed more or less the same as the cavalry, with their respective devices to show rank, but without the *cuera*.

The women wore short skirts and a belt. Above the waist they wore a chemise reaching from the neck to below the belt. This chemise had short sleeves. Under the skirt they wore a woolen petticoat, and under this another and still shorter skirt of fine muslin or coarse cotton cloth, according to the means of the wearer. The very poor wore only a coarse flannel or sacking petticoat next to the skin. All wrapped their heads in a *rebozo*, or muffler, when they went away from their home, and this was as fine and costly as their means permitted. Over the breast they wore a handkerchief of silk, linen, or cotton, coming from over the shoulders with points crossed over the breast and fastened at each side of the belt.

I was fifteen or sixteen years old when I first saw women wearing ornamental combs of tortoise shell or some less costly material. The women always wore low shoes, some with heels and some without. The ones without were usually known as slippers, and were used by dancers.

The children usually wore little coats or short shirts until they were six or eight years old. Those whose parents could afford to do so, began earlier to put little pants on them of *nankeen* or corduroy, or some other heavy material. After the age of eight they wore little pantaloons of *chamois* or coarse woolen cloth or of *baize* or *nankeen*. This last was the material most generally used, not only for boys but also by poorer men.

The parents in better circumstances put shoes on their children while they were small, but generally the boy did not begin wearing shoes until he was old enough to go to work. The same was the case with the girls, although naturally more care was taken to furnish shoes for females. It was a rare thing to see a boy with a hat before he was twelve or fourteen years old. The women did not wear a hat unless they were traveling some distance on horseback.

The dress of the men underwent some change after 1832 or 1833, when the *calzoneras* came in. These were pantaloons open on the outside from the bottom up.

At the top of the opening there was inserted a long strip of colored woolen cloth, blue, black, or some other color. In the lower part of the opening there were buttons and buttonholes to fasten over the insert. Some wore the pantaloons stitched from the hip to the middle of the thigh; others wore them buttoned. Below were the boots or leggings, which everyone wore since they were in style.

48

In later years European styles were being introduced, and from 1846 on all began to dress in European fashion excepting perhaps some old people who preferred the old styles. On the *ranchos* the cowboys always gave preference to the short pants over the pantaloons as being more convenient for their work. In traveling or in the country we used the *serape* or *manga*, which was nothing more than a narrow blanket with an opening in the middle through which the head could be thrust. It served as a protection, without preventing the use of the arms.

To protect both the short and the long pants we wore a piece of *chamois* (made by tanning skin in a special way to keep it soft) reaching from the lower part of the body to the middle of the leg, and fastened to the belt with stout straps. The chamois opened down the middle and was secured to each leg with straps. This kind of apron, which we called *armita*, kept off the dust, and also prevented the wearing of the pants by the *riatas*.

Those who could afford them wore socks, and those who could not went without them, which was nothing strange, since some white people went without shoes, either not having them or being too old to put them off and on.

When we went on a long trip, we usually carried very little with us; that is, in the way of food. If we did not wish to stop along the way, we might take a little parched corn, a piece of meat or a roast chicken, and *tortillas* and bread.

If we could not cover the entire distance in one day, we asked the hospitality of the mission at nightfall, or of some ranch if there was one. There the traveler was furnished lodging, bed, food, or supper; and next day, or when he wished to continue his journey, he was supplied with animals if he needed them, and even provisions if the trip was to be long. Of course not a cent was taken for anything.

The usual custom was for a person going on a long trip to take the animal he would ride, and in addition one or more for a change on the road. Travelers who did not have friends along the way and who did not wish to inconvenience anyone, took the horses they thought they would need, and also provisions and clothing. Some took servants and ten or twelve or even twenty animals. But for the most part horses were plentiful and people were disposed to accommodate the traveler, never minding if he lacked horses or provisions. There was never any charge for any of this.

My longest trips were generally to San Diego or Santa Bárbara, and I made them nearly always in one day and part of the night, as a result of taking one or two horses for replacement.

The *padres* had rooms in the missions for lodging travelers. If a traveler borrowed a horse, he returned it on the trip back, and took his own which he had left. This was repeated several times on occasion; and when the travelers returned their mounts were always returned to them. Great pains were taken to give back the same animal that he had left. In those days nearly all Californians were bound to each other by ties either of blood or of friendship, so that the traveler could go from one end of California to the other without costing him anything in money, excepting gifts he might wish to make to Indian servants at the missions or on the *ranchos*, and so on. This was the custom.

I can say but little about the régime the *padres* followed in the missions, because I never lived in any of them, and visited them very rarely. I went to San Gabriel perhaps two or three times in the year to hear Mass or take part in some Church *fiesta* in Holy Week or Corpus Christi Day, or Saint John's Day. But I saw the work at this mission, and the way the neophytes were treated.

The mission had various workshops; for example, for weaving, carpentry, soap-making, iron-forging, shoe-making, and belt-making. In these were also made bricks, round tiles, adobes, earthenware, basins, leather straps, plows, carts, yokes, and other articles and utensils most needed at the mission. There were orchards of all kinds of fruit trees, vines were cultivated, and various kinds of grains, such as wheat, corn, beans, peas, chick-peas, lentils, and also potatoes, squash, watermelon, and cantaloupes. The mission made great quantities of wine and brandy and other liquors, including vinegar.

The *padres* looked after the morals of the neophytes, and taught them the principles of the Catholic religion. There was Mass in the mission church every day in the week, and the attendants there were Indians who could not work, such as the aged, the blind, or crippled. The other Indians attended Mass on Sunday and other prescribed days.

Many of the married Indians lived in houses inside the mission walls, and others lived in communities on the mission *ranchos*, since the number of converted Indians was very great. The single men at the mission lived in a separate building, and at night when they retired to their quarters the door was locked and the key delivered to the *padre*. The women who were not married lived in still another building, called the "nunnery," which was in charge of a matron day and night. When they were rounded up at night they also were locked in, and the key was taken to the *padre*.

Early in the morning the local *Alcalde*, or town head, under the direction of the *mayordomos* or overseers, assigned the Indians among the various labors. The *Alcalde* also freed the unmarried youths from their lockup, and the matron did the same for the single women.

Before those unmarried ones went to their work they went, along with a good many of the married Indians, to the *pozolera*, or cookhouse, where they were given breakfast at daybreak. This meal consisted of *atole* and *pozole*. The *pozole* was a sort of stew of corn, beans, and meat. The *atole* was merely cornmeal porridge.

The married Indians were given a ration each week of corn, wheat, beans, and a good piece of meat. The meat was sometimes fresh and sometimes dried.

After breakfast each Indian man and woman went to the work assigned. At half past eleven the ones who worked near the *pozolera* went there for food. At one o'clock they returned to their tasks, and these lasted until sundown, when they were given the third meal, which was like the others in being *atole* and *pozole*.

As I did not live in the mission, I can only say that I understood that the neophytes were well and abundantly fed. They were also permitted to go to the hills to collect the seeds which had been their food in their days of paganism, such as acorns, *piñóns*, *guata*, *islay*, *chia*, and so on, along with certain herbs. To gather these they went once a year, the old men and women usually being the ones to make the trips, searching in various directions. Generally dependable Indians went with them as a guard, as they needed to be protected from ferocious animals, which were numerous.

Each Indian man and woman was given a blanket every year, and if it wore out before the year ended another was supplied. Each man was given a breech-clout and a coat of *jerga*, a coarse cloth woven on mission looms. To each woman was given *jerga* for a skirt. Later, when the missions were able to obtain goods through commerce carried on with ships, they began to give the Indians calico, muslin shirting, shawls, and large striped and flowered handkerchiefs in bright colors, these latter pleasing the Indians greatly.

As a general thing, the Indians who worked on the distant *ranchos* lived there, and there was a cookhouse there to give them food.

The mission had a number of *mayordomos*, each of which was charged with a certain responsibility or a certain *rancho*. These *mayordomos* were Californians of education, but they had *caporales*, or foremen, selected from the more intelligent Indians who understood a goodly part of the Spanish language.

The *caporal* was a sort of interpreter, and transmitted the orders to the Indians that did not understand Spanish. They also assisted the community leader and the *mayordomo* in the policing and in the work generally.

Each mission also had a number of *vaqueros*, or cow-keepers, who for the most part were Indians of that mission. These cow-keepers had charge of the animals. They were the ones who broke horses, mules, and male animals generally, managed the *rodeos* and *capazones*, all under the eye of the *mayordomos* and *caporales*.

The heavy work of the field was done by the men. Women who were not employed in the weaving or in the houses were put to work on the lighter tasks that were near the mission. Nevertheless, it was not uncommon to employ women in field labor, because there were nearly always more of them than there were of men.

In addition to working at the looms, the women were busy in sewing, and general cleaning of the buildings connected with the mission, as well as of the mission itself. In most of the weaving rooms there was an educated director and as many strong Indians as were needed.

Indians belonging to the missions could not leave them without special permission, and this was seldom granted. Frequently, they were sent to work in the towns or the *presidios* under contract. They were not paid for the work they did, but the *padre* received it for the benefit of the community, as he said; but we did not know what part of these receipts reached the community.

A few Indian boys received a slight education. They were taught to read, to sing, and play instruments, in addition to the duties of the weaving establishments. Some of them learned to assist at the Mass, and generally these were servants of the *padres* and were better clothed and treated.

Speaking of the cattle-tenders, I must say that some of them rode with saddles and some rode horseback. To the former the mission gave the saddle and trappings, the bridle, spurs, boots, and shoes. To the others, nothing more than was given the other Indians—a spear, a coarse shirt, a breech clout, and a blanket. No Indian who was not a cow-herder was permitted to ride a horse. This riding a horse was considered a grave crime from the days of the Spanish government.

San Gabriel Misión had an Indian orchestra comprising flutes, guitars, violins, drum, triangles, and cymbals. But then all the missions had orchestras and singers, who performed more or less badly. I remember that all who played in the church were known as the *minuet*.

At every mission there was a guard, composed generally of a commander and four soldiers, for the maintenance of order and protection of the *padres* and other persons living in the mission. In San Gabriel there was almost always a large force.

The minor faults which the Indians committed, the kind that would come into the category of faults that the father of a family would punish, these the *padres* were permitted to correct themselves, always knowing that they could call for aid from the soldiers if necessary. The serious faults, or crimes, came under the authority of the district to which the mission belonged. The duty of the mission was to investigate the case, safeguard the person of the criminal, and then send notice to the commander of the _presidio_.

I do not know how many lashes a _padre_ could order given an Indian. I believe that it was not more than twenty-five. I do not know whether or not the _padres_ sometimes exceeded their authority in delivering punishments. I do know that they frequently castigated the Indians who had committed faults with lashes, confinement, and chains. On some occasions I saw Indians working in foot-chains, and I also saw them in stocks.

San Gabriel Misión was threatened several times with invasions by _tulare_ or mountain Indians; but they never carried their threats into action. Once, however (I think it was in 1833), the Indians of San Bernardino, savage and Christian, seized the _padre_ (I believe it was Fr. José María Salvidea or Fr. Tomás Esténega) who had gone to this _rancho_ to attend to his religious duties, and they took him by force to San Gabriel. It must be said, though, that they seized him first and then set him free. The Indians carried off all the sheep, horses, and other belongings on the ranch. This ranch was almost like a mission. On it they were raising many grains, and in the years 1830 and 1832 they were constructing a very large house and other buildings. These were not completed, because of the uprising of the Indians, and the difficulty in guarding them at so great a distance from the mission.

For cultivating the land the missionaries and private land-owners had only plows and mattocks. The plows were of wood and were made by the Indians themselves or by other persons in this country. At the tip there was a bit of iron. The plow had a long beam which was joined to the yoke which united the oxen. It was fastened to the yoke by a strip of braided leather or of twisted fiber, commonly called _barzón_. To each plow was hitched a pair of oxen in charge of a driver.

With this plow the earth was worked up both ways and soaked with water before being leveled for seeding. Furrows were made, and in these were dropped the corn or beans. The wheat was sowed by hand on land cleared of grass and then plowed and dragged.

The mattock was used as it is today. The clearing of the land was done as it is now done, pasturing cattle, horses, and sheep on it, and raking and piling the grass or brush to set fire to it.

The planting of corn, beans, peas, lentils, squash, cantaloupes, and watermelons was done in this part of California in the months of March, April, May, and even in June. The harvesting was done in August and September according to the maturity of the corn.

The wheat and barley were sowed generally in December and January, but sometimes as early as November, which was really when it brought the best yield. The barley was harvested in May and June, and the wheat in July and August. As a regular thing, land was reserved especially for the production of each of these important grains.

The peas could be planted at any time of the year, and they grew abundantly.

In harvesting the wheat it was cut with a medium-sized knife, and with common sickles that had come in with ships. It was piled in heaps, from which _carretas_ took it to the place where it could be ground. The grain was separated from the straw after it was ground by winnowing it, and to accomplish this use was made of wooden shovels or rakes. The first winnowing was done with the rake and the second with the shovel. Generally it was winnowed only twice.

The grinding was done by piling the wheat in a circular place called the _hera_. Into this was driven a herd of mares to trample it while it was being turned over and over. After collecting all the grain that was not yet ground, it was thrown again into the circle to be trodden upon, and finally some which remained still unground was beaten with clubs. The corn, beans, peas, lentils, and so on were separated from their husks with clubs here in California in these times. For the corn, peas, and beans, great heavy sticks were used, and for the others smaller sticks were used.

After winnowing the wheat went to the granary, which was built so that the grain would be well protected. Those who did not have granaries put their wheat in leather sacks called _tanatones_, which held from three to six Spanish bushels, according to the size of the sack, which was generally of horsehide. There were some sacks of cow or sheep hide, but usually those who had these preferred to reserve them for sale, since they had some value, while the sacks of horsehide had none. It was only occasionally that there was a sale of horsehides, and the most that would be paid for one was six *reales*. Four or five *reales* were the ordinary price for a horse skin, while the skin of a cow or sheep would bring from twelve *reales* to two *pesos*. A large skin was worth more than a small one, but when a great number were sold all brought the same price.

The corn was kept in the ear in great *tropes*, or granaries. The part that was used in making *tamales*, bread, *tortillas*, and so on, was shelled by hand; but when a great quantity was to be sold, it had to be shelled by blows with stout clubs.

The beans, peas, chick-peas, and lentils were kept in sacks or *tanatores* [*sic*], or in dry and secure places.

The enemy of all these products was the weevil which attacked them while in storage; but there were not so many weevils then as now. The rats and mice also took much, but the worst eaters were the squirrels, the gophers, or moles, and the birds we called magpies and crows. It was necessary to keep bird-catchers constantly to frighten away these pernicious birds or catch them in traps or shoot them with small arrows. The same methods were adopted with the squirrels and the gophers and moles.

Until 1825 or 1830 the cultivation of grain was on a very small scale on the lands of individuals, merely enough for their own needs or to supply the *presidios* of Santa Bárbara and San Diego. There was no other trade. The missions produced grain in great quantities, but they had to feed their numerous neophytes. Later the missions increased production near the ports because they were in a position to sell their surpluses such as hides and tallow to the ships which came for them. This trade began during the régime of Don Luis Antonio Argüello from 1822 to 1825, and from then on it gradually increased.

When I was twelve or fourteen years old I used to see *carretas* loaded with hides and tallow headed for the ships at San Pedro.

56

In the North, at San Francisco, Monterey, Santa Cruz, and San Luis Obispo, and so on, much wheat began to be sold to the Russians.

Here in the vicinity of Los Ángeles few people planted wheat as it did not yield well; and as there was not a good outlet for it in sale, people did not take the trouble to grow it.

In my early years very few *ranchos* were owned by individuals, and they were the only ones who could live away from the town. No one else was permitted to live elsewhere than in the town itself.

From the year 1827 on I began to go out into the country. The missions had various stock *ranchos*. On some they kept cattle on others sheep. The horses and mules were on the *ranchos* where the stock was guarded. The mission of San Gabriel also had a great many hogs, some goats, and many chickens, turkeys, and geese. This is the only mission of which I can speak from personal knowledge, as it was the one I visited most. I passed through others, but without stopping to inquire about their affairs.

The first *rodeos* for castrating bulls (when there was a large number of them) came in January. The public and general *rodeos* were held in April, when each owner could gather in his own stock which had become mixed with the stock of the missions or of individuals.

When *rodeo* time came, the *Alcalde* beat a drum summoning his townspeople and issued orders that on such and such a day in such and such a place the *rodeos* would begin. The *rodeo*, or roundup, was presided over by a *juez de campo*, or field judge. The owners who had stock in the region began, each man picking out what he considered his own, and driving it to one of the separating places that had been selected. He had only to steer the animals gradually to the edge of the place and keep them there. If an animal resisted it was lassoed.

After each individual had pointed out which were his, he requested the organizer of the roundup and the field judge to pass upon the matter. If he was found to be in the right, he drove his stock home. No documents were given. None were necessary; and furthermore, in those days there were very few who could write. On reaching his ranch the owner marked the yearling calves with his branding iron. The brand was put on the hip or the hind quarter, and the ears were marked either by slitting them or by cutting out a little piece at the top or the bottom. Each owner had a special branding iron. When a head of stock was sold, the new owner put his brand on the shoulder blade.

*   *   *   *   *   *   *

When I was eight or ten years old, that is, from 1821 to 1824, there were great numbers of wild and very troublesome horses. They would come to the very outskirts of the town and eat the pasturage, leaving the gentled horses without food and even often coaxing them away. The government finally decided, in agreement with the *pueblo*, to have a general killing of these wild horses.

I remember seeing three corrals for this purpose here in Los Ángeles. Two were constructed by the town and one by my father. Corrals were also built for this purpose by other persons in the vicinity of the term. Cowboys, on horseback, drove whole herds of wild and tame animals into these enclosures and closed the great gates. There were some small gates, through which only one horse could pass at a time. Two or three lancers were stationed at each of these gates to spear the wild horses as they emerged, this being done after the ranchers had indicated the animals they were claiming. The slaughter of wild horses continued until none but the animals that had been claimed were left in the corrals. Many thousands of horses were slaughtered in these times. I saw a corral constructed for this purpose on the Rancho de los Nietos.

To make the corral, posts called *estantes* were driven into the ground and the spaces between them were filled with smaller poles tied together with leather thongs. The corrals were round, and in size were as much as a hundred *varas* from one side to the center. A *vara* was less than a yard.

The hides stripped from these horses were staked out to dry, the stretching being done to prevent their shrinking.

With no more treatment than this, they were sold or put to other uses as seemed desirable.

The hauling of hides and tallow to San Pedro, which was the only hauling that I saw myself, was in *carretas*, or carts, each of which could carry fifty hides. The *carretas* were made as follows: the two wheels were joined by an axle which was merely a pole some three *varas* long and six by four inches in thickness, with a hub called a *limón* (a lemon) at each end smoothed and pierced as necessary for the pins or clamps. Midway between the two *limones*, or hubs, was another pole of the same form, smoothed and pierced for receiving pins like those of the *limones*. This pole would have a length of seven *varas*, or shorter yards, and of proportionate thickness, a little stronger than the axle. To this long shaft the yoked oxen were harnessed.

The wheels of the *carreta* were of wood—alder, poplar, oak, or live-oak—and round, with an opening in the center for the axle. The wheel was bare, that is, it did not have an iron rim. In fact, no iron entered into the making of a *carreta*.

The missions and some individuals made these carts, and each person had one or two or more, according to his means and needs. The missions, of course, had a great many.

On the Saints Day or any other great *fiesta* day when the authorities gave permission to the young men to have a bullfight, the town *plaza* on which the houses faced was fenced in so that the houses could be safeguarded. From these the sport could be witnessed.

No stage or seats were placed inside the *plaza* railing, for the very good reason that there were no boards or ways of making them, since no one possessed the tools with which to saw them.

After the *plaza* was enclosed, a committee of cowboys was appointed to go out and bring in the most spirited bulls they could find. Generally, they brought thirty or forty bulls for each fight. They would arrive with them the evening of the day before the fight was to occur. On the day of the *fiesta* the combat began after Mass. A single bull was turned into the *plaza*, and then the youths who were to have a part in exciting the animal entered. Each was allowed two or three turns. These men were known as *capoteodores*, because they maneuvered with a cape, or a shawl or a bright cloth. In Spain they used their capes.

When a bull grew tired they turned him out and brought in another until all were exhausted. Sometimes the bull was killed in the *plaza*, this being done with a *rajón* or stick a *vara* or less in length with a knife inserted in the end. The bull was steered into the desired position and the blow was given between the *llaves* (shoulder-blades). Some hit the vital spot, but some did not. The killing, like that of exciting the animal, was always done on horseback. I have seen the exciting done on foot on rare occasions, but never a killing.

When the bull left the *plaza* for the corral, many of the men ran in a crowd to *colearlo*, an operation that consisted in running behind the animal to see who could be fortunate enough to seize the tail and with a powerful tug, to throw him to the ground. He would then be taken to the corral, and if uninjured would start on the return to the country. These bull-fights usually lasted two or three days, from after Mass to eleven in the morning, and from one to five or six in the afternoon.

On the day of the Patron Saint, those in charge of the *fiesta* gave the authorities and other prominent persons a grand banquet. At night there would be a grand ball, which was attended by all who had a taste for such pleasure. An arbor was constructed, with seats around the edges for the *señoras* and *señoritas*, and if there were any seats left they could be occupied by the older men and dignitaries. The men and the women were never in the same group; they remained separated.

The musicians seated themselves at one end, leaving the center free for dancing. The music consisted of a violin and a guitar, sometimes two violins and two guitars. Sometimes a singer or two would be seated with the musicians.

There was a *tecolero*, or master of ceremonies. Dancing to the tune the musicians were playing, he would direct himself to the first *señorita* in the arbor and invite her to dance by giving two claps with his hands. The young woman would rise, if she knew how to dance and cared to do so, giving two or three turns and then returning to her seat. The *tecolero* did the same with each of the other women. From time to time the dance stopped to give the musicians a rest.

There were different types of dances, for instance:

EL JARABE, which was danced by a man and a woman. After dancing for a short time the woman would retire and another would step forth, and another and another, until the man would give place to another male dancer.

LA JOTA, which was danced by four men and four women, and continued as long as the musicians played.

EL CABALLO, in which two women danced alone unaccompanied by men.

EL PENTORICO, OR SINALOA, which a woman danced alone.

EL MEDIO CATORCE, which was a tap-dance that a man usually danced alone, although a man and a woman sometimes danced it together.

LA TIRANA, another dance for a man and a woman.

EL FANDANGO, danced by a man and a woman. During the dance a song would suddenly enter the music, and some old man would shout, *"Bomba el hombre!"* (*Listen to the man!*). Some dancer would then add a *cuarteta* or a *décima* to the dance. (The *cuarteta* was a Spanish stanza of four lines of eight syllables each. The *décima* had ten lines.)

There were other dances of minor importance whose names I do not recall. It should be understood that each dance had its own music and its own particular steps.

I now remember another dance called *Los Camarones*, which was danced by two men and two women. In the dance, *El Son*, various lines were sung. The following are some of them:

> *El león se fue para España*
> *Y se queja de su fortuna.*
> *Y el águila con su maña*
> *Le esta comiendo la tuna*
> *De la patria Mexicana.*
> *El águila es animal*
> *Se retrata en el dinero.*
> *Para subit al Nepal*
> *Pidio licencia primera*
> *Del Congreso General.*
> *Aunque no venga Bretaña*
> *Que para hacer mi camisa*
> *No necesito a la España*
> *La hare de manta hechiza.*

These lines could be used also with any of the tunes. (The following type of comic lines were often sung:)

> *Yo tenia una rata*
> *Con treinta ratones*
> *Unos sin cabezas*
> *Otros con cabezones*
> *Unos sin orejas*
> *Otros con orejones*
> *Unos sin pescuesos*
> *Otros con pescuesos*
> *Unos sin hocicos*
> *Otros, hocicones.*

This sort of thing continued with variations until the *La Jota* ended.

Lines like the following were sometimes chanted when a couple danced *El Fandango:*

> *Sí mis afectos recibes*
> *No me respondas que no*
> *Sere cuanto tu quieres*
> *Porqué me muero si no.*
> *La Fantasía de mi amor*
> *En su corazón te exhalto*
> *Y sigue en mi pecho esmalto*
> *Sin borrar su pundonor*
> *Sí merezco su favor*
>
> *Sí mis cariños recibes*
> *Sí al querete me aparcibes*
> *Sí por mi arriesdas su honor*
> *Sí mis afectos recibes.*
>
> *No me mates con rigor*
> *No me trates con crueldad*
> *No me niegues su lealtad*
> *No desprecies mi favor*
> *Yo—que soy su servidor*
> *Mi amor a ti se incline*
> *No seas ingrata, que yo*
> *A no olvidarte me obligo*
> *No seas ingrata con migo*
> *No me respondas que no.*

There are other *décimas* that I have forgotten.

The respect in which our parents and elderly persons generally were held was so great that no young man ventured to dance in their presence without first having received permission. From 1831-1832 on, customs became less strict; dances became more exclusive and were usually given in the homes of private persons.

What I have said about dances I learned at long distances from them, for I was never permitted to attend one of them until was twenty- or twenty-one-years old. All the other young men were in the same situation.

It was also considered very ill-mannered for a young man to smoke in the presence of an older person, even though the difference in their ages might be only five or six years. I confess that even when I reached an age when I could attend dances, I went to them merely out of curiosity and never danced or sang.

Dances were generally opened by older persons, and the young people were not permitted by any chance to take part in them unless they happened to be married; and even then it was not often allowed. But when the hour came for the old folks to retire, the older of the young fellows began to enjoy the dance.

I have seen in San José Guadalupe, in the North, a misbehavior by some drunken men who entered the *en-ramada*, or arbor, on horseback and jested in a manner disagreeable to the ladies, but this is a thing I never saw in the South, nor did I ever hear of its happening here.

I forgot to say that when a lady was prominent for her skill and grace in *El Son* or *El Jarabe*, the men placed their hats on her head, one on top of the other, and when she could carry no more on her head she took them in her hands; and when she could take no more they threw them at her feet. Then they threw their *mangas*, or wraps, on the floor for her to honor them by dancing on them.

When she retired to her seat, each man had to ransom his hat or other property with money, giving the lady what he could afford or wished to give. Here entered pride and the desire to shine; and as a result no one gave her less than a *peso*, and some gave as much as ten, fifteen, or twenty *pesos*.

* * * *

My life from the age of sixteen years was purely that of a rancher, devoted almost entirely to work in the field. I went to the town only occasionally, and then it was on some urgent business, and I returned without loss of time. This is why I am so poorly informed regarding events that occurred in this country.

Up to the year 1853 I was in good circumstances. If I did not have cash I had cattle or other possessions of value. I had the misfortune to loan my signature as bondsman for other persons in whom I had confidence, and these, for one reason and another, left me as they say vulgarly, "on the horns of the bull," and I had to sacrifice my property and even the house in which I lived to meet these obligations.

As a greater misfortune, this calamity came upon me when I was seriously ill, and unable for many years to re-build my fortune, or at least gain enough for my own subsistence and that of my family. I have a wife and four daughters. Of these only one is married.

—José del C. Lugo
Los Ángeles
October 30, 1877

[José del Carmen Lugo is believed to have died about 1890 at Pasadena, California.]

II.

MY LIFE IN EARLY CALIFORNIA

BY B. D. WILSON

The following narrative of B. D. Wilson was dictated by him at the request of Hubert Howe Bancroft, who was gathering data of California history, and a copy retained by him for himself and family, from which copy this is taken.

I, Benjamin Davis Wilson, of Nashville, Tennessee, was born December 1st, 1811. My father was born in a fort in the Territory of Tennessee in 1772, in what is now Wilson County. He died when I was eight years old, having lost by bad speculation his fortune, which left his family poor.

We, however, were assisted to some education by our grandfather. When I was about fifteen years of age, I went into business for myself at Yazoo City, on the Yazoo River above Vicksburg, where I kept a little trading house to do business with the Choctaw and Chickasaw Indians. My health entirely broke down, and I was told by physicians I could not live in that country, must either leave or die. Went then up the Arkansas River to Fort Smith, an outer post then of the country. The Company I was told to join did not go, for the reason that the River did not rise in time. From there I went to Missouri, joined the Rocky Mountain Company, and crossed the plains with them. Nothing worthy of mention occurred until we reached Santa Fé, in the Fall of 1833.

Being without money, I joined a trapping party, to go and trap in the Gila and Apache country for beaver. The first year there was no event worthy of record, except that we were quite successful; explored the Gila River and returned to Santa Fé in the spring of 1835. Refitted and returned at the head of a small company formed by myself.

I will now relate events connected with this expedition, and its results. The Apaches up to this time had been extremely kind and friendly to the Americans, but owing to bad treatment of their Chief Juan José by the Mexicans, there was a deadly hostility existing between them, the Apaches and Mexicans, which has lasted to the present day. Juan José was educated originally for the Church, and could read and write, and keep accounts, etc. He was really quite an educated man. The Mexicans murdered his father, which prompted him to leave the whites, and place himself at the head of his people, and wage war against the Mexicans. But his relations with the Americans, both traders and hunters, were of the most friendly character, and he never lost an opportunity to show them his friendship. Whenever by any mistake any animals belonging to American parties were stolen by Apaches, Juan José would have them returned to the owners.

There was an American by the name of James Johnson, living and married to a native woman in Oposura, who had during several years been trading between that country and New Mexico, and had thus secured himself quite a competency; he had been invariably an object of friendly regard from the Apaches, and occasionally when some of his stock had been by mistake captured, the same had been returned to him. Indeed, Juan José desired to maintain the best of friendly, as well as uninterrupted, trading relations with American hunters and traders. The Mexican Governor of Sonora was exceedingly anxious to secure the capture and destruction of Juan José, who had become a terror to the Mexicans; he would send out his men and intercept dispatches, and thus keep himself well posted as to the movements of his enemies.

During the two years that I was in that country, Juan José was frequently in our camp and had mails brought to him to read which had been captured by his men. We thus became informed of the military movements contemplated by the Mexican Government. That Government would not give permission to Americans to trade or trap in their territory; we were there as interlopers and smugglers, and would have fared badly had we fallen into the hands of their forces. Juan José's friendship was in every way valuable to us. Returning to my story, the Governor of Sonora made an arrangement, or promise with James Johnson, to kill Juan José whenever the opportunity occurred for doing so, as it was frequent for Juan José and his men to visit Johnson's camp. It was well known to the Governor that the Apaches were friendly to Johnson and all Americans. Of course it was left to Johnson to effect Juan José's destruction, in his own way.

Juan José was generally hovering on the frontier with a small force of reliable young warriors, of about twenty or thirty. Juan José was known to be a fighting man, but his people deemed him too valuable to allow him to expose his person in battle.

All those Gila Apaches had been Misión Indians during the Spanish occupation; after the Mexican independence, the country became disorganized and the frontier Mexicans treated these Indians so badly, without any effort being made by the Government for their protection, that they rebelled and from that time kept up a warfare against everything that bore the name of Mexican. They were a civilized people, and indeed, many of them could not speak Apache, and felt a strong contempt for the wild tribes of Apaches, known under the names of Coyoteros, Mezcaleros, and Jicarillas. The necessities of the war have since made them more friendly, and have allowed them to intermarry with the others.

There was a party under Eames from Missouri that had gone to Sonora to purchase mules, taking with them William Knight (the same man who gave names to "Knight's Ferry" and "Knight's Landing" on the Sacramento) to act as their guide and interpreter. The party consisted of ten or twelve men. They were unsuccessful in their expedition, could find no mules, as the Apaches had stripped the whole country.

They were returning to New Mexico, and took the route suggested to them by James Johnson, as the nearest one through the Apache country, assuring them that there was not the slightest danger from those Indians. Johnson concocted the plan of murdering Juan José with a man by the name of Gleason or Glissón, who also resided at that time in Oposura. Johnson availed himself of Eames's party who were entirely unconscious of the plot to carry out Johnson's plans. All started together, Johnson being the guide. Some days out from Oposura, near the Gila River, they met Juan José, who had heard of their coming and also the arrangement between the Governor and Johnson, which he had obtained through some intercepted dispatches, but gave no credence to the report, as he could not believe that Johnson, whose friend he had ever been, could possibly entertain any project against his life.

In the camp he told Johnson what he had learned, and the latter, of course, assured him there was no foundation for the report. Juan José then said to him, "Don Santiago, you have never deceived me, and if you give me your word of honor that the report is false, come to my camp with your men, and pass the night with us." Johnson repeated his assurance, and all went to Juan José's camp. After arriving there, Johnson said to the Chief that he had a sack of pinoleto to give to the women and children; the sack was taken out that same evening, and Juan José ordered a man to attend to the distribution of the pinole. But all the men, women, and children collected around the sack. This was a part of Johnson's plan. Johnson had a blunderbuss secured under an *aparejo* which had been brought on mule back. The weapon was loaded with balls, chains, etc. Whilst the pinole was being distributed, Gleason had invited Juan José to walk out to where the latter's fine mule was tied, with the pretext that he wanted to buy the mule.

The plan of Johnson and Gleason was that the former would fire the blunderbuss into the crowd, and Gleason was to shoot Juan José at the same time with a pistol. This hellish plot was carried out to the letter; the blunderbuss was fired into the crowd, killing and maiming many. Gleason shot at Juan José, but did not kill him, the latter cried out to his friend Don Santiago to come to his aid, and clenched Gleason, with his knife drawn; when Johnson approached, Juan José told him in Spanish, "For God's sake save my life, I could kill your friend, but I don't want to do it." Johnson's only reply was to shoot Juan José whilst he was over Gleason with his knife drawn. Juan José fell dead on Gleason. Thus perished that fine specimen of a man.

I knew the man well, and can vouch for the fact that he was a perfect gentleman, as well as a kind-hearted man.

After that occurrence, the party had to keep together and fight their way back, for the Indians by smoke and other means had got together a large party and pursued them. Whilst that villainous act of Johnson and his accomplice was taking place, I and my party were camped some thirty miles from Juan José's camp on the Gila River and about forty miles from Charles Kemp and his party of trappers, who were below me on the Gila.

After the Indians fought Johnson's party into Oposura, they went to Kemp's camp, and killed every one of the party, twenty-two in number. I was on the march returning into Santa Fé, entirely ignorant of what had been taking place, my object being to intercept East of the settlement of New Mexico the caravan bound to Missouri.

When we arrived at the trail, we discovered that the caravan had passed there two days before. We then started with the view of overtaking them by forced marches, but were intercepted by a party of Apaches and taken prisoner, everything we had being taken from us.

We were marched to the Apache camp; there we were given to understand that something terrible had happened between the Apaches and Americans, and that the young warriors were determined to sacrifice us. We expressed our astonishment at the changed conduct of the Apaches, from whom we had never before received so many evidences of unfriendly feeling.

That party did not seem to be fully informed of the causes of the change of feeling. In camp that night the Indians kept up a war dance, to the east of the wigwam where the Chief Mangas kept us confined. That old Chief was opposed to our being sacrificed, as he said that he had received many favors from Americans, and believed it was to the interest of his people to keep up the amicable relations existing till that time.

Our party was at this moment reduced to only three; originally there were six, the rest having managed to steal off and reached the settlements with some of the property, leaving the balance in our hands to be turned over to their friends in Missouri; of course, that was before we were captured.

Mangas had told us that he had been doing his best to dissuade his men from destroying us, but unsuccessfully; finally, at a late hour of the night, Mangas came in greatly excited, and said he had to return to his warriors and one of us must leave, as it was the only way he could save the others. I asked my men what we should do—one named Maxwell had a sprained ankle and could not walk, the other named Tucker was a kind of invalid—he replied that if he was to die, it would be as well to die there, as he could not possibly get into the settlements distant one hundred and fifty miles on foot. So it was concluded that I should go and that forthwith, because from the Chief's intimation, the warriors were coming in a few minutes to take us out and burn us alive, for which they had been already preparing the wood.

I caught up a small buffalo robe, threw it over my shoulders (the Indians had stripped us of all clothing), and left.

The camp was situated at the base of a little stony mountain on the prairie. I started up the hill and had not been out but a few moments, when I could hear a general turmoil in the camp, and the whole country soon swarmed with horsemen who had started in all directions in pursuit of me. I heard them in my rear, and crept into a rent in some large rocks where I remained perfectly still, till they passed me and I heard them all going back to their camp. The mountain was about twenty miles from a deep canyon, the only hiding place in all the country.

I had, therefore, to get into the canyon before daylight, for in that plain a man could be seen from the hill in the daylight at the distance of twenty miles in all directions.

I ran and walked as hard as I could, and succeeded in getting into the canyon just as the day was breaking; got on the ledge, and sat down to rest before hiding myself.

As I had expected, at daylight the plains were full of horsemen. I slid down into the deep chasm or cut among the vines and brush, and remained there all day without food; and what was worse, had the prospect before me of over one hundred miles to march without nourishment. The next night was also a perilous one, having thirty miles of prairie to cross before I could get into the next hiding place. That night I walked the thirty miles and got into the spur of the Rocky Mountains, traveled until daylight, rested a while, and went on in a fine-looking country. I traveled all that day, and kept on after taking a little rest. During the night, and when near daylight on that third night, I unexpectedly arrived at a sheep ranch that I knew nothing of.

I there got some mutton and "*atole*." My shoes were entirely worn out, my feet bleeding. I stayed there the whole day with the herder, who had the kindness to make me a pair of moccasins out of some untanned sheep skins with the wool on them. I continued my journey until I reached the settlements at a place called Mouo, where I procured a pair of shoes and some food.

Finally, I walked in about three or four days' time the one hundred miles or upwards intervening between that place and Santa Fé, where I arrived without money, clothing, or friends, not even an acquaintance, and perfectly worn out. Two days after, news arrived of the disaster to a party of Americans known at that time as the Keykendall party (pronounced Kurkindall), about one hundred and fifty miles south of Santa Fé on the El Paso road at a place called Point of Rocks. Someone approached me, inquiring who and what I was, and upon giving him the required information, he told me they were seeking for someone to go out to the place of disaster with a party of men to bury the dead and do anything that circumstance might call for.

I offered my services, provided they would give me a suit of clothes and an animal to ride. I started the same evening; three or four Americans accompanied me. We had letters from the Governor of Santa Fé to the Alcaldes Río Abajo to furnish us all the men we might need. We reached the scene of the disaster and found twelve dead bodies in a state of decomposition, dug a large pit, and deposited the bodies therein. Found many burnt wagons, but nothing of any value. I returned to Santa Fé and made a report. I had not been back many days when a merchant offered me a clerkship in his store, with wages at $25.00 per month and edibles, which I had to cook myself. I remained with him only three or four months.

Whilst I was there, Dr. Josiah Gregg (afterwards the author of a work on the prairies) arrived with a large quantity of merchandise; wishing to pass on with a portion of his goods to Chihuahua, he engaged me to take charge of the rest of his goods. I attended to all his business to his satisfaction.

This now brings us to the winter of 1836-1837. About this time, Mr. Eames and his party arrived from Oposura, and remained in Santa Fé over the winter. Eames lived with me during that time; he related to me all that passed in connection with Juan José's murder. Johnson met with the retribution that his crime deserved: he received no reward from the Mexican Government. Oposura was besieged by the Apaches so effectively that he could do no business whatever, had to sell his property, left his family there, and escaped.

He came to California, lived in great poverty, and died near Gilroy some years later. I never met him in California, nor did I wish to come again in contact with such a wretch.

His act of treachery caused the destruction of a large number of Americans, and the Apache war has continued from that day to this. Eames's arrival in Santa Fé brought us the first full information as to the cause of my own, Kemps's, and Keykendall's disaster.

My two men, Maxwell and Tucker, were not killed; they got away, but I never saw them again. I learned that Tucker died some years later; I also learned that Mangas the Chief had a row with his people, who broke his arm. He frequently visited me in Santa Fé afterwards, and in consideration of his services to me and my companions, was a pensioner of mine.

Myself and my expedition, six men all told, once found ourselves absolutely without anything to eat; the only result to us was a great weakness. On the evening of the sixth day, getting off our mules we felt so weak that we became very much alarmed about our condition, so I had no other recourse but to shoot dead my faithful mule that I had ridden over a thousand miles, it being the only animal that showed any flesh. I feel sorry about that mule yet, the killing of which occurred some forty-two years ago.

On our return, as before mentioned, to intercept the Misión caravan, after crossing the Del Norte at the head of Jomacta going eastward to the River Pecos, we had the misfortune to find no water until the fifth day at night. On the fourth day, crossing an arid sandy plain leading North to South between two parallel mountains, we saw to the North of us in the midst of this plain a large building which encouraged us to believe that our water trouble was at an end. We went to the building and found it to be a large Church. On the northern side of the building we saw evidences that there had been on that site a very large town. The Church itself was built of stone, and stood almost in a perfect state of preservation, while all the other buildings had decayed. We spent the whole day looking for water without any success.

Just at night I discovered on the eastern side what satisfied me were the remains of a concrete aqueduct. Camped there that night; next morning I endeavored to trace the aqueduct, which led easterly to a mountain range. Spent the whole day in tracing it to ascertain which was the gorge it entered, believing we should find water there. Our hopes were gratified and our terrific sufferings ended. I had already had the experience of six days without food, and one of five without water, and state the suffering caused by the former bears no comparison with that of the latter. No living man unless he has had the opportunity of feeling it or seeing it with his own eyes could realize how much flesh a man may lose in five days without water. Every joint in our bodies ached, our eyes sunk in our heads as if we had been dead a week, and the bones seemed to be pushing through the skin. After my return to Santa Fé I narrated our discovery of that building, and some enthusiastic men went in search of it; they called it the Grand Quivira. Those men dug for treasure and reported that they had discovered some five miles from the building, a place where extensive mining operations had been carried on by some civilized people, yet the best informed of the Mexicans could give us no information on the matter. The whole thing was involved in mystery.

I forgot to mention while speaking of my first expedition to the Gila country under Keiker, a remarkable place some twelve miles from where the Little Red River (Colorado Chiquita) leaves the mountains; there was a village built on a sugar loaf-like mound near the banks of the River which left on the mind the impression that the mound was made by human hands, as it was entirely alone in a perfectly plain country within the bounds of what had been an extensively cultivated field. The *zanja madre*, or main ditch, some ten or fifteen miles in length, was plainly visible, covering a plot of ground some one thousand acres, as near as I could judge, the *regaderos* or cross ditches were also clearly seen. In the mound several feet above the base was a row of buildings, or rather rooms, in a perfect state of preservation, and the rooms seemed to serve as the roofing. In the rooms we found a great quantity of dried corncobs. About two miles easterly lie some spurs of the Sierra Madre Project, and are pretty much covered with junipers and other cedars; the soil of a very sticky red clay.

At the foot of these hills our mule herders found a quantity of stone-like bullets, of about the average musket ball size; they brought them to us, saying that they were very large quantities of the same kind. Our curiosity led us to go and examine them for ourselves. We thought there must be wagon loads of such bullets, so great was the quantity strewn upon the ground. We were thoroughly convinced that those bullets were the work of men, as many bore the appearance of having been molded, with the necks still on. My impression is that they were molded from red clay, and age had petrified them. I leave a wiser man to explain.

I deem it proper to record, now that I remember it, some additional names of the parties that crossed from New Mexico with us, which were omitted in speaking of our journey to California. Dr. J. H. Lyman, of Northampton, Mass., stayed in California about eighteen months, returned home, and married. I saw him some three months since; he now resides in San Francisco. He brought with him his family, one member of which I saw, who is also a physician. On the River Sevier in Utah Territory, Dr. Lyman and myself had stopped behind the train to fish. It was in the evening, the

76

Doctor being with his hook and line in the water, the fish biting very well. He spoke to me that a very large fish had bit at his hook and got off. Just as he was talking a ball from an Indian gun struck the ground near him; he remarked very coolly, "That fellow can't hit me, so therefore I will stay and get this fish before I leave," and he did so.

Dr. Mead had been a practicing physician in the West India Islands, and afterwards became a Bishop of the Episcopal Church. He was a Virginian; on his arrival in California after a sojourn of several months, he succeeded in obtaining a passage to China, where he wished to go, I believe on a man-of-war. Dr. Campbell was an ornithologist. He was a very young man at that time, but made himself by his collection on that trip and in California quite an enviable reputation.

He has since become a distinguished man among scientists. He was from Philadelphia, on a scientific expedition from some society. John Behn, a German, afterwards married in this district, where he lived many years. He died some eight or ten years since, leaving several children. Michael White, my neighbor now, and an Englishman by birth, and originally a sailor, had lived and married in California before, and had a family; he was a man of roving disposition. Loomes, who died a few years since, lived as a rancher on the Sacramento near Colusa for many years; a very respectable man.

Daniel Sexton, from Arkansas, now lives in San Bernardino County. John Reed from Missouri, who was married in New Mexico to a daughter of Mr. John Rowland, died a few years ago, leaving only his wife, who still lives on the La Puente Ranch.

There were others whose names I don't remember. They scattered over the country and never made any mark.

In 1837 there was a great revolution in Santa Fé; the Governor, Alvino Pérez, and all his officers, and every other respectable man that had in any way been connected with the Governor, were killed. Armijo, who had until that time been merely a successful sheep-man, headed the Pueblo Indians and the New Mexican rabble, and made that revolution. After Governor Pérez, the three Obica brothers, and the rest had been murdered, the rebels went through the City with the murdered men's heads stuck on pikes, crying, "Death to the Americans, Death to the Gringos." There were besides myself about six Americans; the deceased Major Samuel Hensley was one of them. We shut ourselves up and remained so for six days, till the riot was over.

The rioters tried to get into our store, but the old Indian Chief Pedro León, who was at the head of the Pueblo Indians, and was acquainted with me, saved us by declaring to the others that we were not in the store, so they all went away.

That time I did really expect that our lives were not worth the purchase. Armijo, as soon as the rabble dispersed to their homes, and the Territory was left completely disorganized and without a government, issued a call for the leaders to hold a convention in Santa Fé, and on their arrival there from all parts of the Territory, he had a squad of his own satellites arrest the leading men, thirty-two in number, marched them back on the hill behind the public square of Santa Fé, and the next morning had them all shot. After that he declared himself loyal to the Mexican Government, and soon his commission as Governor of the Territory arrived. He was the man who in 1841 captured Col. Cook and his company, one of whom was Mr. Geo. Wilkins Kendall, one of the editors of the *New Orleans Picayune*.

The fellow who betrayed the Cook party received no other compensation from Armijo than a few hundred dollars, and a peremptory order to leave the territory. Armijo had promised to reward him with an office in the Custom House, but afterwards told him that he could not trust a man who had been a traitor to his own people. This I learned afterwards from a source entirely reliable, Mr. John Rowland, who had obtained the facts from Armijo's own lips. Rowland died here in Southern California a few years ago at the Puente Ranch, which he owned.

I remained in charge of Dr. Gregg's business some two years, and then bought out the remainder of the goods, and remained in Santa Fé till the fall of 1841. Mr. John Rowland and William Workman, who were old residents of that country at Taos, and had been in correspondence with prominent parties in Texas, learned that a party or expedition was being fitted out to come and take New Mexico, as part of Texas. They were convinced that the plan might succeed, but, in the meantime, prominent foreigners in New Mexico would probably be sacrificed to the fury of the Mexicans. As it was, Armijo had information that the Texans were coming. This was in the summer of 1841.

It was even whispered that we were in correspondence with the Texans. One day, as Armijo was haranguing his rabble to rise to a man and meet the foreigners who were coming to destroy their customs and religion, an American French Creole from near St. Louis, who was a bold gambler named Tiboux, made some insulting remarks in a stentorious voice. This came very near to being the destruction of all of us, for the whole wave of the rabble moved toward us, but fortunately Armijo called them back, promising to punish the offender; however, he was not found out, and came out to California with us in the fall. Under the circumstances, Rowland, Workman, and myself, together with about twenty other Americans, including William Gordon and William Knight, concluded it was not safe for us to remain longer in New Mexico.

We formed a party and were joined by a large number of New Mexicans. In the first week of September, 1841, we started from our rendezvous in the most western part of New Mexico, a place called "Abiqui," for California; we met with no accidents on the journey, drove sheep with us which served us with food, and arrived in Los Ángeles early in November of the same year.

As far as I am able to judge, Rowland, Workman, Gordon, Knight, and most of the foreigners of our party came here with the intention of settling. I had no such idea; my plan was to go to China, and from thence return home. But after three different journeys to San Francisco in search of a ship to go to China, I arrived at the conclusion that there would no chance for carrying out my original intention, and so I finally purchased a Ranch in 1843 called the Jurupa, and stocked it with cattle. That place is now Riverside. In the spring of 1842 Mr. Rowland and myself went to Monterey to see Governor Alvarado.

Mr. Rowland had obtained from the priest at San Gabriel, and from the Prefect of the Second District, certificates stating that there was no objection to the granting to Messrs. Rowland and Workman the Ranch of La Puente, which they had petitioned for, as such a grant would not be prejudicial to the Neophytes.

Upon the presentation of the documents to the Governor the grant was made to the petitioners, who were entitled to the privilege under Mexican law, being married to Mexican wives, natives of New Mexico, and having made application for Mexican citizenship.

I never got any grant of land, as I could not apply for Mexican citizenship. The Jurupa Ranch I bought from Don Juan Bandini. I am under the impression that the law did not forbid the owning of land by a foreigner, provided it was at a certain distance from the sea coast. I am not sure whether it was from twenty to twenty-five miles. This was either a law or regulation issued by the Supreme Authority of México.

After many unsuccessful efforts to leave California, and receiving so much kindness from the native Californians, I arrived at the conclusion that there was no place in the world where I could enjoy more true happiness and true friendship than among them. There were no courts, no juries, no lawyers, nor any need for them. The people were honest and hospitable, and their word was as good as their bond; indeed, bonds and notes of hand were entirely unknown among the natives. So as I said I settled upon the Ranch, and led a rancheros' life for some years.

In 1844, I married Ramona Yorba, a daughter of Don Bernardo Yorba, one of the owners of the Santa Ana Ranch, which had about thirty leagues of land. No event of any serious import occurred in my rancher's life, except the following—in the fall of 1844, my ranchman reported that a large bear had been close to the ranch house and killed one of our best milk cows.

I took an American named Evan Callaghan with me, and went to hunt for the grizzly. We separated, and he went one path, and I went by the one leading from the cow's carcass. I followed the track a few hundred yards, and it went under an elder bush covered with wild vines. Thinking the bear had passed out on the other side and going around the bush myself, I became entangled in another bush. In that condition the bear rushed from under his cover and bounded on behind me, bringing both the horse and myself to the ground; he bit me on the right shoulder into the lung, and once in the left hip. By this time my dogs came up and the bear left me, a *vaquero* was coming to me when I managed to get up, and walked a few steps into an open space. I told the *vaquero* to take the saddle and bridle off the horse, as I supposed it was dead, but when the *vaquero* approached the horse, he raised his head, looked around, sprung to his feet, and ran home at full gallop with the saddle and bridle. Upon examination he was found entirely unharmed; his instinct had told him to feign death as long as he thought the bear was thereabouts.

It is well known that the bear is not a carrion beast. I was carried home and laid upon a blanket, where I bled so that I lost my sight and speech, though I still retained the power of my senses. A few native Californian women came to my assistance, and by their judicious nursing I was soon on my feet again. But I still carry on my shoulder the marks of that bear's tusks, in the form of a large hole which can hold a walnut.

The bear in question remained on the ranch, killing cattle almost every night. As soon as I felt myself able to move around, I advised my *vaquero* to kill a calf and drag it through the bush near where the bear lurked, and leave it under a certain sycamore tree. I then took a servant with me, both well-armed, and repaired to the tree; at the approach of dark the bear made his appearance and commenced eating the calf; myself and my man both fired at him out of the tree, and both hit him, and the bear made three attempts to climb to us, but my man's shot crippled one of his hind legs, my shot having struck him through the ribs behind the shoulder. He went away, and we returned to the house. The next morning I called all the neighbors, servants, and dogs, and everyone that I could find, and went to hunt that bear. We trailed him to a marsh after diligent search for him, and almost despaired of finding him, when my attention was called to a hole in the mud no larger than a blackbird. When I became satisfied that it was the bear's nose, I got off my horse to give him a deadly shot in the head. He jumped out with the rapidity of lightning and made for me, who stood about twenty feet from him. He came very near catching me a second time; a general flight followed, and the beast was finally put to death.

I have mentioned this part of the occurrence to corroborate what I have been told by others, that bears have the sagacity to seek the healing of their wounds with application of mud.

In 1845, about July or August, the Mojave and other Indians were constantly raiding upon the ranchos in this part of the country, and at the request of the Governor, Don Pío Pico, who had promised me a force of eighty well-mounted men, well-armed, I took command of an expedition to go in pursuit of the Indians.

I organized the expedition in San Bernardino, and sent the pack train and soldiers (less than twenty-two which I retained with me) through the Cajón Pass; myself and twenty-two men went up the San Bernardino River through the mountains, and crossed over to what is now Bear Lake. Before arriving at the Lake we captured a village, the people of which had all left, except two old women and some children. On the evening of the second day we arrived at the Lake, and the whole Lake and swamp seemed alive with bear.

The twenty-two Californians went out in pairs, and each pair lassoed one bear, and brought the result to the camp, so that we had at one and the same time eleven bears. This prompted me to give the Lake the name it now bears.

We pursued our course down the Mojave River, before we met the balance of the command. Then all together we marched down some four days. I was in advance with one companion some two or three miles, with the view of looking for signs of Indians.

I saw ahead of us four Indians on the path looking towards us; noticing that they had not seen us, I went down into the river bed, and continued on my course until a point was reached that I supposed was opposite to where they would be, and then went up on the bank again. My calculation was correct, the Indians were right opposite on the plain, and I rode towards them. I spoke to them and they answered in a very friendly manner. My object was not to kill them, but to take them prisoners that they might give me information on the points I desired.

The leading man of the four happened to be the very man of all I was seeking for, *viz.*: the famous marauder Joaquín who had been raised as a page of the Church in San Gabriel Misión, and for his depredations and outlawing bore on his person the mark of the Misión, that is, one of his ears cropped off, and the iron brand on his lip. This is the only instance I ever saw or heard of this kind. That marking had not been done at the Misión, but at one of its ranchos (El Chino) by the Majordomo.

I entered into conversation with Joaquín; the command was coming on, and he then became convinced that we were on a campaign against him and his people. It was evident before that he had taken me for a traveler. Immediately he discovered the true state of things, he whipped from his quiver an arrow, strung it on his bow, and left nothing for me to do but shoot him in self-defense; we both discharged our weapons at the same time. I had no chance to raise the gun to my shoulder, but fired it from my hand; his shot took effect in my right shoulder, and mine in his heart.

The shock of his arrow in my shoulder caused me to involuntarily let my gun drop. My shot knocked him down disabled, but he discharged at me a tirade of abuse in the Spanish language such as I have never heard surpassed. I was on mule back and got down to pick up my gun; by this time my command arrived at the spot. The other three Indians were making off out over the plains. I ordered my man to capture them alive, but the Indians resisted stoutly, refused to the last to surrender, wounded several of our horses and two or three men, and had to be killed.

Those three men actually fought eighty men in open plain till they were put to death. During the fight Joaquín laid on the ground uttering curses and abuse against the Spanish race and people. I discovered that I was shot with a poisoned arrow, rode down some five hundred yards to the River, and some of my men on returning and finding that

83

Joaquín was not dead, finished him. I had to proceed immediately to the care of my wound.

There was with me a Comanche Indian, a trusty man, who had accompanied me from New Mexico to California. The only remedy we knew of was the sucking of the poison with the mouth out of the wound. Indeed, there is no other remedy known, even now. I have frequently seen the Indians preparing the poison, and it is nothing more than putrid meat or liver and blood, which they dried into thin sticks and carried in leather sheaths. When they went on hunting or campaigning expeditions they repeatedly whetted their arrows with this stick; when it was too dry, they softened it by holding it near the fire a little while.

By the time I got to the River, my arm and shoulder were immensely swollen; at once my faithful Comanche, Lorenzo Trujillo, applied himself to sucking the wound, which was extremely painful. He soon began reducing the swelling, and in the course of three or four days it had entirely disappeared, and the wound in a fair way of healing; it never gave me any trouble after, although there was left in the flesh a small piece of flint, which I carry to this day. As I was unable to travel while the wound was healing, I kept with me five men of the command, and ordered the rest to proceed down the River on the campaign, till they found the Indians; they went under command of my second, Enrique Ávila, a native Californian and resident of Los Ángeles.

After an absence of over two days, they returned to my camp, and reported that about ten leagues below camp they had struck a fresh trail of Indians; pursuing it up a rocky mountain, they found the Indians fortified in the rocks, attacked them a whole day, and finally were obliged to leave the Indians in their position and come away with several men badly wounded.

I had to abandon the campaign, as besides the wounded men, the command had all their horses worn out. On the return by the way of Bear Lake, the same twenty-two men that went with me to that Lake, repeated the feat of bringing eleven bears to camp, making twenty-two killed on the trip. We all returned and had our rendezvous at my Ranch of Jurupa to refit with new horses, provisions, etc., for another campaign. Some twenty of these men for wounds or other causes left, and the command was reduced to about sixty.

Our march this time was through the San Gorgonio Pass, where the railroad now runs, down into the Cahuilla country, our object being this time to capture two renegade San Gabriel neophytes, who had taken up their residence among the Cahuillas, and corrupted many of the young men of that tribe with whom they carried on a constant depredation on the ranchmen of this district.

Nothing of note occurred on our journey, till we arrived at the head of the desert, in the place called Agua Caliente (Hot Springs). We were there met by the Chief of the Cahuillas, whose name was Cabezón (Big Head), with about twenty of his picked followers, to remonstrate against our going upon a campaign against his people, for he had ever been good and friendly to the whites. I made known to him that I had no desire to wage war on the Cahuillas, as I knew them to be what was said of them, but that I had come with the determination of seizing the two renegade Christians, who were continually depredating on our people. He then tried to frighten me out of the notion of going into his country, alleging that it was sterile and devoid of grass and water, and that ourselves and our horses would perish there. I replied that I had long experience in that sort of life, and was satisfied that a white man, by placing the Chief and his party under arrest and taking away their arms, [would be safe]. He became very much alarmed, and cried and begged of me not to arrest him, as he had always been a good man.

I assured him that I would avoid, if possible, doing him or his people any harm, but had duties to perform, and I intended carrying them out in my own way. I then sternly remarked to him there were but two ways to settle the matter; one was for me to march forward with my command, looking upon the Indians I met as enemies, till I had got hold of the two Christians; the other was for him to detach some of his trusty men, and bring the two robbers dead or alive to my camp. He again protested, but when he saw that I was on the point of marching forward, he called me to him, and said that he and his men had held counsel together, and that if I would release his brother Adám, and some twelve more of his people whom he pointed out, himself and six or seven more remaining as hostages, Adám would bring those malefactors to me, if I would wait where we then had our camp.

I at once acceded to his petition, released Adám and the other twelve, and let them have their arms.

I told them to go on their errand, first asking how many days they would require to accomplish it. They asked for two days and nights. We stayed there that night and all the next day with the most oppressive heat I had ever experienced; it was so hot that we could not sit down, but had to stand up and fan ourselves with our hats; the ground would burn us when we attempted to sit.

Late the following night, the Chief called me and asked me to put my ear to the ground, stating that he heard a noise as if men were coming. I did as he desired and heard a rumbling noise which at every moment became clearer. In the course of an hour we could begin to hear voices, and the old Chief remarked to me with much satisfaction that it was all right, he could tell by the singing of his men that they had been successful in their errand. I ordered thirty of my men to mount their horses, and go to meet them to see if all was right, as it was possible those Indians were coming with hostile views.

In due time, the horsemen came back and reported that they believed all was right. I then had my men under arms, and waited the arrival of the party, which consisted of forty or fifty warriors. Adám ordered the party to halt some four hundred yards from my camp, himself and another companion advancing, each one carrying the head of one of the malefactors, which they threw at my feet, with the evident marks of pleasure at the successful results of their expedition; Adám at the same time showed me an arrow in one of his thighs which he had received in the skirmish that took place against those two Christians and their friends. Several others had been wounded, but none killed except the two renegade Christians.

By this time day was breaking and we started on our return. The campaign being at an end, I left the Indians with the two heads at Agua Caliente, after giving them all our spare rations, which were very considerable, as they had been prepared in the expectation of a long campaign.

After we reached our homes and dispersed, there arrived at my Ranch of Jurupa some ten or twelve American trappers (it was in the same summer). I related to them how our campaign ended down the Mojave with the defeat of my force.

They manifested a strong desire to accompany me back there. The Chief of that party was Van Duzen. I at once wrote to my old friend and companion Don Enrique Ávila, to ask him if he would join me with ten picked men, and renew our campaign down the River Mojave. He answered that he would do so, "*con mucho gusto.*" He came forthwith and we started for the trip, twenty-one strong.

Some seven or eight days after we reached the field of operations, myself and Ávila being in advance. We described an Indian village. I at once directed my men to divide into two parties to surround and attack the village. We did it successfully, but as on the former occasion, the men in the place would not surrender, and on my endeavoring to persuade them to give up, they shot one of my men, Evan Callaghan (mentioned before), in the back. I thought he was mortally wounded, and commanded my men to fire; the fire was kept up until every Indian man was slain.

We took the women and children prisoners. While the fighting had been going on, a sad accident occurred between two Mexican servants that had charge of the pack train and loose animals. My servant had my double-barreled gun that I had given to him to carry; he had handed it to the other man to hold while he was righting a pack mule, but hearing our firing, he demanded of the other man to hand him back the gun, which the latter declined. Both men were on horseback; my man grabbed the gun and the other punched back at him with the breach, the hammer of the lock struck my man in the forehead just above the eye, the gun went off, shooting the man that held it, and the two ball charges entered his body just below the heart; he died in a few hours.

After burying the dead man, we found that we had to remain camped there all night, owing to the suffering of our wounded, Evan Callaghan. Fortunately, the next morning he was able to travel and we marched on our return home, bringing with us the captured Indian women and children. We found that these women could speak Spanish very well, and had also been neophytes, and that the men we had killed had been the same who had defeated my command the first time, and were likewise Misión Indians.

We turned the women and children over to the Misión San Gabriel, where they remained. Those three short campaigns left our district wholly free from Indian depredations till after the change of Government.

I will now relate the part I acted in the campaign between the Micheltorena and California parties in 1845.

General Micheltorena's officers and men were all well-known to the people of Los Ángeles, for they had been here several months before they went up to Monterey. Whilst Micheltorena and a few of his officers were unobjectionable men, there were at the time a majority, much the larger number of them, who were a disgrace to any civilization.

They had made themselves obnoxious by their thefts and other outrages of a most hideous nature. Hence, when it was announced that a revolution had broken out in the North against Micheltorena and his rabble, and that they were on their way here in pursuit of the California Revolutionists, all classes joined the movement with great alacrity, to get the country rid of what was considered a great scourge.

I was on my Ranch of Jurupa at the time, in the early part of 1845. I had been for several years, and still was acting as the Alcalde of the district. I had at first refused to accept the duties; not being a citizen of México, I was not obliged to perform municipal duties, but at the request of friends and for the defense of my own interests, I had finally consented, and was acting as such Alcalde when an order came to me from the Prefect of the District (I think it was Abel Stearns) to summon every man I could find on my way into Los Ángeles. I obeyed, and arrived as early as possible with some twenty or thirty men, and found on my arrival in the town great excitement; almost every man I knew— among them John Rowland and William Workman of La Puente—were armed and determined to do everything in his power to prevent Micheltorena and his scum from entering Los Ángeles. All provisions were made, and ammunition prepared that night for us to march out early the next morning.

Accordingly, we did all leave the town for the Cahuenga Valley. Mr. Workman had some Americans under him. We joined our forces without regard to who commanded; our joint force of foreigners then consisted of about fifty men, determined to give the enemy a regular mountaineer reception. Although José Castro was ostensibly the Commanding General of the forces, the brothers Pico, Governor Pico and Andrés, had the actual control of the people of this end of the country. We arrived in the Valley of Cahuenga, and Pío Pico heard that Micheltorena had camped the night before at the Encino, about fifteen miles above.

We took our position and awaited the enemy's arrival; this was about noon. Both parties began firing their cannon at each other as soon as they were in sight. I think that no one was killed or hurt; one horse, I believe, had his head shot off. Mr. Workman and myself, having learned that the Americans and other foreigners in the Micheltorena party were commanded by some of our old personal friends, and feeling convinced that they had engaged themselves on that side under misapprehension or ill advice, and that nothing was wanting but a proper understanding between them and us to make them withdraw from Micheltorena and join our party. We sent our native Californians to reconnoiter, and ascertain in what part of the field those foreigners were. We soon obtained the desired information of their whereabouts. It was at once decided between Mr. Workman and myself that I was to approach them if possible under a white flag, as I had a personal acquaintance with the leaders. Captain [Henry] Brandt and Major Banot, who had been an old Army officer in the United States service, had chief command of the foreign force.

Mr. James McKinley of Monterey volunteered to accompany me with a white flag. They were stationed in the same ravine that we were in, but about a mile above us. We succeeded in getting to the point we started for, and raised our white flag, at which time we were fired upon by cannon loaded with grape shot, but no one was hurt and we had gained our point; the Americans on the other side had seen our flag.

We dropped down immediately into the ravine, and waited awhile for the coming of someone from that side. Brandt, Hensley, John Bidwell, and some two or three others came to us. I at once addressed myself to them saying, that they were on the wrong side of this question, and made the following statement:

> We in the southern portion of California are settled, many of you are settled, and others expect to be settled. This rabble that you are with of Micheltorena's are unfriendly to respectable humanity, and especially to Americans. The native Californians whose side we have espoused have ever treated us [well]. If the Micheltorena rabble hold their own in this country, that will constitute an element hostile to all enterprises, and most particularly American enterprises.

Captain Brandt remarked that thus far I was right; that he could see the point. But many of his young men that were with him had been induced to join Micheltorena by his promise to give them land, of which many already held deeds, and how would Don Pío Pico feel towards these young men and their land grants if they aided to raise him to the position of Governor of California? I replied that in the same morning I had had a talk with Don Pío on this same subject, and that he had said that the thing could be easily arranged.

Furthermore, that Don Pío was there, where I could have him advised of what was going on, and he would in a few minutes join us, if these gentlemen desired to see him. I was asked to send for Governor Pico, and he came in a few moments. I knew and so did Pico that these land questions were the point with these young Americans, before I started on my journey or embassy.

On Don Pío's arrival among us, I in a few words explained to him what the other party had advanced, and he said this:

"Gentlemen, are any of you citizens of México?"
They answered, "No."

Then your title deeds given you by Micheltorena are not worth the paper they are written on, and he knew it well when he gave them to you. But if you will abandon the Micheltorenas cause, I will give you my word of honor as a gentleman, and that of Don Benito Wilson and Don Julián Workman, to carry out what I promise you, *viz*:
I will protect all and each one of you in the land that you hold now, in quiet and peaceful possession, and promise you further, that if you will take the necessary steps to become citizens of México, I under my authority and the laws of México will issue to your people proper titles.

He also added that they need not hurry themselves to become citizens of México, and he would not disturb them in the possession of their lands; but advised that they should become such citizens, for then their titles would be invulnerable.

I interpreted to them what Pico had said; they bowed and said that was all they asked, and promised not to fire a gun against us, and, at the same time, expressed the desire of not being asked to fight on our side, as they had marched down with the other party, to which we all assented. Brandt and his companions returned to their camp. McKinley and myself went to ours and the Governor to his headquarters.

Micheltorena had discovered (how I don't know) that his Americans had abandoned him. He at once, about an hour afterwards, raised his camp, and flanked us by going further into the valley towards San Fernando, marching as though he intended to come around the bend of the River to the City.

91

The Californians and we the foreigners at once broke up our camp, came back through the Cahuenga Pass, marched through the gap in the Feliz Ranch on to the Los Ángeles River, till we came in close proximity to Micheltorena's camp. It was now in the night, as it was dark when we broke up our camp.

Here we waited for daylight, and some of our men commenced maneuvering for a fight with the enemy, when a white flag was discovered flying from Micheltorena's front.

The whole matter then went into the hands of negotiators appointed by both parties, and the terms of surrender were agreed upon, one of which was that Micheltorena and his obnoxious officers and men were to march back up the creek to the Cahuenga Pass, down to the plains west of Los Ángeles, the most direct route for San Pedro, and embark at that point on a vessel there anchored to carry them back to México.

After that campaign we all went home perfectly satisfied with the result.

I returned to my ranch and devoted myself entirely to stock raising till 1846, when war was declared between México and the United States, and Commodore [John] Sloat raised the white flag over Monterey. But prior to that event the so-called "Bear Party" seized Sonoma, making prisoners of some of the officers residing there. The news of these events caused general uneasiness in this part of the country. But the excitement here culminated in the summer, when the American forces were reported on the march to Los Ángeles. I was still discharging the duties of Alcalde, or Justice of the Peace, in my district, when I received a communication from the Governor, asking my most active cooperation to raise forces, wherewith to repel the invaders.

I replied that I must respectfully declined, being an American citizen and not a military man. I was then menaced with arrest if I did not comply. I gathered around me about one dozen Americans who had left town, when it was unpleasant and even unsafe for them to be there at that time. I did say to someone who came to make known to me that I would either have to act or be arrested, I believe it was Felipe Lugo, or one of his brothers, that I would not allow

92

myself to be arrested; and sent a message to Governor Pico not to make the attempt to arrest me, for I would resist. But if he would consider that I was not a Mexican citizen, nor a man disposed to do military duty, and to allow me to remain quietly on my ranch, I would pledge my word to be peaceable and do no act hostile to the country.

That pledge of mine seemed to have been satisfactory, as I heard nothing more until Commodore [Robert F.] Stockton had arrived with his squadron in San Pedro Bay, when I received a private friendly note from Governor Pico, requesting me to come and see him, as he was desirous of holding some conversation with me.

I came immediately to Los Ángeles and waited on the Governor, who received me as usual, in the politest and most friendly manner. After the salutations, he said, "My time here as Governor is no doubt very short. You have always been a friend of mine, and are married to a daughter of one of my warmest friends. What can I do for you?" He asked me if there was no tract of land that I would like him to grant me whilst he had, as he thought, the power to do it. I answered laughingly, declining, as I was not a citizen, to which he remarked with a laugh, that everyone thought I was, even if I was not. Governor Pico went on to say that tomorrow would probably be his last day; that he was going to leave, for he gave no credence to Castro's assertions of intending to attempt repelling the American forces

I had frequent interviews with the Governor till the hour he left, and on my taking leave of him he said with a smile, "You go tomorrow, meet Stockton, wherever he may be, *y dele muchas saludes de mi parte*, tell him of my intention to abandon the country, and that I hope he will not ill treat my people." I went the next morning accompanied by John Rowland and others to meet Commodore Stockton, to whom I communicated the news that José Castro had broken camp and left, and Governor Pico had departed from Los Ángeles, intending to make his way to Sonora. When I had given this information to the Commodore, he held in his hand Castro's bombastic proclamation of the previous morning and requested me to read it to him. I read it, and assured the Commodore it had been issued by Castro to give time for his own leaving. On my way down, I was requested by one of the Domínguez to present to the Commodore with his compliments his favorite saddle horse, equipped for the Commodore's personal use, which had been led down by Domínguez's servant. After a short conversation I invited the Commodore to mount his steed and come with us to the City, assuring him that there would be no danger in his doing so, and his troops might march up at their leisure. We rode into town together and had a pleasant time. His mariners arrived late the same evening. Everything was perfectly quiet, and everybody seemed perfectly satisfied. All knew that Governor Pico and General Castro, with a certain number of followers, were on their way out of the country. The natives had dispersed, and returned to their usual avocations.

I remained a few days about the town of Los Ángeles visiting the Commodore frequently, and rendering him such friendly services as were in my power. On my last visit to him before leaving for my Ranch, I told him that I had done all I could for him, and must go to look after my private affairs. He answered with some seriousness, laying his hand on my shoulder (Stockton is a politician as well as a soldier), "I don't think we ought to place too much reliance on Castro's actual leaving for Sonora; he may go to Sonora, or he may only go to the frontier and await for a rabble of Sonorans to come back and retake the country, and it is my duty as Commander, and for the interest of this country, that I should have someone on the frontier watching events." He added that upon inquiry, my friends had told him I was a proper man to perform that important service. I replied, assuring him of my willingness to do all in my power to meet his views, but that I was a civilian and did not wish to engage in military service. He laughingly said, "That is nonsense. You have a Ranch on the frontier, there is no other person in whom I can trust who knows the people or understands their language. Therefore accept a Captaincy from me, and make up your own command of as many men as you please." He knew there were many Americans thereabouts that I could bring into service.

I then replied to him, that if he would give me his promise verbally, that I should not be required to leave this district where my family and interests were, I would then accept his commission and do the service he required to the best of my ability. He delivered me the commission, and directed me to stay over another day, and pick up as many men as I could find fit to enlist, and he would assist me. I did remain over, got some fifteen men, and reported to the Commodore. I assured him that I would be able to fill up the camp to at least twenty or thirty men. I left for my Ranch Jurupa with my squad, and on the road increased the number to twenty-two.

I did not see the Commodore again till he returned to Los Ángeles, after the actions of the 8th and 9th of January, 1847.

On my arrival at home I reported that I had availed myself of all information, and learned positively that José Castro had crossed the river at Yuma with a small squad, and had gone into Sonora. The Commodore answered that he was going to depart, as he did not think there was any danger of disturbances, and would leave Lieutenant Gillespie with a small force in Los Ángeles to whom I could communicate anything worthy of being reported. I concluded as there was nothing for me to do around my place, and having the men on my hands, I would go further up the frontier and have friendly palavers with some Indians that I knew. I went to the mountain after visiting the Indians, and instructed them to keep a lookout and advise me forthwith if they saw any movements or troops, and all about them. We went upon our hunt in the mountains; after a few days hunting and shooting a messenger arrived with a letter from Mr. David W. Alexander and John Rowland, advising me that they were then on my ranch, having fled from the Pueblo, and from their homes with others, that there was a general revolt of the Californians and Mexicans against Gillespie and all Americans, and that there was the devil to pay generally and to hasten down. I received the information in the evening and started at once, marched all night, and arrived at the Jurupa by daylight. I found there Alexander, Rowland, Rubidoux, and others. They verbally detailed all occurrences to the time of their departure from Los Ángeles, that Gillespie's course towards the people had been so despotic and in every way unjustifi-

95

able that the people had risen to a man against him. I also had letters from Gillespie summoning me to come as fast as I could to his aid. He had established very obnoxious regulations to annoy the people, and upon frivolous pretexts had most respectable men in the community arrested and brought before him, for no other purpose than to humiliate them, as they thought. Of the truth of this I had no doubt then, and have none now.

The people had given no just cause for the conduct he had pursued, which seemed to be altogether the effect of vanity and want of judgment. When I met Alexander and Rowland, I mentioned the fact that in the mountains we had wasted most of our ammunition. That reminded them that they had a letter for me from Cal Williams, of the Chino Ranch. On opening this letter I saw that Williams had invited me to come to his place with my men, assuring me that he had plenty of ammunition. We at once saddled up, and in great haste repaired to the Chino. On our arrival Williams advised me that an officer and some soldiers of the California Brigade had just been there and taken all the ammunition he had. I then called all my men to hold counsel, and told them that we had but little ammunition to fight or stand a siege, and in my judgment it was best that we should go to the mountains and make our way to Los Ángeles by following the edge of the mountains, when we found ourselves threatened by a superior force. But the majority of them being new in the country, had a very contemptible opinion of the Californians' courage and fighting qualities, and seemed of the erroneous opinion that a few shots would suffice to scare away any number of them should come to attack us. They seemed to hint that any attempt on my part to avoid meeting the Californians face to face would be deemed by them an evidence of lack of courage in me. I remarked that I had hoped they had not underrated the natives, but in obedience to their opinion I would remain with them, and as we were all volunteers, would not attempt to exercise any authority over them, and that we would see where the real courage was.

This was on the 26th day of September, 1846, in the evening. Very soon there appeared from eighty to one hundred men on horseback, some of my men among them. Isaac Callaghan volunteered to go ascertain who these men were and their number. Callaghan soon returned with a broken arm, stating that as soon as he had approached the Californians, several shots had been fired at him, one of which struck him on the arm. He added that among the Californians he had seen one of the Lugo brothers, who was apparently commanding one of the owners of San Bernardino. I suggested once more to my men if it would not be more prudent that we should march out whilst we had the opportunity under the cover of night. They answered "No," we can whip all they can bring against us, so we had to await the coming of events, keeping guard, etc. At break of day, we found ourselves almost surrounded by cavalry. We were in the house, which was an old adobe built in the usual Mexican style, with a patio inside entirely enclosed by rooms, with only one large door for entrance to the main patio or square. The house was probably over three hundred feet long, and had on the northern side only two or three windows. There was a knoll on the west side, on which the Californians were arranged, making their plan of attack.

As they moved from there in their divisions, we had no chance to fire but two or three shots apiece (we had no breach loaders or repeaters), before the larger portion of them were under the protection of our walls. They immediately set fire to the roof, which was made of cane covered with asphaltum; fire was applied in several places. The Californians were in position where we could not see them, neither could they see us, but awaited the result of the fire. The house burnt rapidly with a great deal of smoke and bad smell. As soon as they were satisfied that the fire would force us out of the building, the Commander of the Party, Cérbulo Varela, came to the main door where I could be near enough to converse with him through it. On asking him what he wanted, he inquired if I knew who he was, and I answered, "Yes, Cérbulo Varela." He then told me he commanded those men and wanted me to surrender to him, assuring me of his friendly disposition in these words. "You know I am your friend, neither you nor any of your friends shall be injured," adding, that as an old soldier, he knew what were the laws of war respecting the treatment of prisoners. I informed my men at once of what Varela said, and they unhesitantly answered that if he would send his men away, they would come out and deliver their arms. He assented saying that he would send his men to the rear to put out the fire, whilst we marched out the forward door. We threw the broad door open and marched out, Cérbulo directed us to stack our arms against the walls, and we did so. We were then ordered to another building distant about four hundred yards to the south, belonging to the same Ranch, and called Casa de la Mantaza.

Varela ordered us all to be mounted, I being allowed to keep my horse and saddle, and to ride by Varela, while the others were ordered to march forward in charge of the second command, Diego Sepúlveda. We all started, the Californian Chief saying that they had to be in town that evening. Varela, the Commander, remained back talking with some persons, I at his side, the rest went on and were about half a mile ahead. We then followed slowly along. About one mile from the house, these men who were in charge of the prisoners made a sudden halt, which attracted the attention of Varela; he put spurs to his horse telling me that some deviltry was going on there, and to follow him. As soon as he got near enough to make himself heard, he gave the command to stop. The prisoners had all been placed on one side for the purpose of shooting them. But Varela rode up quickly and placed himself between his command and the prisoners, declaring that he would run his sword through the first man that attempted to harm a hair of the prisoners, that he had given his word as a gentleman and as a Commander to save the lives of the prisoners, and if they wanted to shoot anyone, they might shoot him; his voice was stentorian and his deportment very gallant, and his conduct on that occasion made him worthy of our admiration and respect.

On many occasions he was arrested for breaking the peace, and some American would immediately pay the fine and thereby obtain his release; he never was permitted to be in prison.

We all arrived that evening on the Mesa south of town now known as Boyle Heights, without any further oc-

98

currence, except the suffering and groans of my poor wounded men.

I forgot to mention that in the fight at the Ranch, one Californian named Carlos Ballesteros, a very good man, and one who had ever been among my best friends, was killed outright whilst charging on the house walls; half a dozen or more were wounded, two of them very badly. Among my men I have mentioned, Isaac Callaghan, Joseph Perdue, Mat Harbin, William Skene (an Austrian) were also wounded, Perdue and Skene very badly.

The only names besides my own that I can now remember as belonging to our party are: D. W. Alexander, living; John Rowland, dead; Isaac Callaghan, dead; Evan Callaghan, dead; Joseph Perdue, dead; Mat Harbin, living in Northern California; Geo. Walters, living in Los Ángeles; Michael White, living in San Gabriel; William Skene, killed in California; Louis Rubidoux, dead.

In "Boyle Heights" we were all placed in a small adobe room; the first thing after we were placed in there, a priest came in bearing a large cross, and after salutations, asked if any one amongst us wished to confess. Rubidoux, who was huddled in a corner answered, "Yes, I do," adding, "My God, men, they are going to shoot us, the priest coming in is a sure sign." The priest, understanding some English, remarked, "My mission amongst you has nothing to do with the Government's intention in regard to you. I heard that some of you were badly wounded, and I did not know but some might be in jeopardy; for this I came to tender my services." This quieted our men, and Rubidoux sat down again. Immediately after the priest left our room I was instructed to walk out of the room, that the Commanding General ([José María] Flores) wanted to see me. As I went out I met him, and we walked to one side and sat down.

He addressed me as if he felt the importance of his position, saying in a mandatory voice to me, "I desire you to address an open letter to Captain Gillespie—" (who was then camped on Fort Hill in back of town)—"informing him of what you have seen, and that you and your men are prisoners. Say to him that General Flores is a Christian as well as a soldier, and wishes to avoid the spilling of blood unnecessarily; that my men are very anxious to attack him, and one charge from them would cause the destruction of himself and all his soldiers."

That was true, for many of the old Californians who had been ill-treated by Gillespie felt revengeful. Flores's proposition to Gillespie, as conveyed in my letter, was that he would allow him to march out the next morning unmolested by any Californian forces, and to proceed to San Pedro carrying their arms, and there embark. Flores demanded an immediate answer, adding that if the answer was in the negative, he would not be responsible for the consequences. I believe that if Gillespie had refused the terms he would have been attacked that night, for a large portion of the Californians were drinking deeply, and expressing themselves against Gillespie personally. His answer accepting the terms came back early the same night. Flores had directed me to state in the some note, as coming from myself, my impression as to the state of things. I had done so, giving Gillespie my conviction that it was for the interest of himself and all Americans in the country, whether prisoners or not, that he should accede to Flores's demands and leave forthwith. Gillespie then left early the next morning, which must have been the 28th of September.

Myself and my associates were all marched into town and placed in a building then standing on the site now occupied by the St. Charles Hotel, on Main Street. On my being placed there, a Doctor was for the first time allowed to attend our wounded. Doctor Richard [Somerset] Den was the physician and he is still living in Los Ángeles. An old Spaniard named Don Eulogio Célis, whose widow and family now reside in Los Ángeles, came to our prison where we had no comforts, no beds, blankets, or clothing.

He saluted me whom he knew very well, and cast his eyes around as if he were counting the prisoners, saying but few words. He went away and returned in a few minutes with two or three servants loaded with blankets, clothing, and other articles for our comfort.

I think he gave one suit of clothing and two blankets to each man, and then broke out looking at me, "Carajo, these fellows must all chew tobacco"; he then ordered one of his servants to go and fetch him a box of tobacco, *"para que la comare."*

Looking around then and noticing that the men who guarded us seemed to consider us as so many criminals, Célis delivered a severe rebuke to them, asking if they were barbarians to treat prisoners of war as criminals, that only barbarians did so, that civilized warfare demanded that prisoners of war should be kindly treated. It is a satisfaction for me to state these facts, of one who although not of our nationality, had the courage as well as humanity to stand for us, whilst several of our own countrymen who were close around us did not even come to see us.

Gillespie and his men were gone. As the Californians thought their country rid of all Americans but ourselves, who were prisoners in their hands, Flores the Commander and many of the prominent ones came in and manifested great friendship to us personally; saying, if I would sign for myself and men a parole of honor, that none of us would again take up arms, or use our influence in any way during the existence of hostilities between México and the United States, they would then and there give us our liberty. I replied that I would accept the offer, provided the condition was added that our obligation should not go beyond such time as we were exchanged. They would not agree to it, and we remained prisoners. In the course of a few days we fully expected our release through the arrival of Captain [William] Mervin[e] in the U.S. Sloop of War at San Pedro. Soon after our hearts were all made light by hearing the firing of cannon in the direction of San Pedro, but that was of short duration, for in the evening we learned that a force under Captain Mervin[e], including Gillespie and his command, had attempted to march to Los Ángeles, been defeated, and forced to retreat and return on board their ships.

The deportment of General Flores towards prisoners now changed entirely, and in a few days we heard of the hellish plot concocted by Flores and Henry Dalton (whose wives were sisters) to send us as prisoners and trophies to México, having its conception in Dalton selling the remnants of an old store to Flores as Commander in Chief, for the pretended purpose of clothing the soldiers, and Flores giving to

101

Dalton drafts for large amounts against the Mexican Treasury.

Dalton was to go in charge of the prisoners and others, to present us to the Governor of México as evidence of Flores's great military achievements. William Workman of La Puente Ranch, an Englishman, having heard of the plot at once came into town, and determined to defeat the villainous plot. He at once put himself in communication with the leading Californians, among the most prominent of whom was Don Ignacio Palomares, using the line of argument that if they stood by and allowed us and others to be sacrificed to the cupidity of Flores and Dalton, they would be held by the Americans responsible in the future; that all Flores and his accomplice would have to do would be to flee the country when the hour of danger came, and the Californians would be left to bear the whole brunt.

The Californians saw through the whole thing, and resolved to undo the plan. They at once organized a revolution against Flores, and when everything was made ready with the utmost secrecy, one night Flores's headquarters was attacked, the Californians' side being led by Workman, Palomares, and other prominent Californians. The whole plan was known to us previously, hence we, during the firing with cannon and small arms in the streets, which was kept up for many hours, were in the greatest anxiety, as our fate hung on the result.

At a late hour in the night the firing ceased. Workman rushed into our prison, bringing us the glad tidings that Flores was a prisoner and in irons, and his and Dalton's plot broken.

The next day Palomares, who was now virtually Commander, took us out of prison and furnished us horses, and we all went to the Misión San Gabriel, where we remained for several days breathing fresh air. A compromise was made by the Californians and Flores, for the former to recognize the latter as Commander-in-Chief, upon written conditions that we were to be treated as prisoners of war, with humanity, and not to be sent out of the country. We then went back to the prison in town, but were thereafter treated with more kindness and allowed greater liberty—

indeed, we were permitted to arrange for our food at the respectable house of Don Luis Arenas.

Things went on smoothly for a short time, then news arrived that Commodore Stockton was coming with a powerful force, and with determination to put a stop to all further resistance on the part of the people here.

One day Don José Antonio Carrillo, who was temporarily in immediate command of the Mexican forces around Los Ángeles, came to our prison and made known to me a plan that he had in his mind to take us all to Temple's Ranch (Cerritos, now owned by Bisby & Co.). We all marched down to said Ranch. This was, I believe, early in November, 1846.

After arriving there, Carrillo took me aside and said that he had now a good deal to talk to me about; he began by saying that they knew that Stockton would soon be in with his ships, and that he felt very unfriendly to many of the Californians for their revolt; then he uncovered to me the following scheme:

> That when Stockton should reach San Pedro, and begin to land his forces, I have you brought down here, and will take you personally and place you on the Mesa of San Pedro Landing. You will there remain along with a Sergeant; when I want you to raise a white flag, I will signify it to you by sending you the order. You will bear this message to the Commodore from me, that I hope no more blood will be shed on either side during the pendency of the War in México, when the fate of this country must be decided upon. You can bear personal testimony to the Commodore that American interests in this country are safe, and that on my part I wish to make him this proposition; that I will guarantee as a gentleman and an officer, and as one who has the power to enforce it, that all Americans and their interests shall be duly protected and respected in this district; and that he, the

103

Commodore, may land and take all his supplies needed for his forces, and hold the sea and landings unmolested.

Ask him, in the name of humanity, not to march forces through the country, as this would cause the spilling of blood, and engender bad feeling between two people who in all probability will have to live together.

I was to depart and return with the Commodore's answer, either written or verbal, under my parole, pledging myself not to give any information beyond the message I was instructed to deliver. In accordance with this arrangement, I was placed under charge of a Sergeant, and carried to the place designated, near the old San Pedro Landing on the Mesa, where I was to wait Carrillo's orders. On our way we passed Carrillo's command, of some four or five hundred men all mounted, where they seemed to be collecting on Domínguez's Ranch, all the scattered horses they could secure—they already had a large number together. The Sergeant and myself having stationed ourselves as above, I looked back in the gap where the road leads through from the Palos Verdes to San Pedro Landing, and saw an immense dust raised by a large "*caballada*" mixed with mounted soldiers. This immense band of horses and cavalcade occupied several hours in passing through the gap, down a short distance where there was a low depression in the same hills, and passing back through this depression or gap, going up again to the same gap and passing through again.

This gave the impression and appearance of an immense mass of mounted cavalry, as no one at a distance could distinguish through the dust if all the horses had riders or not. At the time I took my position, I could see that the Commodore's flagship was loading boats with war materials, which boats, some four in number, left the ship's side and came ashore crowded with Marines. By the time that the cavalcade stopped its maneuvers, the boats were signaled, as we supposed from the ship, for they all returned to her, leaving nothing on shore.

104

As soon as everything was reshipped, the frigate lifted her anchors and put to sea. I have seen it stated in a book which purported to give the lives and acts of American Commodores, that Stockton landed at San Pedro, marched with his Marines three miles to Palos Verdes, there met the Californians, with his well-trained eye fired at them several shots and slew a number (how many he could not tell, as their friends carried them away), but having no cavalry, he thought it imprudent to advance into the interior without it, and concluded to go to San Diego and there improvise a cavalry force. The whole thing is a fabrication, I assert from personal observation—that Stockton did not land, but that four of his boats came to the water's edge and returned to the frigate without having effected a landing at all.

The Commodore did good and gallant service, and fame needs no fictitious aid. Carrillo then sent orders to the Sergeant to bring me where he was. He saluted me, saying that he had deceived himself in endeavoring to make a demonstration to Stockton of his forces, in order to secure a favorable response; in other words, he had made too great a demonstration and driven Stockton away. Therefore, there was nothing left for me to do but go back to my Ranch prison.

We remained there over night, and the next day came to town and went again into our prison. We had now the prospect before us of a long monotonous imprisonment. But excepting the fact that we had to sleep in prison, we were allowed every other liberty, and treated with uniform kindness by the natives.

Our life was not a monotonous one—the campaign ground had been established by both parties in San Diego County. Nothing worthy of mention happened in Los Angeles. We had reports that Col. Frémont was marching with a battalion from the North, and Commodore Stockton would soon come up from San Diego. Then we heard that [Stephen W.] Kearney had arrived from New Mexico and been badly defeated at San Pasqual.

These events bring us down to the sixth of January, 1847, on which day Don Andrés Pico and other prominent Californians came to our prison and said, "All our troops march tomorrow to meet Commodore Stockton and General Kearney, who are near Santa Ana on their way up—you must give your parole and leave your prison for your own safety, as we have no spare force to guard you or to protect you from the rabble." Pico added that the next morning early he would bring two Blancos, one for Mr. Rowland and one for myself; those two horses were considered the fleetest in the country. We promised to make all ready for the next morning to disperse. He brought us the two horses fully equipped the next morning in person; the one intended for me had on his fine silver mounted saddle and bridle. "Take this horse, and you will be perfectly safe, there is no other horse in the country that can overtake you; if I fall in battle give it to my brother Don Pío." I expressed some sympathy for him, mentioning the hope that he would take no extraordinary risks. He replied jocosely, but with tears in his eyes, "*No Andrés, y no muero.*"

Mr. Rowland and myself mounted our horses, the other men went and scattered themselves among the various vineyards, so as not to be seen in the streets. My family was in Santa Ana at the residence of my wife's father, Don Bernardo Yorba, and Mr. Rowland's at the La Puente—we joined our respective families that same day.

On my way down I passed the American forces, but avoided speaking to them or to anyone on the route.

Knowing that on the 8th the contending forces would meet one another near the San Gabriel River, I came back skirting the hills of the Coyote Ranch, before I could get a view of the two armies. Remaining in view as long as the fight lasted, I saw there had been nothing decisive except that the Californians rather gave way. Rode back to the Rancho where I remained all night. The day of the 8th a portion of the Californians made charge and seemed for a time to have broken the American lines, which gave me much alarm, but as soon as the dust cleared away, I saw the Californians retreating, and from what I learned afterwards, had the charge been simultaneous of all the Californian forces, the American lines would have been broken, and there is no telling what the end might have been.

Our forces rallied and closed ranks. The Californians retired over a hill a short distance. I knew from the position of the two forces that the fight would be resumed the next morning. The Americans camped that night on the field of that day's fight.

The ninth of January I started out to view the fight but on my way out I met some Californians, friends of mine and relations of my wife, who I knew had been in the actions of the preceding day; they told me that in the morning Flores and his Mexicans had refused to continue the fight, confining themselves to firing a few guns, and that they were running away to México, by way of San Gorgonio Pass, inviting all that wished to follow them.

Hearing that news, I made up my mind to spend the day in the hills back of La Puente Ranch, and wait for the night to come to Los Ángeles through La Puente, where I would obtain some definite news. But that night it rained in perfect torrents, the night was black as pitch, and I lost my way; I had no other recourse but to sit on my horse and wait for daylight.

Early in the morning I went to the house of Mr. William Workman; after waking him up and having some conversation, he told me there were two very important persons in one of his outhouses with some fellows—he could not tell who, or how many. We talked a great deal in a few minutes, and Mr. Workman told me that those persons were Monterey men, and I probably would know them; Workman felt in doubt as to the condition of things, whether it would be safe for me to see them or not, or how far he would be compromised by harboring them. We did not as yet know the actual results of the fight, and of course were unable to foresee events.

The information I had the day before was not such as I could give entire weight to, as none of the men that communicated it were officers of note, though men of character who would not knowingly deceive me. I then asked Mr. Workman (as I was still a prisoner on parole) to go and speak to them himself, learn their names, ask them if the fighting was really over, what had been the result, and where were Flores and his Command. Workman did so, and returned in a few minutes confirming what I had learned the day before from my own friends, and that Flores and his Mexican forces (two or three hundred perhaps) were by forced marches going out of the country. The two chief men there harbored were the La Torre brothers.

I then concluded there was no impropriety in my seeing them, and asked Mr. Workman to let me go and have an interview with them. Mr. Workman went to the room where the Torres were, and told them Don Benito Wilson wished to see them. They came out, remarking that above all, I was the man they wanted to see. We met, had a very warm salutation and shaking of hands; for I had been on very intimate terms with Joaquín and Gabriel de la Torre in Monterey. I said, "Is it possible these are my friends Joaquín and Gabriel?" They, like myself, had been out in the rain the night before, and we all looked like so many drowned rats. I hastened to make inquiries about the state of matters as they understood it.

They reported that on the morning of the ninth, after the skirmish and retreat of Flores, they accompanied him all day till night came on, still on the march. They and a few of their friends, all Californians, fell out under cover of night and made a hasty retreat to La Puente, adding that they would rather be shot in California than go to México. They begged me to go to town in person and intercede with Commodore Stockton. I said, "No, I am sick of this thing, have been in prison three months and want to see an end to this trouble."

I was clearly of the opinion that the course best to pursue was for them, the brothers Torre, to mount their horses and come with me to town. I called Mr. Workman in English, requesting him to order my horse, which he did. The two brothers ordered their horses immediately and had them saddled. They gave some directions to their comrades and sent some messages to their families in Monterey in case they were shot, for they really expected such might be their fate. After a good, warm breakfast the two brothers and myself started for Los Ángeles, they having left their arms with their friends.

It took us a whole day to reach Los Ángeles, where we could have gone in a couple of days, but in consequence of the constant apprehensions manifested by them at almost every half mile, and resolve not to deliver themselves up to be shot. At every stopping I had to argue the question again and again, assuring them that the course advised by Mr. Workman and myself was the safest one for them. Finally, they arrived in town—they were still in great fear. I succeeded in getting them dismounted and to the foot of the stairs of the house where Commodore Stockton had his quarters.

The Commodore was yet Commodore-in-Chief, the command had been conceded to him by General Kearney, in consideration of the great services he had already rendered in California, and for other reasons. Stockton, on or about the third day of his arrival in Los Ángeles, went away to rejoin his flagship, the *Congress*, at San Pedro, to which port he had ordered her from San Diego.

Kearney then assumed the Chief Command. I went up and saluted Stockton, being the first time I had met him after the day when he commissioned me as a Captain, told him in a few words the condition of things, and informed him there were two more unfortunate than I was at the foot of the stairs who were anxious to see him. He asked who they were and I gave their names; he then tried to put on a stern countenance, but I could detect under the frown a look of satisfaction at having these two important persons again at his mercy. He replied to me, "Let them come up."

I went down to the foot of the stairs and requested them to come up. They showed considerable anxiety to know how the Commodore felt towards them. I said that I thought all was right, although he had not said so. We went up together to the Commodore's presence. The Commodore stood up and saluted them but showed a good deal of sternness in his demeanor, but not more than was proper for him to show. Some hasty allusion was made to the past, and the two brothers begged the Commodore not to mention those particulars; they had violated the laws of war in breaking their paroles and were there at his mercy.

The Commodore then said very sternly, "You have given me a great deal of trouble, but neither the Government of the United States nor myself wish to treat harshly the native Californians. Can I rely upon you, if I again give you your liberty?" They emphatically answered, "Yes, we are tired of the war, and have paid dearly for our errors."

Stockton then asked, "Will you proceed at once to Monterey, your homes, if I give you passports, and allay some existing discords threatened up there?" They said, "Yes sir, and we will neither stop to sleep or eat on the way, if you so order us." The passports were then and there issued to them, and they departed that same evening for Monterey.

I never saw them again, but I understood that they fulfilled all their pledges, and were ever after during their lifetime good and loyal citizens.

In the meantime we heard that Andrés Pico and the small force under him had met Colonel Frémont at San Fernando, where he made capitulation and delivered up his arms. This gave rise to no little dissatisfaction to Commodore Stockton and General Kearney.

On the eleventh, learning that Andrés Pico was in the upper part of town, I repaired there and on the way up met a man with a message for me from Don Andrés. I was still riding his favorite "Blanco Chico." I found Pico, and in answer to his anxious inquiries gave him all the news, particularly that relating to the Torre brothers. He informed me that he had capitulated to Frémont, but still showed himself conscious of the fact that there were men of higher rank than Frémont in town and insisted after the good fortune the Torres had met with, I should accompany him to the Commodore, which I did.

On arriving at the Commodore's quarters, the Commodore did not hesitate to give Don Andrés to understand and very positively that neither his (Pico's) nor Frémont's courses were in order, as he, Pico, after the fight of the eighth and ninth, and being enough of a military man to know his duties and be aware to whom he should surrender, had gone out of his way to surrender to a subordinate officer, and not to the Commander-in-Chief. It was generally known

110

that Frémont had designedly delayed on his way from Santa Bárbara, by taking circuitous route on the mountains, so as to keep himself out of danger from the Californians.

Commodore Stockton had sent dispatches to him by one Daniel Sexton and others, at great risk to the carriers, through the mountains, urging him to hurry his march and meet him south of Los Ángeles with his command. The Commodore did not expect with his few Marines and sailors and a handful of volunteers that he would withstand the whole force of the Californians, who were probably the best horsemen in the world and all mounted on fine horses, probably the finest cavalry horses in the world at that time, for their fleetness, endurance, and easy management to the rider.

Daniel Sexton, whom I have mentioned above, went from San Diego on foot with a knapsack on his back to near San Buenaventura, where he met Frémont. To fulfill his mission he had to travel on foot through the mountains some two hundred miles, occupying about ten days. All this trouble and suffering, as well as those of others, went for nothing, as Frémont made no effort to comply with the Commodore's wishes.

Commodore Stockton was exceedingly angry with Frémont's conduct from beginning to end, and did not hesitate to express it in the strongest terms of all, particularly to Don Andrés, who had unfortunately got himself into the false position of ignoring his undoubted authority. Don Andrés felt humiliated and tried to apologize. The Commodore, who was as generous as he was gallant, said to him, "Whilst I do not recognize any authority, or even justification in Frémont, for making to you the pledges appearing in his agreement at San Fernando, I, as Commander-in-Chief, say to you, that we do not wish to have any ill feeling shown to anyone, and much less to the natives of California, who in all probability will have to be citizens of our common country, and in that spirit I will make known, that if you have come in real earnest, and in good faith to yield and surrender yourself and comrades, there will be no punishment for past acts." I may not have given above the very words used by

111

the Commodore, but I am certain that I have given the substance of what he uttered.

I should have mentioned before, that almost before the salutations had been gotten through between the Commodore and Don Andrés Pico, the latter manifested his good faith by telling the Commodore where the cannon was concealed with which he had fought at the action of the eighth and ninth. The Commodore asked me what kind of cannon they were; I told him they were common, short, heavy cast iron guns, to which he answered that they were not worth looking after, and would not send for them. I told him then that if he would give them to me I would make them posts to keep the *carretas* off the entrance to my store; he gave them to me, and being told by Don Andrés where they were, I hired a man with a *carreta* to bring them in and placed them at the head of Commercial Street at the junction of Main Street in the City of Los Ángeles, where they may be seen to this day.

At that interview Commodore Stockton told Pico to go among his people and keep them orderly, assuring them that they would receive no harm at the hands of the Americans, if they conducted themselves peaceably and minded their business. "What I have already done to you and to your brother officers should be received as sufficient evidence that we mean well by you," or words to that effect.

He directed me to mount my horse, go among the people and ascertain what was going on, and if everything was quiet. I did so, and returning in the evening, reported that all was quiet, and that it was reported that Frémont was marching with his force towards the Misión of San Gabriel, where he purposed to encamp.

Up to this time Frémont had not reported to Stockton. The streets were full of rumors that Frémont did not intend to recognize the authority of Stockton or Kearney. When I reported these things to the Commodore, he broke out, "What does the damned fool mean?" He then had a few words of conversation with me, and said, "I must go away, I am in an unpleasant position, and only by courtesy of General Kearney the Commander-in-Chief." He felt that he was the head officer as long as he remained, because Kearney had told

112

him, "As long as you are here, you are Commander-in-Chief; after you are gone, I will be."

He gave me to understand that if he was to remain he would bring Frémont to terms, but as he was to leave the next day, he would let Kearney settle the matter with Frémont. The latter was still claiming to be Military Governor of California, under the appointment given him by Stockton himself in the previous year 1846.

After Stockton's departure (which I think was on the next day) with all his officers and men, General Kearney had with him a mere body guard of dragoons, some fifteen to twenty men, and one officer, Major [William H.] Emory, now General. Kearney had seen me several times with the Commodore, and sent for me to come to his rooms.

I obeyed his summons. He asked me what was going on, and was informed that nothing of importance was occurring. He asked me if I was in no haste to leave town, as he desired me to stay with him; he had then no one with whom he could trust, and who knew the people.

He followed up his conversation, saying, "Frémont's course towards me is very extraordinary; he declined to recognize me as Commander-in-Chief. I have no power to enforce my authority. Frémont has a large force with him of undisciplined men, and I hear all kinds of rumors of his intentions and acts. I only now propose to remain here a few days to give Mr. Frémont full time to deliberate; perhaps he will then acknowledge my authority—if not, then I will leave."

He repeated several times the same words, and requested me to communicate with my friends, and we all kept him posted as to what was going on. These conversations lasted about two days.

In the evening of the second or third day, he sent for me and said he was going to leave in the morning, prefacing the information with the remark that he had heard no word from Frémont; he wanted me and some of my friends to ride with him. Next morning I waited on the General with two or three reliable native Californians; I think that among them were Don José Sepúlveda, father of Judge Ignacio Sepúlveda, and one of the Lugos. I was much surprised to

113

find the General after we were out of town on the road bound to San Diego, under some apprehension of foul play to his person by some of the Frémont party. This produced a most disagreeable impression in me, though I then, as now, believe his apprehensions unfounded. I was anxious to leave in the evening for the first day's camping time for my Ranch, but he asked me particularly to camp with him that night, saying that "we are not far out enough from those fellows," meaning Frémont and his party.

I accompanied the General as far as the Santa Ana River, there I bade him goodbye, and he expressed himself very thankful.

In the same fall of 1847, I moved up all my stock, about two thousand head of cattle, passed through the Tulare Valley by way of Cajón de las Uvas. There was not a white man living on the route from San Fernando Misión to Sutter's Fort. Passing by what is now Stockton, I learned from some friendly Indians that Charles Weber was coming there to settle on his Ranch, which he got from Mr. [William] Gulnac. I swam all my stock without losing any across the Sacramento River at the place now called Knight's Landing, and drove up the foothills north of Cash Creek at the place known as Lone Trees, and then left them in charge of my companion-at-arms, Mat Harbin. I returned to Los Ángeles City, where I was engaged in Merchandising.

Nothing worthy of mention happened till 1849, when a convention was called by General [James] Riley to form a Constitution for California. At this time this part of the country was much depopulated by the rush to the gold placers that had been discovered in the spring of 1849. We held a public meeting and selected the best men we could find: Abel Stearns, Manuel Domínguez, Stephen C. Foster, etc. We had no direction to give our representatives, except that we wished not to be a State as yet, but if we had to be a State, although most of us were Southern men, we were very positive that we wanted no slavery. We had enough of a variety of races, and the character of the country was not favorable to any but free labor. The following year California having been voted in the constitution a State, we held a convention of the Southern country in Santa Bárbara, at which I

114

was a member, for the purpose of sending a protest to Congress, that in case California was admitted as a State of the Union, the Southern portion would be allowed to form a Territorial Government, and allowed to remain as a Territory of the United States.

Our efforts proved unavailing. After the State was organized, I was elected the first Clerk of the County of Los Ángeles, making the condition with my friends that I should not serve personally, but would appoint Doctor Wilson Jones, now of Arizona, my deputy, to run the office and have all the emoluments. When the town of Los Ángeles was incorporated as a City, the people elected me as its first Mayor. I only served a few months, and then resigned. My wife, Ramona Yorba Wilson, died March 21st, 1849.

In 1852 I was appointed by President Fillmore Indian Agent for the Southern District, accompanied with a letter particularly requesting my acceptance, to help arrange Indian affairs in California, in conjunction with General [Edward F.] Beale (then Lieutenant), who had been appointed General Superintendent for the State. I did accept and accompanied Beale, and assisted to lay the Reservation at the Tejón, passing through the Tulare Valley and holding council with different Indians, and then returned home by way of Santa Bárbara.

During that trip and subsequent events, I became thoroughly convinced that I could not continue in the office in harmony with the Superintendent and others, especially in regard to the moneys appropriated by the Government, so I resigned. My commission bears date September 1st, 1852, signed by Millard Fillmore, President of the United States, and by Daniel Webster, Secretary of State, and bears the seal of the United States; term of office, four years from date. On February 1st, 1853, I married Margaret S. Hereford, widow of Dr. Thomas Hereford. In 1855 I was elected State Senator and served out my term, and again served in 1869 and 1870. Since then I have spent my time as a horticulturist in Los Ángeles County at Lake Vineyard. My family consists of a wife and three daughters, one by my first wife and two by my second wife, all living, and four grandchildren, and I hope to pass the remainder of my life in peace with God and man, as well as with myself.

—B. D. Wilson
Lake Vineyard, California
December 6th, 1877

NOTE

Mr. Wilson died on March 11th, 1878, being survived by his widow and three daughters, the eldest a daughter by his first wife being Mrs. J. DeBarth Shorb, and the other two, Annie Wilson and Ruth Wilson, by his second wife. Ruth Wilson married George S. Patton on December 10th, 1884, and there were two children by this marriage, General George S. Patton, Jr. and Anne Wilson Patton.

III.

CALIFORNIA'S GOLD RUSH DAYS

A CONTEMPORANEOUS ACCOUNT OF A VISIT
TO NORTHERN CALIFORNIA IN 1851

BY ALEXANDRE HOLINSKI

TRANSLATED BY MARY TERESA COREA

TRANSLATOR'S PREFACE

The present study is an annotated translation of portions of a French work describing conditions in California during the Gold Rush. It will be seen that Alexandre Holinski, the author, was a well-educated and seasoned traveler. He displays for the new state an enthusiasm equal to that of our most ardent present day "Californiacs." Attracted to the new El Dorado as were so many thousands at that time by the cry of gold, he came however not as a miner nor a trader; nor was he here in an official capacity as an investigator sent by his government.

Four of the chapters treating of California have been selected for translation: San Francisco, The Gold Region, The Climate and Soil, and The Importance of California. Certain tedious transgressions, having no bearing on the subject, have been omitted.

Listed in the bibliography are the works which were consulted in an attempt to discover the sources used by this little known author in his *California and the Interoceanic Routes*. Helpful they were above all in comparing his views and statements with those of his contemporaries who witnessed at its height that phenomenal migration which during

117

the early fifties of the last century, made California the center of the universe. The experiences of the two authors especially were interesting to compare with Holinski's. These were M. de Saint-Amant, sent by Napoléon III on a tour of investigation, and M. Ernest de Massey, a young nobleman attempting to retrieve his fortune. Both were Frenchmen, both in San Francisco at the time of Holinski's visit (October 1, 1851 to January 1, 1852), both recorded their impressions in French for readers in France.

To Mr. Everett R. Perry, the librarian, I am indebted for the permission to translate Alexandre Holinski's book which is the property of the Los Ángeles Public Library; to Miss Laura Cooley for her kindness and courtesy in pointing out interesting and helpful works among the treasures in the "Californiana" room. I wish also to express my sincere thanks to the members of my committee, Dr. Owen C. Coy, Dr. George P. Hammond, and Dr. René Belle for their valuable assistance and advice. Deep gratitude I owe especially to Dr. Coy who by his inspirational seminars has made my work in California history an interesting and fascinating study.

TRANSLATOR'S INTRODUCTION

Little is known of Alexandre Holinski whose book is here translated in part. Only two references to him have so far come to light. Lorenz's *Catalogue General* states that this writer was born in Lithuania in 1816 and lists three more of his works, while the *British Museum Library Catalogue* mentions two translations by "Holyński" and an additional work, *Nubar Pasha in the Light of History*. All further information regarding his nationality, education, profession, and purpose in writing must be drawn from his own statements in the book before us. Concerning his stay in California we learn of his arrival on the *Tennessee* in San Francisco from New York, by way of Panama on October 1, 1851,[1] and of his departure for Europe three months later (January 1, 1852), on the *Pacific* via Nicaragua, after an absence of five years.[2] Speaking of his extensive travels, the author says:

118

> Spending my life continually touring around the world as I do, no one is happier than I to travel by steam while awaiting the use of balloons. I go from Europe to America and from America back again to Europe with as little concern as the Parisian goes from Saint-Germain to Saint-Cloud....Had I been obliged to travel by sailing vessels, my journeys would have been more toil than pleasure.

His only complaint was that little leisure was affronted him for exploration by the steamers hurrying from port to port. In all probability he was one of the large number of intelligentsia whom succeeding political changes in Europe sent into voluntary or forced exile, and who were caught up in the great wave of immigration rushing to California's shores. But unlike the majority of these travelers, he was a man of leisure and came not to dig gold, but merely to observe and record.

Obviously an enthusiast for democracy (in reality socialism), he untiringly compares European conditions with the government of California where, according to him, no restrictions existed.[3] He observes:

> Thus, self-government results, that is the government of the province by the province,...the township by the township, the group by itself, and in fine man by himself.[4]

> Even gold is purified in the American atmosphere....The lust of gold in a republic does not exclude high sentiments. This lust, so corrupting in a monarchy, is purified in a republican atmosphere.[5]

So strong was Holinski's resentment against all centralized governments, in fact against any organized body whether political, religious, or social, that he frequently denounced them in long tirades, calling upon the nations to re-

119

bel and have recourse to civil wars which "cause only a ripple of disturbance and bring political freedom."[6] He was apparently that type of a radical unwelcome here today by the government. He would probably be given free transportation in a "sealed" train and hurried out of the country.

Though born in Lithuania, and described on the title page of his book as "American citizen," still his sympathies are all French. He writes in French, is thoroughly conversant with French life and customs, and deeply concerned about the misfortunes of France. Was his family perhaps among the number that were driven out of Poland in the troublous early decades of the nineteenth century and took refuge in Paris only to witness more upheavals and repressions? That might have been the origin of his bitter radicalism.

Holinski gives evidence of having received some religious training; he is familiar with the Bible which, however, he quotes in an irreverent and at times blasphemous manner. Priests and physicians are to him the cause of all man's sufferings.[7] Toward the Franciscans he is hardly fair in blaming them for the backwardness of the Mission Indians, while in Sutter's Indians he attributes the same deplorable condition to a racial characteristic.[8] Radical though he was on the subject of religion, politics, and society, the author was doubtless an accomplished classical scholar and a careful student of modern authors. He quotes and discusses works written in many languages and dialects. In tracing the derivation of names, he records with care the variations and corruptions as used in the different parts of the world he visited. Likewise in the field of the various sciences as known in his day, he gives evidence of familiarity.[9] In fact where his strong prejudices do not come into play, he is capable of accurate and intelligent observation; his statements often agree with those of reliable contemporary authors, as is shown in the footnotes accompanying the translation from his book.

Besides the portion dealing with California, his work of four hundred and fourteen pages comprises an introduction, four other "books," on Cuba, Panama and the Mexican Coast, Nicaragua, and the Meeting of the Oceans. The table of contents is placed at the end, following an appendix of three lengthy notes dealing principally with slavery. The volume under consideration is the second edition of the work, and was published by A. Labroue in 1853. Both editions appeared in Brussels, the work being prohibited in France. This is not surprising since the author makes Napoléon III, then reigning in France, the target of bitter criticisms and accusations. Nevertheless later works of Holinski's appeared in France after Napoleon's fall.

The "book" here translated is preceded by one on Cuba and one on Panama in which the author pleads the cause of the slaves. These are followed by three "books" devoted in part to the controversial question of the interoceanic canals in which he gives the preference to the Panama route. It will be remembered that in 1851 slavery and the canal project were both vital questions. As stated above, Holinski, notwithstanding his vagaries on certain subjects, was a keen observer and a persevering student. On some points his predictions have since proved to be strikingly accurate, though they were uttered at such a distance of time. He foresaw the "Fulton of the air" crossing the Atlantic in almost the exact number of hours that it took the "Spirit of Saint Louis." He hails the airplane as a fraternizing medium.

"Agent of freedom of movement destined to set at naught the laws invented to separate nations and thus perpetuate baneful race prejudice!...Aeronauts affirm that in favorable conditions a speed of 160 miles an hour can be attained. New York would be twenty hours from Liverpool according to this reckoning, and *thirty-two hours away* if we take the ordinary velocity of the wind as base of our calculations....I have a presentiment that the "Fulton of the air" will appear somewhere in America."[10]

He foresees air trips of discovery to the North and South Poles, of exploration over deserts and jungles! He lauds the Americans who so wisely "settle their differences by discussion," but adds: "The only time blood will be drawn in America will be over the question of slavery."

Regarding the purpose of this book he has this to say:

The noblest mission of the nineteenth century traveler is to bring back ideas of the future, to observe the signs of social regeneration in countries whose greatness still escapes the attention of Europe...The study of these facts is the most efficacious of all propaganda, for it is based on facts and not on hypotheses.[11]

"The Union of North America is destined to become the union of all peoples of the two hemispheres..."[12] With the abolition of slavery, and the cutting of the interoceanic canal, there will soon follow the establishment of the Federated Republic of the Universe. Then will be completed "the work of fraternity and love so happily begun by the thrice blessed land of California."

1.

SAN FRANCISCO

The Bay of San Francisco[1] from a maritime standpoint has no rival in the Old World or the New. The navies of all nations, both civilized and barbarian, could with ease ride there at anchor; and this statement is by no means an exaggeration.[2] This incomparable harbor consists of two salt lakes formed by two peninsulas, one coming from the north and the other from the south and leaving but a narrow passage between them. [102] The lakes are encircled by hills and sheltered from the winds; the northern, into which flows the Sacramento River, is called the San Pablo Bay; while the southern, where San Francisco rises at the tip of a strip of land, takes its name from the future commercial metropolis of the world.

What struck me there at first was the imposing sight of five or six hundred ships, the majority of which were stationed along wooden wharves or shut up in docks where anchorage was easy and safe. Our steamer, so stately in the solitude of the ocean, was lost to view when anchored in the midst of masts like a tree hidden in a dense forest.[3]

With characteristic North American impetuosity the passengers rushed forward to land. The custom-house officers stationed at the exit do not submit them to the long, minute, inquisitorial inspection which Europe has made a part of civilization. They confine themselves to opening the large trunks and nearly always let through untouched the little valises in which it would appear absurdly small to look for petty smuggling. O model customs, thy good common-sense alone would suffice to reveal the profound wisdom of the institutions of the New World! In passing through thy hands in a minute or two one has not, as in England and France, the time to theorize on the freedom of commerce. Thou, o most reasonable customs-office, wouldst never think of feeling about men's pockets and disrobing women whose figure might appear to be artificially formed. Why this difference in sisters? Because the former are imbued with vexatious monarchial sentiments; [103] while in thee republicanism, liberal by nature, has modified whatever might have been repugnant to the dignity of a citizen.[4]

When the crowd had dispersed I prepared to leave my floating dwelling.[5] It would have taken four or five porters to carry my luggage; it was only later that I learned that a cart would have cost me only a dollar and a half from one end of the city to the other. A coachman offered to take me and another traveler with our belongings to the hotel of our choice for the trifle of ten dollars (fifty francs).

"Ten dollars," said this other passenger who was from Siberia, "ten dollars is not dear. Not long ago that sum was charged, I am told, for taking a single trunk."

"Let us take the carriage," I answered.

At the *Oriental Hotel*, a large, three-storied wooden structure, the owner could not—or would not—give us single rooms. It was the same at the other inn, a smaller one called *Rassett's Hotel*. Finally we succeeded in getting suitable accommodations at *Jones' Hotel*.[6] The room which fell to my lot was twelve by eight feet. It was neat, and besides a spacious bed it boasted of a porcelain basin and pitcher, two chairs, a table, a chest of drawers and a small mirror. The walls were papered and the ceiling was covered with cloth to conceal the cracks between the boards. [104] *Jones' Hotel* was, as one has surmised, a wooden palace. My room and board, without wine, cost twenty-five piastres a week, or five a day, just as one chose.

When the time came to pay the coachman:

"It is thirty dollars," said the scoundrel in a decided and determined tone. "And pay me without delay, for I am in a hurry to get back to the steamer."

"What, thirty dollars for twenty minutes?"

"It is not a question of minutes but of three trips. From the wharf to the *Oriental*, ten dollars; from the *Oriental* to the *Rassett's*, ten, and from *Rassett's* to *Jones'*, ten; total thirty dollars. Is that not correct? But so as not to waste my time in arguing, I am willing to take twenty-five dollars."

The demand was all the more preposterous as the three hotels were almost next door to one another. Moreover the cabman had not informed us on his first stop that he intended to act in this manner. But he was an individual with whom the soundest reasoning would have been of no avail. He threatened in a loud voice to take one of our trunks if his pay was not immediately forthcoming. Such conduct disgusted me and I was inclined to fight rather than yield.

Then the Siberian gave his opinion:

> I would be delighted to administer a sound thrashing to the wretch. But we are not within the realm of the Czar where we could, without fear, settle our account in full in this manner. I will pay my twelve and a half dollars. [105] Do the same, for a fight might prive fatal to us, especially if this moujik should pull from his belt a 'Californian protector' with its much dreaded, keen-edged blade. For my part, I should be rather pleased to preface my impressions of the Gold Region addressed to my friends in Irkoutsk by these words: The carriage which conveyed us from the steamer to the hotel cost us twenty-five dollars! That would give my compatriots a higher idea of California than all they have read about it in the *Abeille du Nord*.

Convinced by this eloquence, I took his advice.

Accursed brood of drivers of public conveyances, accursed in all countries where they exist! The Russian *izvoschtchik* combines in his person all the most glaring and the basest vices of his race. He is as knavish as a judge, as deceitful as a courtier, as intemperate as a Greco-Russian pope. Capable of all baseness and infamy, he steals when he can and murders when he dares. The German *Kutscher* takes pleasure in torturing his passengers by his systematic sloth; he imbibes from his intoxicating beer an immeasurable dose of stupidity, apparent in his grumbling, his cursing and coarse remarks. The French *cocher* loses in the exercise of his trade his characteristic lively wit, and displays a morose temper. He is typical of the coachman class. The Italian *vetturino* is in league with the innkeepers against his clients and so is the Spanish cochero with the highway-robbers. The surly and proud English coachman treats men—except in the case of a lord or a bishop—with less consideration than he does his horses. The American driver cultivates preferably bad Yankee habits. He keeps constantly in his mouth a quid of tobacco, which without a word of warning, he spits around him in the faces of his passengers. This marks him clearly as a ne'er-do-well loafer. [106] Regardless of nationality the cabman stands out conspicuously among other public officers for his incivility. How is this to be explained? Probably by continual contact of the man with the horse; a contact which effects a change in the two natures; while the brute becomes humanized, the man takes on somewhat of the nature of the brute in a manner which may some day be explained by magnetism. But, to this cause insufficient in itself, must be added the habit of absolute power, as depraving to him on the box as to a potentate on his throne.[7]

From outside the Bay one gets an unfavorable view of San Francisco. The central and elegant district is hidden by the harbor and the hills that rise on all sides. The first impression is one of confusion, the houses looking like scattered houses of cards that a child would place on a table without order or system. This is however an optical illusion produced by the unevenness of the ground. San Francisco is, like all cities and villages of the United States, built on an admirably regular plan.[8]

We now come to the shipping district built entirely on pilings and, like Amsterdam and Venice, reclaimed from the swampy plain.[9] Steamers and sailing vessels anchored on both sides of long piers form as it were a double row of houses, of dry goods stores, hotels, and barrooms as far as one can see; carts go back and forth and passersby jostle each other. Such is the aspect of what one may call the entrance to San Francisco.

Leaving the water front from which anyone not partial to the odor of tar or stagnant water is eager to escape, one enters the long and fine Montgomery Street. [107] It is the Broadway of the business section. There the stores display a Parisian elegance. The restaurants attract epicures vying with one another in cleanliness and splendor. All the prominent money-changers who are at the same time bankers have here their offices from the respectable and universally respected Rothschild firm to the savings bank of some shrewd Yankee who attracts the miners by means of striking signboards in English, French, Spanish, and even in Chinese. All these brokers of gold-dust, offer the highest prices, making none the less enormous profits for themselves. In their monthly shipments to the United States and to Europe to be divided among a dozen firms, they handle five or six million dollars.[10] They now pay seventeen dollars an ounce for unpolished gold worth during the first years sixteen or even fifteen.

Clay and Washington Streets lead to the Plaza which would be easier of access though less picturesque if it were not situated on such a steep slope. This square, the meeting-place of the idle as well as of pleasure seekers, contains the pretty *Jenny-Lind Theatre*.[11] In California this name is popular and has been given to steamers, shops, streets, bears, etc. The theatre, a brick building decorated in the interior with the best of taste, puts on English plays every evening not excepting Sundays. [108] Serving as a branch of this theatre is the *California Exchange* next door, a hall whose exact size I could not give but which in London or Paris would be considered quite vast. Twice a week fancy-dress balls and masquerades are held here. The ladies most of whom are Magdalens, often appear on these occasions dressed in bloomers, a charming costume adopted from the harem of the Orient with appropriate modifications.

The *California Exchange* is also a barroom and a gambling den. In this respect it is less popular than other establishments of the kind. To mention only two situated on the same square, we have the *El Dorado* and *La Belle Union.* These "hells," as they are called by the English, resound from morning to night with the clinking of gold and silver. Monte, thirty and forty, baccarat, lansquenet, pharaon, twenty-one, roulette, etc., etc.—games to suit every nation, taste and whim.[12]

By artificial light the appearance of these places of perdition bearing fascinating names is truly fairylike. The walls are hung with erotic paintings placed there to encourage the winning of gold. At the gambling tables women most elaborately dressed preside, and with lascivious wiles entice the loafers to try their fortune. Impossible for them to resist these allurements with their reason already befuddled by alcohol and dizzy from the light, gay and ravishing music which seemed to repeat in every tone: Gold is but a chimera!

These bewitching sirens come from Paris and must be able to remember the late Frascati who, as everyone knows, died on January 1, 1838. Superannuated as they are they are nevertheless attractive thanks partly to their dress and make up, and partly to the prejudice in their favor on the part of the miners so long deprived of the society of women. They reap a plentiful harvest of octagons (fifty dollar gold pieces) and I could mention more than one who by their charms have amassed yearly from fifteen to twenty thousand dollars. [110]

In gambling dens women bartenders are paid a hundred and fifty dollars a month. They are on duty only six hours in the evening...

Though the cost of luxuries is high, the cost of the necessaries of life is comparatively low.[13] Without leaving the public square let us stop at the *Lafayette Restaurant* which is typical of the better kinds of restaurants. A liberal

127

menu card is submitted to the guest, and the dinner of his choice costs only one dollar and fifty cents; breakfast, one dollar. These meals by the week cost sixteen dollars. [111] A bottle of very good light Bordeaux wine is served for a dollar. Cliquot or Aï champagne costs two dollars and fifty cents. Bad or adulterated wines are rarely seen on the California market.

There are other restaurants in San Francisco where a workman who wishes to economize spends in a week not more than one day's wages. Such a restaurant is the *Dime House* near the harbor which serves food at ten cents a dish.[14]

"Man does not live by bread alone," says the Bible. No maxim is more indelibly engraven on the American mind. At La Piazza alone there are three or four book stores and many others are scattered about the town.[15] Every steamer brings the papers and magazines and inexpensive publications of Harper and Brothers, of Putman, Scribner and other popular American editors. Dickens, Bulwer, Douglas Jerold, Reynolds, Eugène Sue, Dumas, Georges Sand, etc., are to be seen in the most distant mines and form as it were a mysterious link between the old world of thought and the new world of action. The *New York Herald, Tribune*, and *Times* and the *United States Courier* publish specially for California a semi-monthly edition selling at twenty-five cents a copy. The circulation of these popular papers is increasing steadily throughout the country. [112] The *United States Express*, I hear from reliable sources, ships to San Francisco two thousand copies by each mail. French emigrants generally prefer this independent paper published under the standard of liberty to those of the censored Parisian press. However, one bookstore keeps the *Débats*, the *Presse*, and the *Charivari* sold at a franc a copy, but it not a paying enterprise.[16] German emigrants rely for news of their Fatherland on the *Allgemeine Zeitung*, not from Augsburg but from New York. Those of Spanish extraction give the preference to the *Diario* from Valparaiso.

The local press has flourished in California. San Francisco alone has seven or eight newspapers including the *Alta California* of the size of the *English Times,* which enjoys well merited popularity.[17]   Other cities, Sacramento, Stockton, Marysville, Nevada, San Jose, etc., publish each one or more newspapers.   The *Alta California*, and one or two other papers, to return the compliment to the *United States Express* print special editions for the United States on the days the steamers sail.

To the North American, literature, politics and science are inseparable. He likes to view in retrospect the progress made in the past; for him this lifts the veil of the future. A marvelous nation this, knowing whither it is going and seeking to discover the shortest road to its goal—social well-being.

Here is a city started scarcely four years ago on the high-road to civilization already opening a valuable agricultural, mineral and industrial exhibit: the Shelton Museum opposite the *El Dorado*.[18]   It contains a herbarium of hundreds of plants, nearly all native of California, several bulbous roots including one which can be used as soap; vegetables of enormous dimensions; potatoes weighing seven and a half pounds, onions three or four, tomatoes, two pounds, etc.; specimens of gold and other metals, articles of home manufacture, etc.   Art is likewise represented there by beautiful daguerreotypes, and as an antique in the printing line, the first book published in San Francisco: *California As It Is, and As It May Be; or, A Guide to the Gold Region*, by F. P. Wierzbicki, M.D.[19] [113]

To this Pole is due great honor, and in the name of Poland I thank him for beginning California literature by a work which will always be read and referred to with interest and pleasure. In keeping with the high prices in vogue at the time of its publication, this book of seventy-eight pages in 8° sold for five dollars a copy. Its author made the sum of eight to ten thousand dollars on two editions. It is now to be had for twenty-five cents, not that it has been discredited, but because this country is changing so rapidly that what is written of it today becomes ancient history in six months time.[20]

The admission fee to the museum is a dollar. In order to increase its attractiveness Mr. Shelton has lately added an exhibit of savages from New Holland, who are a strange contrast to the native savages here. It is to be hoped than an enterprise displaying such indefatigable energy will develop more and more. [114] Californians will find it a field for useful emulation; new arrivals, casting a glance at the products of nature improved by the genius of man, will understand in an instant as by magic what many books, journeys and investigations would fail to convey to them as clearly. Such a study can but be agreeable and profitable to all.

The citizens of a free and happy America succeed in accomplishing loyally and wisely what the monarchical governments of Europe try often in an aimless and foolish manner.

Mr. Shelton has stood out alone as the promoter of Californian agriculture and manufacturing. At a solemn meeting on November 15, 1851, he presented two prizes awarded by competent judges: one, a silver cup, to Mr. Horner for his display of vegetables, and a small gold hat to Messrs. Boyd and Dolsen for the best California-made hats. On this occasion Mr. A. Williams made an eloquent speech in which he dwelt on some interesting details concerning California.[21] As a proof of the astonishing fertility of a land which so far has attracted universal attention only by its minerals, he cited the following facts on the testimony of the most trustworthy citizens of Santa Cruz County:

> On the James Williams property an onion gained the enormous weight of twenty-one pounds. Land owned and cultivated by Thomas Fallen produced a cabbage measuring thirteen feet, six inches in diameter; a redwood tree in the valley, called Frémont tree has a circumference of fifty-one feet, and a height of three hundred. [115]

The speaker added that from his own knowledge there grew in Stockton a turnip that weighed one hundred pounds, and that in that same town twelve people dined off one single potato and consumed but half of it.

The products of the north and south are combined in the delightful valley of Los Ángeles where the banana, the

130

orange, and the lemon grow side by side with the peach, the pear, the cherry, and the apple.

"Lately," said Mr. Williams, "I was informed by one of our adopted celestials, whose phrenological development of the "auri sacra fames" outweighs his "amor patriae," that our soil, our climate and our resources were eminently suited to the cultivation of tea."

After having gone around the square, stopping to read some curious sign-boards, such as "Mesdames Napoléon et Comp. Costumer," we returned to the *California Exchange*, the center of continual movement. It is the only place where hired cabs are stationed. These have no fixed rates, but usually cost twenty-five dollars a day or ten dollars for half a day. This custom is not scrupulously adhered to as has been noted in my own case. All stage coaches and omnibuses start from the *California Exchange*.

Profiting by the throng of passersby an industry, quite Parisian and up to now unknown in America, has spread itself along the sidewalks.[22] A dozen or more shoe blacks offer their services at twenty-five cents a shine. They are all French, most of them engaging in this lowly and least gainful occupation in California because they are recovering from an illness, or have not the means to go to the mines. Shoe blacking brings in enough to live on: one or two piastres on week days, and four to five on Sundays. [116]

Kearney Street runs across the plaza and is parallel to Montgomery Street both having about an equal number of shops and crowds flocking there. Between these two principal thoroughfares is the pretentious and gay Commercial Street where the traveler finds himself right in the "Heart of France." This is the favorite walk of the "grande nation" as it was—not without reason—formerly called. The French language is heard in this street from morning to night; the signboards are French. Here, for instance, is the *Bonhomme*, a French hairdresser, the equal of the best in Paris; there *Madame Payot*, a French *café* and billiard-room.

Most prominent among establishments of the kind is the brilliant *Polka* gambling-house, run by M. Baroilhet, a brother of the famous singer of that name and president of newly organized French benevolent society.[23] The dense crowds you see thronging into the spacious and magnificent hall are drawn, not so much by the god of chance or the choice drinks served there. Two queens of beauty preside inside, now at the counter, now at the gambling table. One is called La Belle Lucienne and appeared formerly at the *Variétés Théâtre* in Paris; the other is the beautiful Madame Touchard. The charm of these two women turn the heads of miners who in some respects have become Oriental in their tastes. There is no need for further details. [117]

Kearney Street boasts of a club whose members, prominent merchants and lawyers meet there to read the daily papers and play whist or billiards. Through this strip of neutral land I pass from France over to China.

Nearly all the subjects of the Celestial Empire dwell in Sacramento Street, where they build Chinese houses, sell Chinese wares, run Chinese laundries, and serve, in special restaurants, Chinese dishes. The emigration of these Asiatics increases monthly in spite of the ukase of their emperor who is as little disposed, as is the Czar of Russia, to tolerate foreign travel. This magnanimous sovereign threatens his subjects with his paternal wrath and warns them that the Yankees have bored deep holes in the California soil in which they force all foreigners to work without pay, forever deprived of daylight.

But these celestials are not so unworldly wise as they appear to be, even into their minds the spirit of incredulity, to which man owes his glory and his progress, is beginning to seep slowly. They do not believe the forbidden fruit as bitter as reported; the weekly arrival of a large shipment of these Asiatics is a proof of this. Most of them go to the mines where they are noted for their untiring patience in the slow and tedious process of gold mining; they become industrious workers, digging either for themselves or hiring themselves out to others for four or five piastres a day.

Being an enemy of oppression in any form whatsoever and wherever it may descend on a race like a hideous vulture, I am happy to see that in California no one has thought of taking advantage of the ignorance of these Chinese to bind them by contract to five years of veritable slavery as is done in Peru. I do not know how far the American laws, merciless to Africa alone, would have permitted such an abuse towards Asia. [118] But it might have been attempted and it has not been. As free as the other inhabitants in California under the banner of the Union, the twelve or fifteen thousand Chinese scattered throughout the land very promptly inform themselves of their rights which they understand perfectly and take care that they are understood by their newly arrived compatriots. The Decree alone is hard to understand.[24]

These men said to be in their own country deeply demoralized and who in their wretchedness and abjection no doubt deserve their unfortunate reputation, these men, when raised to a life more worthy of rational beings become honest and peaceable citizens. Let kings and their tools hurl anathemas on thee, holy Liberty! Each step in the journey of time shows me that the hatred of the race comes solely from the fact that in thee they see the home of virtue. And it certainly is not on virtue that iniquitous power is based.

I cannot quite explain why there should be only three or four women among the large number of Chinese settlers who seem to have no thought of returning home. Is it due to their reluctance to expose the weaker sex to the vicissitudes of an unknown country? [119] Or is it the unwillingness of the sex to leave the native land?

The only Chinese woman I have seen in San Francisco is one very much in vogue, not with her compatriots who do not cultivate her acquaintance, but with Americans who besiege her door from morning to night. At home she is seen in her national costume, in the street she appears in European attire. Though not actually pretty, she is attractive. It is a pity she lacks, to be a perfect type, the tiny feet of women of the celestial empire. But, as I have been informed, that is a privilege of the high aristocracy obtained by much care, art, and torture. Miss Atoy, who was probably a lowly ferry-woman at Canton or Hong Kong, although not provided with extremities as well developed as those of northern women of both hemispheres, is yet far from having the dainty feet of the Andalusian and the Limean.[25] Chinese modesty is shocked at this courtesan's flirtation from her window or door with the "barbarians" of all nations. They

133

sent recently a deputation to the famous *Vigilance Committee* entreating it to put an end either by deportation or by any other form of punishment, to the tricks of this lively creature. It goes without saying that the complaint was not seriously considered; the committee, organized to deal with thieves, incendiaries and assassins has no time to bother with such comparatively harmless trifles.[26]   The scrupulous Chinese were given to understand that in Miss Atoy's case an exception could not be made to the tolerance shown by the San Francisco police to hundreds of American, French, German, and Spanish women whose conduct is hardly more edifying. [120]   The deputation, although disappointed withdrew greatly impressed by the impartiality of the "barbarians" tribunal which could weigh in the same balance all women in the town, regardless of nationality.

Barbarians! They would have every right to call us that, seeing us surprised that the lowliest amongst them can read and write. Barbarians! How could we be anything else in their eyes when they compare the frugality of their lives with the intemperance of the Christian population? Grave, calm and composed they smile with contempt at our state of feverish excitement.[27] One peculiar mania, however, arouses them from their habitual composure: they never miss an opportunity to fire off rockets and crackers skillfully manufactured by themselves. So elaborate is their celebration of the Fourth of July that one would think that American independence was declared mainly in their favor.

Starting on the heights of the city, Dupont and Stockton Streets run across it parallel to Montgomery Street. Although lined with numerous shops, barrooms and other public places, these streets lack the glitter, life and animation of those nearer the harbor.

On Dupont Street there is a French theatre open on Sundays. It is owned and run by four actresses, the Misses Alexina, Racine, Adelbert, and Eleonore. [121] The fortune amassed by these women, three of whom on landing at San Francisco had not twenty francs between them, is a proof of the great ease with which women, when at all experienced, can get along on this distant shore.[28] A rich mine indeed is the mine these Parisians own in this Gold Region! Eleonore,

134

Adelbert, Racine, and Alexina lead in California a life of ease, elegance and luxury which must compensate for their exile from the banks of the Seine. They live under the protection of some of the most important business-houses, assured for the present of a good income and of ample savings for the future—that cold and wrinkled future that comes all too soon whenever it comes.

In the theatres short, lively vaudevilles of the boulevards are put on, and the actresses as well as the actors perform their parts to the utmost satisfaction of an audience of French people ready to applaud were it only through patriotism.[29] Though the hall is small the receipts usually amount to seven hundred piastres a performance. The box seats cost four piastres, the orchestra, three, the gallery, two. In California these prices are not considered high and are the same as in the two American theatres.

Dances are sometimes given in the French theatre. They are necessarily lacking in gaiety, there being scarcely one woman to every ten men.[30] These women are in great demand by the eager dancers, and have to multiply themselves.

Stockton Street extends along the summits of the hills commanding a view of a most beautiful panorama below. With its cross-streets it is as peaceful a district as one could wish to find. It is remarkably salubrious being beyond the reach of the noxious odors of the harbor. [122]

On one of these streets that climb to the hill-tops the Spanish people have grouped their flimsy wooden houses. As the Chileans predominate here, the section is called "Little Chile"—a veritable South America in customs, dress, and amusements. Though on the whole lacking in education these people are noted for their exquisite innate courtesy. The men go about with their comfortable cloak called a *serape* in México and a *poncho* in South America. The women throw over their flowing dresses a beautiful, costly *pañuelo* (silken shawl) of brilliant colors. Both men and women smoke incessantly from morning to night and sometimes from night to morning, the men showing a preference for cigarettes and the women for large cigars. Many of the latter have come from Valparaiso for a sad and degrading trade. In

California at least they are not reduced to starvation but are given liberal compensation.

The barrooms of "Little Chile" resound at night with the lively stamping of the fandango and the *samacueca,* the Spanish-American national dance. The North-Americans take part in these *tertulias* (reunions), real Jupiters in pursuit of Danaës. They pay for admittance by offering sacrifice on the altar of monte, a gambling game that continues uninterruptedly throughout the evening. Like the Chinese with their fondness for fireworks, the Chileans also have a childish passion imported from their native land. They amuse themselves by the hour in flying kites betting among themselves the while on the outcome of the game. [123]

The time has now passed when the streets of San Francisco used to become deep marshes during the rainy season.[31] They are today all covered with planks and provided with sidewalks of stone or marble, but more often of wood. The mud in which the carts were sucked down, and the horses drowned is now but a tradition in the memory of the old inhabitants of 1849. The mud today is less miry than that of New York or Paris.

The architecture of the city presents a pleasing appearance by the elegance as well as by the variety of its styles. These include red brick houses such as are seen in the United States, wooden cottages in the English style, open dwellings resembling Italian villas, or real Chinese buildings constructed and used by the Chineses themselves. Then there are cast-iron edifices, and from Canton a merchant has just ordered granite houses all ready-made. Many large wooden hotels were imported from Boston in the same way.[32] The architecture of San Francisco is an index of its cosmopolitanism.

In viewing the innumerable dwellings placed in rows above one another, I could never have believed, had there been any room for doubting, that four months before my arrival (October, 1851) on this spot an immense void had been created by fire. Of the devastating fury of the flames that had spared no street, not a trace is to be seen. In a few short weeks brick buildings have been erected and wooden structures have sprung up overnight. This incredible haste to re-

136

build the town on warm ashes and smoking ruins is stimulated by the high rents paid at this time.[33] A house brings in thirty-five to seventy-five percent.[34] Such rates of interest encourage investors to risk their capital without the guarantee of insurance companies. [124] It will be some time before these are formed owing to the risk of fire in a town built almost entirely of excessively combustible materials and exposed to violent winds that drive the sparks from one district to another. The exception is an English agency which now insures well built brick houses for two thirds of their value. Few proprietors have taken this wise precaution which would reduce their risk to a mere trifle when compared with advantages derived from it. San Francisco has experienced six fires, but the phoenix at each resurrection has reappeared in a richer plumage.[35]

On the whole the people here display a neatness and good taste in dress as is seen in European capitals only among the privileged classes. At San Francisco everyone considers himself a gentleman, a well-bred man, and does his best to appear such.[36] A few miners are still seen with red shirts in public places, but most of them on arriving in town cast aside the livery of labor and are soon metamorphosed from head to foot at little cost in one of the numerous clothing establishments in competition with one another. The Jews and the Germans are especially interested in this type of business which has become most risky since the fall in prices. By bargaining awhile one can have a frock coat for sixteen piastres, an overcoat for sixteen to twenty, a pair of trousers for six, etc. These garments come from New York, Paris, or Bordeaux.

The miner objects to being encumbered with heavy baggage; he discards with disdain old clothes; consequently the streets are strewn with flattened hats, garments of every variety and heavy shoes. How fortunate would not the Parisian rag-picker esteem himself had he all these objects within his reach. [125] How gladly would the beggar in the Old World adorn himself with this cast off apparel! But in San Francisco there are neither beggars nor rag-pickers. The inhabitants enjoy real comforts; no able-bodied man runs the risk of lacking the necessaries of life. Poverty, for which a government refusing to recognize man's right to work or to emigrate is more responsible than is the individual suffering from it, exists here only among the temporarily disabled. Bureaus of charity organized to take care of the sick who are in need will probably succeed in preventing even such occasional misfortune.

Worshipped as goddesses, the women display in their dress the most attractive fashions of the day. They take from each country its specialty: hats from Paris, silks from China, laces from England, and create a rich and tasteful costume. Numerous jewelers are busy setting for them imported diamonds in the beautiful local gold. Surrounded by so much luxury how could they fail to be attractive? What matter to a crowd of bachelors that these ladies be no longer young or beautiful? They will be fascinating as long as each one can claim a score of admirers. In a population of thirty thousand San Francisco has only twelve to fifteen hundred women![37]

Oddly enough, the Californian population consists mainly of men between the ages of thirty and forty who have left in their native country their wives and children, and come all alone to seek a fortune which hope always pictures to them as near at hand. Planning to return home after a brief absence, these men, with few exceptions, live "as birds on a branch." [126] There is consequently, aside from a very small number of married couples, no family life in the whole length and breadth of the land, and no social activity in the towns.[38] The men live either in hotels or boarding houses in which the bedrooms are occupied by one or two, a common room being reserved for evening gatherings. There, in the absence of the virtuous mother and reserved sisters, the conversation, when not turning on the speculations of the day, can scarcely be expected to remain within the bounds of refinement. Women are admitted to these gatherings. Whatever their influence may be in other ways, it is not a refining one in social intercourse.

The wise maxim dating from the creation of the world: "It is not good for man to be alone," is beginning to make itself felt among the miners, many of whom are speaking of going home to get their better halves. The presence of women living within the marriage bond will change the

138

moral tone of California. A brilliant society will rise in San Francisco composed of numerous races in which the various characteristics will be combined in a new and interesting fusion. A few years hence the traveler will not, as now, when tired of hearing of the value of gold dust or the price of land be compelled to frequent monotonous theatres, gambling dens or to wander around the streets.

Then too, of only out of consideration for the ladies and their frail offspring, steps will be taken to light the streets which are now without lamps and have holes in many places. [127] In dark nights when there is no moon it is extremely difficult to avoid these dangerous places. I barely escaped injury on stumbling into one of these pitfalls. I might have broken a leg, but escaped with a cut on the knee. Such accidents are of frequent occurrence.

The inky darkness in some districts is so intense that robberies could easily be committed there. Imagine for a moment Paris or London without street lights! How many bandits would hold up passersby demanding their money or their lives! Well, in San Francisco this rarely happens. In 1849 some rascals banded together and paraded the streets, breaking windows, insulting people and molesting women. Under the significant title of "Hounds" they terrorized the peaceful citizens for some days. Seeing the powerlessness of the authorities, the people rose as a man and arrested all the culprits who were sentenced to hard labor. This vigorous measure put an end to public disturbances of this kind.[39]

Moreover, few burglaries are committed in this town. Objects of small value are utterly disdained by the thieves. In the boarding house where I lived for two months I left my door open with impunity in spite of the presence of fifteen other tenants and several servants. Notwithstanding some newspaper accounts which make of California a den of thieves, I do not believe that in proportion to its population the average of criminal element is as high as that of old civilized countries.[40] Most of the murders that unfortunately disgrace this new country are not the result of premeditation. Sudden anger or revenge are the common motives of these odious crimes and they are usually committed by drunkards or gamblers. [128]

The people of California, far from being as has been asserted by some, unusually lax in morals, manifest on the contrary an exaggerated sense of justice. They seem unable to tolerate in their midst crimes against the property or the person of their fellow citizens.[41] Such actions, not having elsewhere the excuse of poverty, are considered unpardonable. Consequently the spontaneous creation of the "Vigilance Committee" which, under the pretext of making a salutary example of them, take away the culprits from their legal judges, submit them to a summary trial and carry out their own decrees. This tribunal, upheld and sanctioned by the voice of the people, although usurping power, has not been guilty during its four months of existence of abusing this usurped authority. Nevertheless, it is an infringement on legal justice and one which only unusual conditions in a new country can sanction as a temporary abuse to avert still graver abuses.

Taken thus, the Vigilance Committee is a regulated, modified and improved form of the Lynch Law. When one sees inland mob rule in its most brutal form one can only congratulate San Francisco for having introduced a more orderly form. The Vigilance Committee is composed of honest and respectable citizens who, except on rare occasions, make it a point to observe the strictest justice. But for this committee, popular indignation greatly excited on two occasions within a couple of months, and prompted by as praiseworthy sentiments as those which excited the brewers of London against the wife-beater Hyman, this noble and virtuous indignation could have had most disastrous consequences. [129] The first case was that of Captain Watterman, commander of the clipper *Challenge*, accused by his sailors of having subjected them to most infamous treatment. The second case, that of another captain named Ellis who after having undertaken to bring from Sydney to San Francisco Smith O'Brien, the hero of Irish freedom, was said to have frustrated this plan of escape by denouncing him to the English authorities of that city. Thanks to the committee, Watterman was brought before a regular tribunal and Ellis was protected against the anger of some of the Irish colonists.[42]

It is, after all, not so strange that a people to whom acts of violence are revolting should be themselves inclined to punish them with undue severity. Man is all too disposed to avenge crime by imitating it. This tendency is seen in the laws of old nations as much as in the summary justice of budding governments. It was not possible for California to escape this general law.[43.]

The growing spirit of fraternity manifest in the planning of charitable institutions about to be created in San Francisco is a clear proof that high sentiments may very well exist side by side with the greed for gold. This cult, so utterly corrupting in a monarchy, is purified in a republican atmosphere. Boston, the millionaire city of the United States is a case in point. Nowhere is wealth more lavishly shared with the needy. San Francisco is destined to follow this noble example.

Meanwhile, the worship of gold does not exclude religion. In San Francisco there are fifteen Christian churches, two Catholic and thirteen Protestant. The Jews have two synagogues and the Mormons a chapel. [130] The Chinese sometimes meet one of their houses to take part in religious services conducted by priests in flowing sky-blue robes.[44]

In the midst of so many different sects in close contact with one another, religion tends naturally to lessen its tolerance. To the great regret of some fanatic clergymen the Sunday is not observed in San Francisco with the exaggerated strictness of Protestantism. It would be impossible to stop business for a whole day in the busiest place in the world. Some of the shops are open in the morning, and if most of the gambling dens are closed, the theatres on the other hand reserve for that day their most brilliant performances. After church time the streets are deserted. Cabs, omnibuses, all manner of vehicles take the crowd to the Mission Dolores two miles from the city. An excellent road paved partly with planks and partly with macadam leads to it.[45] Elegant country houses, fields under cultivation bringing in fabulous sums, little restaurants along the road, all testify to a progress that seems more rapid than thought.

A traveler who left California in 1842 and returned in 1851 was telling me lately that such a transformation had

141

taken place on this road that it seemed to him like dream.[46] Ten years before, instead of passing between two rows of houses, the traveler had to follow an uneven path in a labyrinth of bushes. Instead of a continual stream of carriages, riders, pedestrians, there reigned a dreary solitude broken only rarely by the apparition of a monk riding on a mule, or of a ragged, dull Indian whom the Catholic Church claimed to have civilized by teaching him the principal doctrines of Catholicism and feeding him on acorns—slender dole both moral and physical given as salary for arbitrarily imposed labor.[47] The Mission, and adobe building, was founded in 1776. It has not been inhabited by the Spanish friars since its secularization in 1831.[48] But in order to retain something of its Spanish customs, bull-fights are held there regularly on Sundays. This spectacle is very much to the taste of mixed Castillian and Indian blood and is usually attended by a motley crowd. It is hard to account for the throng of *serape* clothed men and *reboso* covered women very rarely seen on any other occasion. [132] The features of both men and women betray their mixed origin. The latter though not pretty have beautiful eyes. And what a gleam in those bright eyes when the bull charges, and when it receives from the matador the death blow, what an expression of cruel delight. Thus is drawing to a close Mexican California always eager for excitement. Its traces will soon be lost in the international fusion of a universal California and with it will disappear these cruel games, a sad legacy of a barbarous age which will be repudiated with other remnants of Spanish rule.

The Anglo-Americans and the Europeans take little interest in these bull-fights. If they attend them it is reluctantly and at most out of curiosity to see a combat between a bear and bull tied together and forced to fight until blood flows. This hideous sight is a specialty of the country. From Mission Dolores one has a good view of the immediate surroundings of San Francisco. Except for glimpses of the ocean, there is little to charm the traveler.[49] The land stretches out in monotonous rolling hills unbroken by abrupt elevations or interesting formations. No rapid stream, no dense forest relieves the monotony of the landscape. The

142

water flows slowly between prosaic banks. So sparse are the trees, that a group of half a dozen is a rare sight. But the farmer has no fault to find with a soil which the artist views with indifference if not disdain. Nature has provided California with the useful; to man has been left the task of creating the agreeable.

2.

THE GOLD REGION

From the Sierra Nevada to the Pacific Ocean and from Oregon to the city of Los Ángeles, the land of California is exceedingly rich in gold.[1] The mining region is watered by two principal rivers, the Sacramento and the San Joaquín, which unite before emptying their waters in a large sheet into San Pablo Bay, the vestibule of San Francisco Bay proper. Many tributaries flow into these two rivers, which like the waters of the Hudson and the Mississippi are plowed by magnificent steamers.

The Sacramento is the high road to the northern mines; the San Joaquín, to the southern, according as the mineral deposits are located in the neighborhood of one or the other of these rivers. [134] The Sacramento is navigable for ninety miles from San Francisco, as far as the city of Sacramento, built on the site of a ranch which Captain Sutter had established there under the name of New Helvetia.[2]

By its thriving commerce, its population of fifteen thousand, and its marvelous prosperity, Sacramento ranks as the second city of California.[3] Ocean-going ships discharge here their cargo to save the cost of trans-shipment. Half a dozen steamers keep it in daily communication with San Francisco, others by the Feather River with Marysville, its suburb. Stage-coaches bring it near to the surrounding mines of which it appears to be the triumphal gate. In Sacramento the same amusements are to be had as in San Francisco: theatres, luxurious architecture, the same variety of faces, languages, costumes.

It could not be otherwise in a place through which all nations must pass in their rush to the richest of California's gold mines. Far from inspiring the terrifying phantasmagoric of the mythologic tales, the entrance to these treasures revives hope by its pleasant appearance, redoubles courage and excites the imagination. In crossing Sacramento the idea which these modern Argonauts have of the *Golden Fleece*, a share of which each one expects to gain, takes on gigantic proportions; for is this not a city born of a few cuttings of this Fleece? They are all confident of success, these enterprising paladins! Some of them, alas, return from their great venture sad, thoughtful, comparing what had appeared to them a triumphal gate, to Dante's portal of despair on which these famous lines are inscribed:[4] [135]

> *Per me si va nella città dolente,*
> *Per me si va nell alto dolore,*
> *Per me si va tra la perduta gente.*

Let us hasten to add that this disillusion is the exception. Its victims can blame themselves, their imprudence, their misconduct, their insatiable greed, rather than Fate.

Navigation extends, if I am not mistaken, for a hundred and twenty miles from San Francisco up the San Joaquín and is stopped only by the Stockton Slough at Stockton, a city which is progressing more slowly than Sacramento;[5] for the southern mines to which it leads are not nearly so rich as those of the north. It has a population of five or six thousand souls. The mud of its unpaved streets compels its citizens to wear heavy boots over their trousers in the old San Francisco style. Stagecoaches run between Stockton and the Sonora and Mariposa mines.

The mining camps become cities with surprising rapidity. The process by which this transformation takes place is very simple. A few men pitch their tents in a spot where the soil appears to be auriferous. If they are successful in striking gold the news is soon spread abroad, exaggerated as it goes from mouth to mouth, and gold-seekers, anxious to abandon their barren diggings or eager for a richer yield than they are obtaining, hasten from all sides. Dozens of other tents soon surround the first tent. [135] After a few months of this pastoral life, it suddenly occurs to a few of the inhabi-

144

tants that wood provides a better shelter than canvas. Fir trees are soon felled and made into boards and for awhile all are busy erecting for themselves as comfortable a shelter as possible. The largest of these dwellings hoists the American flag and declares itself a hotel. Small shops open their doors and sell merchandise in the overstocked markets of San Francisco at greatly reduced prices. When the settlement numbers a thousand inhabitants, a newspaper, if only weekly, is deemed necessary to the interest of the place.[6] The editor, a former innkeeper, butcher, or traveling preacher is ready to resume his original occupation should his literary venture prove a failure. The Yankee can adapt himself to everything except slavery.

The fame of the new city spreads and soon the arts begin to be exercised; musicians are engaged by a proprietor bent on outdoing his competitor who in turn likewise hires musicians, and a Frenchwoman besides, to preside at his bar. She is often the only woman in the neighborhood; one can judge of the sensation created by her presence.

A woman and an orchestra! In California these mark the transition from rough camp life to more orderly city life.

But no sooner are a few fortunes made and is general prosperity increased than a thirst is felt for the relinquished pleasures of civilization. Bear-dancing and bull and bear fighting become insipid spectacles. Then some speculator anticipates the wishes of the public and builds a theatre, or some traveling company of actors puts on a series of performances. Houses of worship have preceded the building of places of amusement.[7] A post office has long been established, and public conveyances run regularly from the new city to Stockton or Sacramento. [137] Scattered along the road leading to these two centrally located cities one sees small inns; the little place numbering a thousand inhabitants today, may soon boast of three, four or five thousand.

With the "go ahead" principle of the North American one can never tell where a movement once started will stop.[8] The suddenness with which towns have sprung up at the gold fields cannot fail to give a false impression to those who have not seen them. You would expect to find a disorderly mass of rustic houses thrown here and there. Not so. A regular plan, symmetrical streets, city houses, that is what one sees in Coloma, Nevada City, Downieville in the north, Sonora, and Mariposa in the south.[9] And how many other mining towns already started or to be started are destined to compete with those mentioned above!

Accounts by North Americans who have no feeling for the picturesque had given me the impression that the mines were reached through smiling landscapes. This is an illusion common to these men in whose eyes all land valuable for agriculture or mining is, for that reason alone, possessed of dazzling beauty. The fact is that the Sacramento Valley on the way to Sonora is truly monotonous. Here and there one passes through desert land with vegetation similar to that of the Texas prairies, the steppes of Russia and the pampas of South America. Occasional oak trees stand in the distance like solitary islands in an immense ocean. A few trees border the rivers between which the almost complete absence of vegetation is explained by a total lack of water. The traveler may have to go two or three miles without quenching his thirst. Some relay horse owners are obliged to fetch their water on foot from a distance of a mile or two; others showing Yankee resourcefulness sink a well a hundred feet deep or more.

The public conveyances are jaunting cars without springs. Usually the seats with room for two passengers accommodate three. It would be difficult to drive any other kind of vehicle on roads covered with muddy pools during the wet season from April to November [actually, November to April]. Even these often break down, but they are easily repaired because of the simplicity of their construction. This way of traveling however slow it may be—four to five miles an hour, discounting accidents—is yet a great improvement when compared with the journey on foot common among poor or economical miners, or on horseback which is almost as slow since the horses have to stop every few minutes to get their breath. The stage coaches have well organized relay stations.

Along the thirty, forty or fifty miles of uninterrupted desert land devoid of all vegetation through which my different explorations took me, it was the animal kingdom that

146

provided me with diversion. Herds of antelopes, deer and elk roam the plains of California. The coyote, a jackal rather than a wolf, although classed with this species, is seen everywhere; he never attacks man but seems to defy him. Not content with prowling around dwellings from which he would gladly carry off a pig or a hen, he loiters along the highway and instead of fleeing at the approach of a carriage, a horse or a pedestrian, he stops and gazes curiously at them, keeping however prudently beyond the range of a gun. [139] The bear is rarely seen in open country: he hides in the wooded ravines where the venturesome gold-seeker suddenly comes upon him. Stories of these terrible encounters are favorite topics in the miners' conversations. But who believes all these hunters' tales?

The region abounds in game. Partridge, wild ducks, grouse, pheasants, etc., vie with one another for the honor of passing from the cares of this world to the transfiguration of the sauce pan.[10] But little variety is seen in the ornithological ornament. What shall I say of the reptiles? There are many rattlesnakes, although none were to be seen. On the other hand I recognized the horned toad that I thought was confined to Texas. From insects out-of-doors I suffered no inconvenience, the temperature—it was in December—was too cold for gnats; but it was otherwise with fleas. Myriads of them tormented me continually at night everywhere in California, excepting in San Francisco, where they spared me, owing to the scrupulous cleanliness with which my room was kept by my amiable hostess, Madame Ducloss. But at Sacramento, Stockton, at the mines, these execrable blood suckers were invariably found. What contributes to their propagation is the unfortunate habit the workmen have of avoiding as much as possible the use of linen or cotton and of wearing instead red flannel shirts for a fortnight at a time without washing them. In the early days of the gold rush exorbitant prices were paid for laundry work.[11] Now, however, the price is reduced to six dollars a dozen inland, and five in San Francisco. This is still too high for men who prefer to add this sum to their bacchanalian libations. Besides, one grows accustomed to fleas as to the other miseries of life, and ends by not noticing them.

147

However limitless the ocean may appear to a tired traveler on a long voyage, it sooner or later breaks against some shore. So also with the pampas, steppes, or prairies, whatever be the name of the apparently never ending plains leading to the *placers*. These wearisome valleys end in a mountain chain called the Rocky Mountains [Sierra Nevada] which before rising to snowy heights spread out in myriads of hills. Numerous rivers wind in and out between them and mingle the waters they bring as a tribute to the Sacramento and the San Joaquín. Deep ravines open out on all sides. The scenery has suddenly changed; uniform before, it now varies. Dense forests of oaks, cedars, firs rise around, overhead and far below. In the heart of these forests, in the depths of these ravines, on the banks of these rivers, on the heights of these hills tents or wooden houses stand out, descend, spread out or climb, forming groups, disorderly when they are camps, regular when they are towns. This soil out of which nature by volcanic action has already created a picturesque disorder, the hand of man has furrowed with ditches, pierced with levels and dug up in all directions.[12] With the shovel, pick, and gunpowder a crowd of people are busy digging in the ground, breaking stones, dynamiting rocks; others with the same, if not greater eagerness wash the sand, the mud or the crushed quartz. Never before was such activity displayed in the accomplishing of a task! What is all this? [141] Where are we? Need I inform you? These are the placers of the modern El Dorado. We are at Nevada City, at Sonora, at Coloma, no matter where, the same description answers for any of these places.

Placer—pleasure. The Spaniard in his melodious tongue means by this word a gold mine, as though by anticipation he experienced that of which the yellow metal is the dispenser. Hope, the promise of pleasure, and pleasure itself, are they not after all the same thing? Does one not enjoy more truly when saying, I shall enjoy, than when tasting the enjoyment? Deeply philosophical is the application of this word. What matter that this word should have arisen for the first time out of cupidity in the presence of undreamed of buried treasures? The most striking truths are not always those consciously uttered.

148

Over a stretch of four or five hundred miles, on a curve running from north to south, California is dotted with placers. One sees nothing but gold, more gold, still more gold. Science is as yet unable to decide to which kind of soil gold gives the preference, for it is found mixed in gravel, limestone, and clay, red or black. The gold runs in veins in quartz; it drops or seems to drop like rain-water suddenly changed into ice from a compact mixture of different minerals; it is mixed as dust or nuggets with the sand of the rivers. All the streams that flow into the Sacramento and San Joaquín are filled with it. It accumulates usually in places where the stream winds around an abrupt projection of the river bank, a projection called by the Americans a *bar*. The Rocky Mountains and these bars are the places where this precious metal is pleased to tarry. [142] But it is found in lesser quantities in the steppe described above and almost on the seashore near Bodega. There does not exist, there never has existed gold mines richer than those of California unless perhaps in a few districts in Australia. The mines of Peru, today exhausted and abandoned, were not nearly so rich; those of Siberia actively exploited by the Russian government are greatly inferior. And these gold mines, the foremost in the world remained unknown until the North Americans came to take possession of the country.[13] Does it not almost seem that Providence had reserved them for a fortune of which they alone were worthy to be the trustees? Of the nations from whom escaped as by a miracle the deposits of this precious metal, none would have put it to good use. Spain would have monopolized it for her idle priests and useless saints; México would have used it to carry on her deplorable wars; Russia, by means of this enormous increase in revenue, would have redoubled her zeal for the destruction of liberty in the two hemispheres. This last came very near being realized.

As one knows, a Russian colony existed on the coast of California from 1814 to 1842.[14] it was under military rule and was despotically governed by commanders appointed by the Russian-American Company. The following conversation took place one day between one of these commanders and a simple laborer on his return from hunting.

149

"I saw in a river," said the man, "a few grains that shone like gold. If Your Highness deems it expedient, a detachment of men could be assigned to explore the river."

"What nonsense! Dismiss such thoughts from your mind," answered the chief, little dreaming that such a thing could be possible. [143] And annoyed at the laborer's persistence:

"Mind the work assigned to you and don't bother with what is no concern of yours."

Further argument was useless, and so the incident ended.

How different might have been the subsequent course of history had this conversation turned out otherwise! Imagine for a moment autocratic Russia instead of republican America the owner of California's placers! There is no doubt that this lost opportunity has stirred the ambitious thoughts of the Czar. The case of Admiral [Ferdinand von] Wrangel's startling disgrace is in all probability the advice he gave to his master to give up entirely Bodega and Ross[15]—just six months before the discovery of gold. M. de Ratcheff, the last Russian commander, entrusted with the evacuation of the colony, transported the inhabitants, willing or unwilling, to Sitka.

It is curious that scientific explorations made from time to time, did not establish the presence of gold in California. Mr. [James Dwight] Dana, the geologist attached to Captain [Charles] Wilkes's expedition, merely remarks that the rocks in the districts of Umpqua and of Shasta resemble in many spots the auriferous rocks of other regions.[16] "But," he adds, "if gold exists there, it is yet to be discovered."

This as we see is not a positive affirmation but simply a guess. Mr. Dana had taken special care to examine the minerals of the country. [144] He went from the Columbia River to San Francisco, across the Sacramento within forty miles of the spot where chance placed the discovery destined to be looked upon by posterity as the most important event of the century and the one that has had the greatest influence upon the destiny of the entire human race.

I assert without hesitation that the year 1848 will affect the life of man less by its numerous European revolu-

150

tions than by the simple fact of the discovery of gold in California.[17]

As though this event was to begin a new era it preceded the "February Days"[18] by a month only. Two workmen, [James W.] Marshall and [Charles] Bennett, were employed by Captain [John Augustus] Sutter to build a saw mill on the southern branch of the American River, about fifty miles from New Helvetia, today Sacramento. The place was covered with oaks, firs, cedars, etc. When the mill was built, it was found necessary to widen the race-way for the wheel. There in a heap of earth Marshall saw something shining.

"It is gold!" he exclaimed. With the assistance of his companion he collected yellow dust to the value of one hundred fifty _piastres_ according to the estimate of a San Francisco prospector who confirmed the statement of the two workmen regarding their find.[19]

In vain did Captain Sutter bind his employees to secrecy, the news flew with lightning speed from mouth to mouth.[20] A veritable fever seized the inhabitants of California, impelling them to desert in large numbers the cities and the ranchos and to pitch their tents in the beautiful Coloma Valley, as the Indians call the site of the sawmill. [145] Yielding to an irresistible impulse, the merchant forsook his shop, the physician his patient, the sailor his ship, the soldier his flag, the rancher his oxen and sheep. Of a population of several hundred in San Francisco there remained only seven inhabitants.

The courts of justice were idle, the judges being the first to be affected by the fever.[21] Even the Governor, Colonel [Richard B.] Mason, and his staff appeared at the mines with pick and shovel. The workers were on the whole very successful in their quest. They made on the average a hundred piastres a day, and some acquired large fortunes. Gold that had lain undisturbed in its secret retreats ever since its formation was found in great quantities during the early days of the gold rush.

The exploration was not long confined to Coloma: the effluents of the Sacramento and the San Joaquín were visited simultaneously by men eager to strike virgin places and willing to brave all fatigue, obstacles and dangers. The passion for wealth, the strongest of all passions, urged them over inaccessible paths obstructed by virgin forests, perpendicular cliffs, muddy bogs. This passion for wealth dispelled terrors of every kind. The bears of gigantic size might rise, saying: "This is my domain." "Mine it is," would reply the miner as he buried a shot in the furry monster. When the wandering savage protested at the violations of his home by sending arrows whistling past the ears of the intruder, the latter would strike down the Indian and carry off his bleeding scalp. The passion for wealth rendered them careless of comfort and even of necessities of life. Those who happened to strike a rich vein would follow it up with such zest as to forget to eat for twenty-four hours at a stretch. Some having too late thought of replenishing their supply of provisions died of hunger like King Midas at a feast of gold.

All occupations but one being suspended, the cost of living became excessive. The following bill for a breakfast for two, dating from the period, gives an idea of the high prices paid for food:

Box of sardines	$16.00
1 lb. dry bread	$2.00
1 lb. butter	$6.00
½ lb. cheese	$3.00
2 bottles of ale	$16.00
Total	$43.00 [22]

Forty-three dollars—two hundred fifteen *francs*—or one hundred seven *francs* fifty *centimes* each without meat, eggs, or coffee! Another bill of the same date quotes meat at two dollars a pound, eggs at a dollar a piece, coffee at four dollars a pound. A bottle of alcohol sold for forty-eight dollars and a barrel of flour for twenty-four. Twenty-four dollars was also paid for a box of Seidlitz powders and one drop of laudanum cost a dollar. These last two items may be reckoned as food of which they were at that time indispensable correctives. Salted meats and lack of vegetables ruined the digestion of the miners, who to escape scurvy and dysentery, were dependent on medicines.[23] In the early days these two diseases constantly decimated the mining population.

Today however, hotels are established everywhere and the miner pays either a dollar a meal or two dollars a day for room and board. [147] Coats, which he got along without, and boots costing some time before fifty dollars or more are, thanks to sharp business competitions, now almost as cheap here as in New York. I have seen enough dry goods in California to clothe a population ten times as large as that of which she now boasts. Great numbers of speculators have been ruined by this excessive importation of goods.[24] That of course is the other side of the medal.

The news of extraordinary success at some of the mines was not long in getting abroad. It was said that a German with the help of Indian labor had amassed four or five hundred thousand dollars; two Americans, also by means of Indian labor, obtained in two days the sum of seventeen hundred dollars; a canyon of the Stanislaus River furnished an Irishman with twenty-six thousand dollars, and a Frenchman at another river made three thousand dollars in four days.[25]

These stories, repeated and exaggerated, inflamed the people's imaginations in the United States, as also in the rest of America, in Europe, Asia and even in the farthest parts of the world. Emigrants began to arrive from all directions: through the Rocky Mountains, around Cape Horn, by Panamá, by México, from the Sandwich Isles, China, Sydney, etc.[26] Was there indeed any route or place from which none came?

History knows of no other such agglomeration of men of all nations. At the preaching of the first Crusade Peter the Hermit united under his standard only the Christian peoples. More universally venerated than the tomb of Christ, gold drew together all religions, all superstitions, all unbelievers. Divergences in religious and political opinions were harmonized in a common faith, the faith in gold. [148] And marvelous phenomenon! While the old continent, shaken on its feudal bases, was proclaiming Utopian equality, the region of gold was making equality a reality. Education and ignorance, polished manners and rude forms, upper and lower classes were united in the fraternity of labor. Labor! Its rehabilitation was effected in the sight of all. Beneath the red flannel shirt who could distinguish the elegant dandy from the uncouth peasant, the master from the servant, those born to rule from those destined to obey? A leveling indeed of rank and caste! In this suddenly improvised society those social fictions, which everywhere else reason vainly tries to discredit, disappear here of themselves, are automatically annulled, abolished, forgotten. And the same leveling process ennobles through high wages that type of labor usually considered degrading. A Negro cook earned a hundred and fifty dollars a week. A laundress bestowed her hand on a man of high breeding who esteemed himself fortunate in having acquired by this marriage two, at that time, rare privileges, a wife and clean linen.

There is at the present moment no place in the world so democratic as is California. All trades are here respectable and respected. At *Jones' Hotel* in San Francisco I was waited on at table by a professor of Latin and a doctor of medicine. At the *Lafayette Restaurant* I was served by a French count of a *Legistimiste* family and by the son of a Parisian lawyer. Servants are paid a hundred to a hundred and fifty dollars a month.[27]

A year after the discovery of gold there were fifty thousand workers in the mines; there are now between a hundred and a hundred and fifty thousand. [149] Such an influx of people made of San Francisco a large and important city in a very short time. Building lots that had been bought at ten dollars a piece were now sold for three or four thousand dollars. Houses sprang up on all sides, yet rent remained incredibly high. The *Parker House*, a hotel on the Piazza, was rented for two hundred thousand dollars a year.[28]

Sacramento, where up to then travelers had had no other lodging than a dismantled ship, was now rapidly covered with comfortable dwellings. The rise in the price of the lots was the same as in San Francisco.[29]

The principal mines were promptly transformed into cities, and now Nevada City, Grass Valley, Rough and Ready, Coloma, Sonora, and Mariposa number each from three to five thousand inhabitants. Picturesque as well as luxurious with their somber forests and attractive gambling halls, they remind one of the watering places in Germany to

154

the beauty of which both nature and art contribute their share. Nothing so enchanting, for instance, as Grass Valley; I could not help comparing this delightful spot with Baden-Baden.

Then too, one stands amazed in contemplating in the mining region the gigantic work accomplished in less than three years! It appears like an extravagant dream, a phantasmagoria, a reminiscence of fairies and giants. Pits dug to reach the gold in the entrails of mother earth, levels following the winding veins through rocky hills, mills with immense wheels to crush the quartz, rivers turned aside from their course, artificial canals that ascend and descend to carry the water: here is proof of superhuman activity, stubborn perseverance and a daring that baffles the imagination. [150]

Nowhere has the genius of man shown its power as in this marvelous land! The pyramids of Egypt, the Gothic cathedrals, Saint Peter's and other monuments of pride, of superstition and of vanity inspire only contempt when one counts the time it took to erect them, when one thinks of the thousands of unfortunate slaves, serfs and laborers who have sweat blood and water in placing stone upon stone, and when one considers how greatly these edifices have contributed and still do contribute to the enslaving of man's intellect in the stupid respect for the past and vain fear of the future. In viewing the colossal works of the California genius one's admiration goes to *crescendo*, for they stand forth in a region where three or four years ago there reigned the most absolute solitude. Conceived, planned and carried out by free and voluntary association of small numbers of men, they point to that kind of progress that raises man more and more in his own estimation.

The mines are classed according to their nature as "wet diggings" or "dry diggings."[30] In the former the gold is found in the bed of the rivers, streams or torrents, while in the latter is located in the crevasses of the rocks. In the "wet diggings" the gold is found more evenly distributed everywhere and compensates more or less for the miner's labor; the "dry diggings" contain the precious metal here and there accumulated in large deposits, yielding on one day a fortune, and on another nothing at all. In selecting the latter one must rely on chance; with the former one is assured of a reward.

The precious particles are separated from the sand or mud in which they are contained by a very simple process. [151] A tin pan filled with as much auriferous earth as it can contain is tipped into the water. As the stones rise to the surface they are removed by hand, while a gentle shaking of the pan diminishes the semi-liquid mass. Heavier than sand, the gold particles tend to remain at the bottom of the pan where, after a series of baths, it is found in the form of grains or flakes mixed with black soil. This soil the miner removes by blowing it off and he then puts the almost pure gold that remains into a bag usually worn at the belt with a revolver and a bowie knife.

A man working his claim by himself cannot make use of any but his primitive method of gold washing. But when three men are associated together they may use a machine called a "cradle."[31] This is a wooden box built in the form of a cradle, as its name indicates, and closed on all sides except one through which the dissolved earth escapes. The "mouth," one of the closed sides, is provided with a sieve and the box itself is placed on rockers. While one man fills the sieve with sand, the second pours the water and a third rocks the "cradle" gently back and forth.

This method however is far from satisfactory and has been modified in different ways, which would be tedious to explain here at length. So far, no perfect system has been found. It is estimated that by the present methods a third of the gold is lost.

While I was in California a Russian imported a machine in use in Siberia and experimented with it on the banks of the Yuba at Sicard Bar.[32] Will this Asiatic invention be more successful than those of Europe or America? That remains to be seen. [152] It would indeed be strange, though not impossible, that a useful suggestion should come from a country in which civilization has never dreamed of finding improvements. This Russian assured me that by the Siberian method the loss of gold would be less than one fiftieth. Amalgamation with quicksilver has now been introduced. The objection to this scientific process is its costliness.

It is not vain curiosity that leads men to seek to determine by what geological revolution gold was scattered in California's soil. The solution of this question is of real practical value. Investigators are inclined to believe that originally, through volcanic action, gold must have flowed in liquid form, for the El Dorado bears everywhere traces of the action of fire. The abrupt and irregular formation of the rocks, tossed up often in a horizontal [vertical] position, shows that they were violently torn from the bowels of the earth; rivers are bordered with excavations resembling ancient craters. The nature and the aridity of certain plains cannot be otherwise explained than by a cataclysm similar to that of which Judea, among other countries, bears the dreadful marks.[33]

That gold was injected into the quartz in a liquid state there seems to be little doubt. The crevices in the stone which must have cracked during the ebullition are completely filled with the rich metal either in flakes or in nuggets. Both ending as do all molten metals in a lachrymal form, they resemble drops of lead poured into a glass.[34] In washing the rocks the water has carried away and is still carrying particles of gold to the bottom of the ravines and rivers where these particles, by reason of specific gravity, sink until they come in contact with something hard, such as stone, clay or the root of a tree. Their shape as a consequence is determined by the friction which they undergo; they are seen microscopic in size, scaled off in shells, rounded out in leaves, in flat flakes or molded in queer figures.

"Gold stops in this or that spot according to the force of the water, the weight of the particles and the obstacles in the way. The lightest particles are naturally carried further away from their primitive bed. Since the scattering of the gold took place in very remote ages, one meets, as a rule, all these deposits more or less deeply embedded in the sand, gravel, or rock.[35] Strictly speaking the gold does not belong to the rivers; it was brought there from the hills. It is consequently useless to seek gold at the source of rivers that are not surrounded by auriferous hills. Personal experience has taught us this fact."

The logical conclusion from this hypothesis is that the California mines are not, as has been asserted, inexhaustible. Today however, they yield more gold than all the rest of the world, Australia excepted.

The continual increase of workers, the use of labor saving devices, better washing methods, the discovery of virgin deposits will all help to maintain, if not increase for awhile the quantity of metal taken from the earth.[36] Conditions may continue thus for twenty-five, fifty or a hundred years. But there will come a time when the miners will of themselves desert a decreasingly lucrative work; when even efficiently organized companies will fail to defray working expenses in spite of economy of time and labor; when the country having been explored in all directions there will be no more discoveries to make.

There is necessarily a similarity in the history of California's mines and that of others, ancient and modern. Many rivers, streams and torrents have washed down gold in the Old World. The Tagus's reputation in this respect was proverbial. Today, however, so rare have become its gold flakes that it would not pay to collect them. The same can be said of the Danube, the Rhone, and the Rhine. The Potosí mines of which the Spanish kings were so proud, and which enabled the Incas of Peru to make massive gold statues, shrubs of gold and golden gardens, these mines, reputed inexhaustible, were abandoned after half a century of regular exploitation.

Such will be the fate of the California mines.[37] Richer than other mines of the past, they may last longer— that is all. Great numbers of places from which the early miners obtained nuggets in abundance are today worked in vain.

It is estimated that in 1850 the average daily yield of gold was eight dollars *per capita*. But by dividing at this rate the output of fourteen companies comprising 344 members, Mr. D. Woods finds only three dollars and sixteen cents for each man. From first hand information obtained at Nevada City, I concluded that the probable earnings of the miners should be placed at five or six dollars. This sum is accurate, as day labor is no where paid less than four dollars.

158

The usual wages are in fact, five dollars for surface work and eight dollars for underground labor in ditches or levels.

Twenty-five *francs* a day, the pension of ex-representatives of ex-French Republic, nothing less are the wages on which the miner can count, whether he works for himself or hires himself out to others. In the first case he has, as it were, a lottery ticket on extraordinary strikes which are now, however, rare; on the other hand, his daily quota may be reduced to three dollars or less. In the latter case, although the hope of suddenly making a fortune is denied him, yet he is assured of a regular income of which he can easily economize the half. [156]

If we set work days at two hundred and forty, we have the sum of six thousand *francs* per annum, an average salary very easily earned. Consequently in going to California every workman whom competition reduces to poverty in Europe is sure to improve his condition. He does well to emigrate if what he craves is an increase in wages that will permit him in five or six years to accumulate a modest competency. But he is greatly deceived if he expects to find gold heaped in a pile all ready for him to shovel, and if he counts on becoming wealthy in the space of a few weeks or months.

Does it not seem unnecessary to exaggerate the wonders of a land that is in reality as marvelous as is California? Yet most of those who determine to go there indulge in chimerical dreams; taking exceptional cases for the rule, they imagine that a sudden fortune awaits them. Disappointment soon follows this intoxicating hope. Thence bitter grief, delirious despair, sometimes suicide.

Those individuals especially are subject to deep discouragement who by their former occupation or leisure are not equal to the work in the mines, which with inconceivable lack of foresight they considered a mere trifle.[38] The life of the miner is in reality the most laborious imaginable. It requires both physical and moral strength. The body must be able to endure fatigue and the heart disappointments. The miner's work is a combination of different trades; of the farmer, stone cutter, bricklayer and woodcutter; he must be all these in turn. His head is exposed to the burning sun or to the dampness of the dew or of the showers; his feet to the

159

shock of icy water, his hands to the painful excoriations, bleeding, cuts, and to infected wounds. His stomach will have to stand now indigestible food, now devouring hunger. His limbs, exhausted by nine hours of labor in the most difficult positions, will rest on a hard couch where the mosquito, the flea, and the bug will fight with all their might against his sleep.

There is no need of adding here descriptions of accidental occurrences: the contact with a common plant, *Rhus toxicodendron*, the poison oak, which causes a painful skin irritation; the unexpected meeting of the grizzly bear, the dread monarch of the forests of California; the savage lying in wait for the white man who invades his domain. One may also omit the catastrophes by which the miner loses in one day the fruits of several months' labor: thefts which deprive him suddenly of his treasure; floods bearing away his machines, his tools, his tents; fires consuming everything but what he has with him. And these fires, floods and thefts are unfortunately of only too frequent occurrence. [158]

Aside from the many misfortunes, as also from epidemics more or less inevitable, is the ever present temptation of gambling, which robs the miner of far more than does the bandit whom one can oppose with weapons. Apart from all these disasters the miner's life in its normal state is one which a man accustomed to hard labor from his youth need not hesitate to undertake as a means of improvement for the present and of independence for the future.[39] But how can men whose muscles are not inured to fatigue hope to succeed in this laborious career? One can only pity the notorious folly of lawyers, judges, doctors, chemists, writers, soldiers, clergymen, hairdressers and men of leisure of Broadway in New York or of the boulevards of Paris, and other individuals who, while they may be successful in their own calling, are utterly incapable of digging canals, building dikes, boring rocks, crushing stones, felling trees and erecting huts. With the exception of a very small number of unusually adaptable individuals, such men make a complete failure of their venture.

All that was necessary to establish a claim to "diggings" was to take possession of them.[40] Each man was allowed forty-five feet along a river bed and had the right to follow the gold vein as far as it should extend into the neighboring hills. Exploitation on a larger scale necessitated the cooperation of several miners. In the quartz mines the land allotted to each man is not restricted by law. Ownership extends as long as there is work. A tool left on the claim was sufficient to indicate possession. Without this sign, or if the land were left unworked for ten days, anyone was allowed to appropriate it and retain it on the same conditions.

To this simple and at the same time rational system is due on the whole the gigantic extension of the "diggings." Today a miner will begin to exploit a certain spot and is free to move from it to another if he sees fit. No annoying regulations hamper the movement of work which is so alluring in the quest of gold. The North American scorns petty restrictions of individual undertakings under pretext of general welfare. He would not have tolerated the Spanish law requiring a new permit for each claim, nor the autocratic Russian system in Siberia of dividing the mines into immense lots which are accessible only to rich capitalists or stock companies. Monopoly in whatever guise is repugnant to a progressive democracy such as the United States. [160]

In the early days when claims were worked in surface soil by single individuals or small companies of four or five, disputes over claims occurred but rarely. Now, however, the exhaustion of the first layer of gold having led the miners to unite in large companies to exploit the gold veins in pits or in levels, it happens that these pits and these levels meet underground where it is difficult to determine the rights of each party. This occasions lawsuits. Lawyers and judges not needed before are now provided with lucrative occupation by these increasing disputes.[41]

Such is the progress of civilization. Mutual interest, in the absence of laws, in fact by reason of their absence, brings about suitable harmony. But this mutual safeguard against injustice had in California only an ephemeral duration. The Golden Age of the region of gold is not much more than a tradition at present which though indeed a reality, appears after a lapse of three or four short years as legendary as the Golden Age of the beginning of the world,

161

sung by Ovid. With the influx of emigration the character of the miners soon degenerated from its earlier uprightness.[42]

Desperadoes from Texas and Arkansas, convicts from Sydney, *ladrones* from México, thieves from Paris or New York, and other industrials *ejusdem farinae* were soon attracted by the gold, like vultures by carrion. As larger numbers of miners gathered together, thefts, murders, and other crimes called for repressive measures, which were carried out with promptness, energy and sometimes cruelty. Draco seems to have inspired this code which subjects the delinquent to the whip, the cutting off of the ears, to hanging on a summary verdict, as of a provost court, although it is rendered by a popular assembly. The death penalty is incurred not only for premeditated murder, but as the law states: [161]

"Anyone who steals a mule or other beast of burden, who enters a tent or house, steals gold dust, money, provisions, goods or any other article of the value of one hundred dollars or more, shall be hanged. Accomplices incur the same penalty."[43]

Not having witnessed an execution by this inexorable court of justice, I borrow the following account from an eye witness:[44]

"We received word," says this spectator, "that five men had been arrested at the dry diggings in the neighborhood of Coloma and that they were to be punished for theft. The case reported was the following: a young Mexican named López having in his possession a large sum of money retired to his room to sleep, when towards midnight he was suddenly aroused by five men attacking him. One covered him with his gun while the others searched his trunk. Some neighbors, hearing a noise, forced the door and arrested the bandits. The next day they were tried by a jury chosen from the community and were condemned to receive each one thirty-nine stripes the following morning.

"Being curious to witness the carrying out of a sentence imposed by Lynch Law, I came to the dry diggings on a beautiful Sunday morning at dawn. A crowd surrounded an oak tree to which one of the prisoners was attached with ropes ready to receive on his bare back the strokes of a strong cowhide whip. A dozen men covered the other prisoners with their rifles to prevent their flight.

"When all five had received their punishment there arose new complaints against three of their number. They were accused of committing a few months before on the River Stanislaus, another theft with attempt at murder. meanwhile these unfortunate men, two of whom, García and Bissi, were French, and the third, Manuel, a Chilean, being, after their flogging, too weak to stand, were stretched on the floor of a nearby house. It was impossible for them to present themselves to a new judge and jury chosen by a crowd of two hundred men; nevertheless, they were tried in their absence. The accusations of *attempt* to steal and to murder were proved, but no actual deed of theft or murder could be brought forward. They were known, however, to be ne'er-do-wells, and the mob seemed bent on ridding itself of them.

"At the end of the trial, which lasted about half an hour, the judge put the guilt of the accused to a vote. A universal cry of guilty was returned. The question of penalty followed. A ruffian with a brutal expression shouted: 'Let them be hanged.' This expression was then almost unanimously approved.

"I climbed on an elevation," continued the narrator, "and protested in the name of God, of humanity and of justice against such a procedure. But the crowd, excited by drink, would not listen to me but threatened if I did not cease my importunate remarks to hang me likewise. Afraid of meeting with the same fate, and being also convinced of the futility of other arguments, I kept silence and prepared to assist at the dénouement of the horrible tragedy.

"Only half an hour was accorded the unfortunate victims to prepare themselves for eternity. [163] Then at the appointed time they were placed on a cart at the foot of a tree from which hung three pieces of rope. In vain did they try to speak; none of them knew English, but only French and Spanish, which hardly anyone understood. In vain they begged for an interpreter; their cries were drowned by the howling of an infuriated rabble. The eyes of the condemned men were bandaged with black handkerchiefs and their arms tied together, and at a signal, without priest or prayer, the cart was withdrawn and they were cast into eternity.

"Their graves had already been dug and when life had left their bodies, they were cut down and buried in their blankets. That was the first execution I ever witnessed. May it be the last!"

In Europe and even in America the dreadful impression made by the verdicts of the Lynch Law has given rise to the belief that the California mines are the scene of constant tragedy. Such is not the case. If one takes into consideration the size of the population and the mixed elements of which it is composed, one would on the contrary be amazed that so few crimes are committed against property and life.

The prevailing custom of carrying weapons gives a false impression. Life here is not so precarious as it seems. Quarrels caused by gambling and drinking often end in sanguinary fights but here, as in San Francisco, they are confined to gamblers and to drunkards. It is only a case of bandits wounding and killing one another.

It does at times happen, though not often, that a shot misses its mark and strikes some innocent spectator, a victim to his curiosity. While deploring the accident, one is tempted to ask on such occasions: "What business had he there?" The following is an account of a strange case of accidental killing:

The wooden inns scattered along the road are as a rule composed of two stories, the lower used as a refreshment room, parlor for guests, and known in America as the barroom. Above are attic rooms where travelers spend the night. In an establishment of this type on the Stanislaus River a miner stopped one day for a glass of brandy. In carelessly removing his pistol to place it on the table, it went off and the shot pierced the thin ceiling and lodged in the chest of another miner peacefully sleeping in the attic, rolled up in his red woolen blanket. Death was instantaneous. I heard of this strange death on stopping at the inn the day after it took place. The ceiling of the barroom serving as floor of the attic was about four inches thick.

As a rule the different nations that meet at the mines are friendly in their relations to one another. However, some

American citizens, the disgrace and scum of their noble land, have tried to claim a supremacy over foreigners which is quite contrary to the law of equal opportunity in labor. Mexicans, Chileans, and Chinese have been driven at the point of the gun from their placers.[45] Fortunately such abuses are no longer common and the California government, be it said to its honor, when dealing with such cases always rendered equitable judgments. [165]

Some of the companies at the mines are made up of men from the most distant lands. There on the Yuba one could see a Russian and a Chilean together using a Siberian contrivance for washing the auriferous soil. However, as a rule, associations of workers consist of national groups. Similarity of language is the strongest bond between men. Language in a foreign land is an echo from the distant home, and however cosmopolitan they may be, they all love to go back in thought to the events of their childhood.

At each mine then, the different races are grouped in this manner, offering an opportunity to study the ethnography of the four quarters of the globe within the space of a few square miles. The difference of national characteristics stands out very clearly among the men all occupied with the same kind of labor. In this little sphere of work as everywhere else the distinctive traits of the Yankee are activity, a spirit of enterprise and indomitable perseverance in the face of obstacles. The European Anglo-Saxon is endowed with these same qualities, although he allows himself to be outdistanced by his glorious offspring in America.

The German, patient and hard working, is slow but sure in his progress. The Italian proverb, *Chi va piano, va sano*, applies to him. He has not the alert mind of his Yankee cousin, but is just as stubborn in overcoming difficulties.

The Germans, English and North Americans seemed too much absorbed in their wok for me to venture to approach them. But here is the Frenchman; he is only too willing to chat. I could hear him from afar mingling in an odd way snatches of popular songs with fragments of the *Marseillaise*. The sublime and the ridiculous—is there anyone more apt to combine them than is the Frenchman? His principal vice, and also his principal virtue is love of change. He moves around in the mines of California as he is given to changing his government in his native country. He is too revolutionary (I do not say republican), to keep quiet. Consequently he often exchanges the good for the bad, but by sleight of hand as it were, he returns again from the bad to the good. Oh you French, you nation of conjurers! Now it is liberty, now despotism that you juggle away. To count on you is folly, but still greater folly is it to despair of you!⁴⁶

Chimerical hope brings the Frenchman to the modern El Dorado. He has simply put faith in the advertisements of a company with a fine sounding mythological name that distributed generously future millions in exchange for dollars in the present. He believed, naive child, that the shoveling up of gold like sand was all that was necessary to amass an income of fifty thousand francs. And after paying his passage on a boat freighted by the said company and called *Le Pactole*, *La Fortune*, or *La Toison d'Or*, on his arrival he was naturally disillusioned.⁴⁷ Did he give up in despair? Not at all. He was the first to laugh at being so easily duped. If he succeeds in getting along, he is all the prouder of himself; if misfortune continues to pursue him, he has a homeopathic remedy, his witty sayings.⁴⁸

I enjoyed chatting with the French miner who is ever ready to put down his tools when accosted in his own tongue by a newcomer. Intercourse with the French, always amiable and frivolous, took me back as on a magic carpet to Paris, that city which in spite of its frivolousness one cannot but love always. [167]

The Spaniard, including all nations of Spanish descent is, compared with the French, of a decidedly serious turn of mind. Yet instead of being governed by calm common sense like the German and the Briton, he is led entirely by his lively imagination. What after all is the object of this pursuit of gold? Pleasure! In his estimation there is nothing else worthwhile in life. He dreams of women and gives himself up to the feverish emotions, the frenzy of the gambler. What matter that he lose or gain? Like Talleyrand, he thinks it pleasant to lose—when one does not win. The Spaniard and the gambling tables are inseparable at the mines.

166

An impelling feeling of sympathy draws me to a miner of soldierly bearing whose face is covered with heavy moustaches and marked with scars. Just as I surmised, he is a Pole, a veteran of the war of 1830![49] It would be a long story, the history of this patriot—captain at the Battle of Grochow, and later Colonel. Expelled from country to country for singing: "Poland is not lost as long as we are still here," he has been obliged at last to leave a country he believed hospitable. Here he is now, ending his days working in the mines. Alas! how much longer will men be banished from their native land? Resignation is clearly written on the noble brow of this old soldier. Beside him stands a young man whose face is battle scarred but whose eyes glow with hope. In him I recognize a Magyar.

The model of perfect patience is the Chinaman, strange to behold with his long queue, his slanting eyes and high cheek bones. No other miner is as careful to save the smallest flakes of gold as he is in washing the sand. The crouched position necessary for this kind of work seems natural to him; he remains in it even while resting, instead of standing up for relaxation. [168] Withal, he is a good fellow, this docile Asiatic.

Between the Chinese and the Indian I cannot help seeing a resemblance pointing to a similarity of origin, thus reducing to three the principal races of men. To my mind the American savage, from Canada to Cape Horn, belongs to the Mongolian family.[50] He has the same expression, the same high cheek bones, the same copper color. Besides, it is the most logical thing to assume that the New World was populated by an Asiatic emigration, although today the tendency is to reject this rational hypothesis. Morally, the Indian is a Chinaman without his quasi-civilization. He differs from his prototype in his acquired indolence. When he works it is by fits and starts and he squanders his wages on such things as colored ties, glass beads, and dainties. He can be persuaded to work for a gaudy colored garment, a Mexican *serape* or an American uniform; he will choose either one or the other—they are equally pleasing to him. When he has gold in his possession he spends it gambling or on useless trifles. He has been known to pay sixteen dollars for a bunch of grapes,

167

not because he was immeasurably rich in gold dust or nuggets, but because to him it seemed that to satisfy his appetite with the savory fruit was the best use to which his money could be put.[51]

Never before has the world seen cosmopolitan labor as it exists at the California mines today! Nor has progress advanced with such giant strides at any epoch or in any place as today in this country whose name was known formerly only to geographers and navigators, but which today is translated in all tongues spoken by man. [169] Gold has brought about in three years what would normally be the work of centuries.

Whoever has not seen with his own eyes this marvelous civilization rising magnificently at the horizon and shedding its light to the farthest limits of the earth; whoever has not seen with his own eyes this union of nations founding a single society from its divers elements; finally, whoever has not seen with his own eyes the phenomenal vision of San Francisco from his home in the rival cities of Liverpool or New York—he has no conception of the extraordinary progress of which the human race is capable.

The discovery of gold in California opens a new era in history. The events to be recorded in its pages will exceed anything hitherto imagined by Utopian socialists. Reality will surpass fiction. Having at last found a meeting place, the nations brought in contact with one another will rid themselves of the hostile prejudices that separated them; understanding one another better face to face than through the intermediary of their respective governments, they will tend to harmonize, and a lasting peace born of mutual respect of rights will be established between them.[52]

Magnificent perspective! And the golden gate leading to it has already been thrown wide open. In the distance appears a sign with characters that grow more and more legible: *Universal Brotherhood.*

3.[1]

CLIMATE AND SOIL

Placed between the forty-second and thirty-second degrees of latitude, parallel to that part of the Old World comprising Spain, Italy, Turkey, Greece and the northern part of Africa, California enjoys a temperate climate throughout its length and breadth. While the winters are extremely mild, the summers are never oppressive. South of Sacramento snow is a curiosity, and the crisp mornings in December and January can scarcely be said to be frosty. In San Francisco fires are easily dispensed with throughout the year, and if chimneys are now beginning to appear in the new houses it is rather through luxury than necessity.[2] Nothing would hinder the miner from camping in his tent at the foot of the Sierra Nevada if he had to fear only the cold easily excluded by his kitchen fire.

But the serious inconvenience is the torrential rain of the winter season when he runs the risk of seeing his wretched canvas shelter swept away by a downpour of water coming suddenly from the top of the mountain. [205] In the American El Dorado the genius of man is in constant struggle with two destructive elements: fires sweeping the towns;[3] floods devastating the cultivated fields.

Fortunate it is that the inhabitants are, as it seems, endowed with the perseverance of the people of Torre del Greco at the foot of Vesuvius, who continually rebuild their destroyed houses on the warm lava from the volcano. There is this difference, however, that while the Neapolitan peasant confines himself to restoring things to their former condition, the Californian never tires of improving them. Each new disaster gives him a new impetus.[4] Who can tell, by continual progress how far he will finally go?

The fourfold division of the year: spring, summer, autumn, and winter, real in some parts of the world, is far from being applicable to its entire surface. Totally unknown to this, the most beautiful part of our terrestrial globe, is the gradual change marked by the budding of the tree, the blooming of the flowers, and the setting of the fruit followed by the disappearance of all vegetation. Over an expanse of seventy degrees, thirty-five north and thirty-five south, nature never loses her green coat and needs no mantle of snow to hide her nakedness. Further north, as also more to the

169

south, some countries enjoy this perpetual life where the year is divided into two seasons only: the dry, and the rainy.

In California, during five months of the year, sometimes less, heavy showers occur frequently for days at a time. From April to November, on the contrary, it rains but accidentally, or not at all. Speaking from personal observation, I know of no climate comparable to that of San Francisco except that of Valparaiso, and I do not think that the salubrity of these two cities can be surpassed anywhere in the world.

The occasional showers that fall in these two places form no fog, [!] no thick, heavy blanket as in London, no penetrating dampness as in Paris. [206] A cloud crosses the horizon and comes down in a torrent. The streets, cleaned and washed, dry a moment later beneath the bright, hot sun. Even during the worst days there are intervals of mild temperature and blue sky. In the dry season the sky is of a beautiful clear blue and the heat is not felt, thanks to a breeze which regularly blows for several hours driving away any noxious exhalations rising from the wet earth. It must be admitted, however, that the wind is sometimes so strong that it raises clouds of dust not unlike the chamsin of Egypt or even the simoon of the Sahara, but it is not a burning wind. Though the eyes may be blinded by these atmospheric disturbances, the throat is not affected as in the Orient. A day without wind or rain in San Francisco or Valparaiso is, on the other hand, ideally fine weather; it is that happy medium between heat and cold best suited to the human body. The result of this is a superabundance of vitality which enhances the joy of life and lends to the soul, as it were wings to soar above earthly miseries.

The California climate generally dispels melancholy, cures dejection and gilds the illusions of hope. So much for the morale. Its physical effect is to quicken the pulse, to check nervous disorders and impart to the muscles energy and strength. As good a tonic as Bordeaux, it produces occasionally the hilarity of Champagne.[5]

The extraordinary effects of this climate are noticeable in all races of men. The soft, enervated offspring of Asiatics or South Americans feels spring up within him an

170

energy unknown before, when he touches the shores where the Yankee, the German, the Frenchman, without losing any of their racial characteristics, throw themselves into their work as in a favorite game. [207] This magic climate which takes from the Yankee and the German some of their phlegmatic reserve, leaves to the Frenchman his happy lightheartedness.[6] It has been remarked that in California the race of the Spanish settlers has improved, that in the lapse of a few generations it has been growing stronger and taller than in the other Mexican provinces.[7]

Yet, some writers accuse of being unhealthful this climate with which in Europe, only that of Greece and Italy can be compared! A strange assertion indeed, but one easily explained. Among the visitors who in their accounts were pleased to vilify its recognized salubrity, some have held the climate responsible for maladies engendered by excessive hard labor, extreme fatigue and poor food; others have inferred it from certain fever localities—from which no country is exempt—in order to draw a general conclusion. Starting from this viewpoint some English writers have endeavored to establish between California and Australia a comparison, naturally to the advantage of Britain's "Most Gracious Majesty's" colony. Could justice not have been done to the one without undervaluing the other? But how can impartiality be expected from the "shopkeeper"[8] patriotism of our age?

Among these prejudiced travelers is a doctor from a northern state who failing to establish a lucrative practice, as he had hoped, turned to gold digging and a second time being unsuccessful, failed even to amass enough gold to defray the expenses of his journey and stay in California. Embittered by his disappointment, weakened by unaccustomed labor, restricted to a steady diet of salt beef, he fell ill. In a book published on his return to his native land, he does not deign to take into account so many causes injurious to health, and confines himself to condemning the California climate.[9] [208] Oh! son of Doctor Sangrado, you would have no doubt have lauded the climate if less healthful than it is, it has procured you many sick calls at an ounce of gold a visit, for then you would not have been obliged to wield

171

the pick. Your digestion would not have been ruined by coarse foods and you would have congratulated yourself on having returned home in good health while attributing to accidental causes, in no way connected with the climate, the death of the poor unfortunates you would have sent off to the other world...

Dysentery, scurvy, fevers that attack the California miners are due entirely to definite causes, such as intemperance, faulty diet, nervous and physical strain. The climate of the mountainous regions is so good that erysipelas, caused by long exposure, is the only malady mentioned to me in that district. True, the low and swampy banks of the Sacramento and the San Joaquin Rivers exhale deleterious odors; but for that matter, so do many districts in Italy, as for instance the Roman Campagna. [209] In this "American Italy" one sees no livid shadows, a prey to continual suffering, lost souls as it were, harmonizing with the surrounding ruins.[10] The California fevers attack the patient for awhile, but usually yield to a few doses of quinine. It is the Americans themselves who sometimes prolong and even increase these fevers by the excessive use of brandy which they consider a sovereign remedy. The sea coast is perfectly healthful.[11] In no other part of the world have I visited a city in a better state of salubrity than is San Francisco, if one excepts its docks which exhale an odor of stagnant water. The city itself spread out over breezy hills, bathes in air as pure as one could wish.

With the exception of the sandy hills along the coast, the soil of California is unquestionably fertile, although this has not been contested by superficial or prejudiced observers. Agriculture is destined to develop rapidly along the Sacramento and San Joaquín Rivers and their tributaries. But between these two rivers, over an area sometimes of several square miles, water is entirely lacking. Rain hardly makes up for it, and the land, though naturally good, will only be made productive by means of irrigation canals. North of San Francisco one sees vegetation of temperate climates, wheat, oats, corn; and among the districts that are being put under cultivation, the valley of Sonoma is already yielding rich returns to the laborer. Vegetables, as also cereals, grow there in great profusion and are noted for their fine quality as for

172

their colossal size. [210] I have cited above some examples of their gigantic development.[12]

The fruit region is situated south of San Francisco. The delightful valleys of San José and San Juan are veritable orchards where such luscious products of temperate climate as grapes, apples, pears, plums, peaches, melon, figs, oranges, etc., ripen beside the tropical banana.[13] The olive tree abounds south of the thirty-five degrees of latitude and the oil it yields is in no way inferior to that of Provence or Andalusia. The banks of the San Gabriel River which flows through the city of Los Ángeles are covered with vineyards. These produce a wine closely resembling good Canary Island wine. This industry which the Franciscan Fathers directed with predilection, later abandoned and now once more carried on, is destined to thrive and gain great importance. Moreover, from the same grape brandy can be made which will dispense with any further importation from abroad.

The rich and exuberant soil of California is amply fitted to supply the needs of human civilization. In the north hemp grows well. The cultivation of tobacco has lately been tried with marked success.[14] Sugar-cane, cotton, rice, indigo, judging from experiments already made, will not disdain some parts of the land. It remains to be seen whether it will be profitable for California to compete with tropical cultivation. The same applies to tea which, according to some Chinese, enthusiastic over their new fatherland, should find in several localities suitable climatic conditions.

California is eminently suited to the breeding of horses and horned animals in which consisted her sole wealth under Spanish rule and which multiplied formerly at the rate of thirty-five percent. There is no reason why she should not emulate Australia in the production of wool, the republic of La Plata in cattle raising, and Chile in the breeding of race horses.[15]

Is there anywhere else in the world a country which compares with the mineral wealth? I doubt it. Will the rich gold mines recently discovered in Australia hold out as long as those of California? That remains to be seen. Side by side with the most precious of metals, the ramifications of the Sierra Nevada contains silver, copper and lead so free from dross that it can be melted directly into bullets. On the coast saltpeter and sulfur have been found, and near San Diego charcoal resembling anthracite. Even iron has been seen in some places.

The quicksilver mercury mines, operated by the Forbes Company in the neighborhood of San José, are of inestimable value. These deposits will release America from the burdensome tribute she has been paying Europe and will facilitate the working of the California gold. The Rothschild firm, holding for many long years a lease on Almaden in Spain, had the monopoly of the world's quicksilver until the appearance of the new Almaden at a most opportune moment to complete the treasures of this truly privileged land.[16]

4.[1]

IMPORTANCE OF CALIFORNIA

If one considers the manifold benefits bestowed by nature on California, centrally located as it is in an ever expanding world, as a heritage bequeathed to all the races of the human family, one can see at a glance the important part this noble region is destined to play in the scheme of the general progress of humanity. To the natural yearning for social well being, as typified by American freedom, she will rally both enervated Asia and degenerate Europe. The star of civilization, hitherto so slow of progress, has with one bound shot across the Rocky Mountains. It shines on the Pacific Ocean and returns by a magnificent surplus to its point of departure. While the despots of the Old World, emperors and kings, congratulate themselves on the results of their fraud and violence, imagining Liberty to be at last without a place of refuge, Liberty from over here laughs at their bayonets and their cannon.[2]

Transformed in the brain of a small number of farmers, such as Washington, Jefferson, Franklin, the celestial spirit has reappeared more beautiful than formerly in Athens and in Rome. [213] From pagan exclusiveness she has risen side by side with the Christian ideal to universality. A unity and trinity at one and the same time; for Liberty means Fra-

174

ternity, and Fraternity, Equality. Contact with them infuses into the nation a mysterious vitality. Consider what the United States has become during the span of one man's life. Look at America almost entirely freed from the monarchs of the old continent; Love of the thrice blessed goddess engenders irresistible strength. England yields to Washington, Spain to Bolivar, France to Toussaint Louverture, this Spartacus of the Blacks. Liberty which you were pleased to believe dead, oh! emperors and kings, Liberty seated between two oceans holds out her hands to Europe across the Atlantic, to Asia across the Pacific. Why not destroy steam, you wielders of scepters to prevent your subjects from hastening to the love-feast of social regeneration!

Since California has attracted the eyes of all the world to the Federal Republic of the United States, the suffering and oppressed masses are beginning to see and understand the advantages of self-government over governments arbitrarily imposed on them.

"How does it happen," the ignorant and the learned are already asking one another, "that a colony of three million inhabitants at the end of last century now numbers twenty-five million; that a land but recently cleared surpasses in prosperity the oldest existing countries; that a nation without king or emperor sees flourish in its midst order, peace and justice?"

"Does it maintain a formidable army?"

"A few volunteers, numbering eight thousand guard the frontiers against the incursions of savages."

"Has it a strong centralized government?"

"Divided into thirty states that govern themselves as they see fit, that change their constitution when they please,[3] and are bound to the federal government only in the tariff and foreign relations, this nation is free even to its smallest hamlet."

"Has it an official clergy?"

"Enjoying the most absolute religious freedom everyone is at liberty to contribute or not to the cult of his choice."

"At least then, the judiciary is held in high respect?"

[215]

175

"All the more so because it is everywhere elective and in most states removable; the judges are thus under the constant control of the voters and cannot plot against the rights of the people for personal profit or for the benefit of friends...." [216]

"The revolution of 1848 at first triumphant in Paris, Vienna, Berlin, Budapest, and Rome ended by being suppressed in each of these capitals. Yes, unfortunately courage, self-sacrifice, science have all been lavished in vain because instead of borrowing from the United States the basis of their freedom, tested by successful experiment, each patriot sought to create a new system of his own.[4]...What Egypt and Greece were to antiquity Anglo-Saxon America is for the present day: a school of enlightened representative government."

Not indeed from the past must we seek inspiration today, but from the future which the United States is already revealing to us.

Thus it is desirable that both the unlettered and the learned know that a majestic republic destined to point the way to progress is even now growing and developing: [218]

> Without a standing army—
> Without a centralized government
> Without a salaried clergy
> Without an appointive and irremovable
> judiciary—

* * * * * * *

But this digression would exceed all bounds if I included every thought that naturally suggests itself to the mind of a European on comparing the political situation of his old continent with the New World.[5] These salutary reflections based upon palpable facts are far more effective in promoting and spreading democratic propaganda than are mere theories issuing from pure reason. California, by focusing the attention of the nations on the Milky Way of which she is the most brilliant star, will contribute to hastening the hour of a general political transformation throughout the world. [220]

Paris, after all, was but a fitful light (often nebulous, alas), for the nations of the Caucasian race. San Francisco on the other hand will one day be the beacon, ever bright, not only for the privileged races of civilization, but for those pariah Mongol and Malay races which seemed fated never to emerge from the darkness of their ancient barbarism. Within the confines of her immense bay countless emigrants from Europe or America will meet myriads of Asiatics and Oceanians attracted by the lure of gold. These will bear back to their respective countries something more precious than gold: the consciousness of the dignity of man. Such is the exalted mission assigned to California by its geographic position.

As to gold, its abundance will not fail to produce eventually an economic revolution materially furthering general progress. Though not resulting in the social liquidation which Proudhon prophesies with so much assurance that one would think he believed in it himself, the accumulation of currency will cause a diminution of interest on idle capital and will raise the value of labor. Private and public land and stocks and bonds will necessarily rise in price with the increasing need of investments. In spite of the reduced incomes, however, the capitalists will possess by way of compensation greater wealth. Still, this gain will be more apparent than real; depreciation of gold and higher wages for manual labor necessarily bringing about an increase in the cost of living.

The financial reform conceived by California and furthered by Australia is now at hand. The return of emigrants with their sacks of gold-dust has already occasioned, to my knowledge, a rise in the price of land in New York [221] Indeed, speculation in this respect is tending to spread to all the states of the American Union. Capital destined to suffer in the end by this movement, will for many years to come derive from commercial enterprises its highest profits. There are times when daring is foresight. The sudden discovery of gold mines in vast countries on our globe has brought us to one of these epochs. Prudence, financially speaking, has changed its name: today it is the spirit of enterprise and not parsimonious economy as of old.[6]

California although to a certain extent an accomplice of economic socialism is only opposed to that capital which persistently barricades itself in strong boxes or tenaciously clings to patrimonial soil. She repays, on the contrary, with fabulous returns judiciously invested capital. Working the mines, clearing land, breeding stock, building houses, putting money out at interest: in any of these occupations the capitalist can safely engage according to his taste with every chance in his favor of making immense profits.[7]

Mining companies formed on the spot are likely to be eminently successful especially when the craving for individual discovery and gain will have somewhat subsided. And this will not be long delayed. But let people beware of any such companies pompously advertised in European newspapers: they are but organized robbery on a large scale. It is inconceivable how credulous money-lenders in London and Paris have been exploited under pretext of California investment. The shares quoted at the stock-exchange have proved to be mere scraps of paper. The money of the stock-holders, soothed by Monte Cristo dreams, has been spirited into the pockets of a band of captains of industry whose only aim is to coin cold for themselves out of the illusions of their dupes.[8] [222] Most of these companies had no clear titles to their mining concessions, and even in cases of real ownership of mining claims the result was not much better, for the staff of employees of every grade would absorb the entire profits. No such misfortune awaits those who consolidate their capital whether for windmills to crush quartz or for machinery for washing gold and who will themselves watch over their enterprises. Associations organized in this fashion already exist and some are enjoying prosperity beyond all expectation. But in quarry mining chance plays a great part. A more dependable source of income will in time be derived from agriculture in California which is still dependent on Valparaiso for flour and the Sandwich Isles for vegetables. Vast fortunes lie hidden in the fertile land of this country. To be brought to the surface they await only the plough and the ox. The tilling of the fields, precisely because so greatly

178

neglected, cannot fail to enrich in a few years large numbers of intelligent farmers. Unfailing success awaits likewise the herding of stock which with little care multiplies astonishingly.

Were it not for the frequently recurring fires there would be in California no more lucrative investment than the building of houses. The smallest income from a house in San Francisco in spite of the high cost of materials and labor including all costs of upkeep is an interest of thirty-five per cent. In some cases this interest amounts to fifty-five per cent and even seventy-five per cent. That explains the immediate rebuilding of houses devoured by the flames notwithstanding the lack of fire insurance companies. [223] As soon as the custom of building large numbers of flimsy wooden houses ceases such companies will probably be organized. Already brick buildings can be insured in London and some proprietors have wisely taken this precaution which safeguards them from all disaster. There is still a better method of ownership of city property, one that has nothing to fear from fire. It is to buy a lot in a favorable location and rent it for so much a month (from two to four per cent, that is, twenty-four to forty-eight per cent per annum) to some building contractor. No risk is run, for payments are made in advance on the first of each month, and a first mortgage is held on the house which if burned is immediately rebuilt. Many merchants consolidate their funds in San Francisco by renting building lots; they have moreover the prospect of selling them again at great profit a few weeks, months or years later.

The rate of interest on safe mortgages, which must be distinguished from bad ones, is fixed at present (January 1, 1852) in the great Californian city from two to three per cent per month.[9] A French acquaintance of mine was able to double his capital of two hundred thousand francs in this way in the course of two years. None of his numerous transactions turned out badly, he said, thanks to the simple precaution of verifying the title deed offered him.

This California, the mighty battering ram of the democratic and social revolution, will long remain for enlightened capitalists.

179

The liberal professions also are richly remunerated in the cities at the mines. [224] Lawyers have appeared like a cloud of ravenous locusts and are prospering in spite of the keen competition with one another. The chaotic Mexican administration furnishes them with rich pasture in the form of title deed to property. From these they find no difficulty instituting lawsuits. Some who came from New York or Boston destitute are now rolling in wealth. And the doctors, though finding few patients to treat, have nevertheless attained brilliant positions through the high fees they receive. Between five and sixteen dollars is charged for a visit, that is, from twenty-five to eighty francs.

That the city of San Francisco so eminently salubrious should maintain forty pharmacists or druggists may at first cause surprise; but wonder soon ceases when it is known that these forty aides-de-camp of Aesculapius are at the same time perfumers and cigar dealers.[10]

It is evident that a population each individual of which is started off on a steeple chase of fortune can have in the matter of literature little more than journalism; in painting nothing but daguerreotypes; in sculpture only jewelry. Newspapers pay well; portraits made in the bright sunshine find ready sale; gold ornaments give employment to many skillful workmen who earn, not an artisan's wage, but an artist's salary. Pins and brooches representing miners, savages, or bears seemed to me to be of remarkably fine workmanship.

Craving diversion, the people indulge with avidity in music and singing, dancing and gymnastics, drama and comedy. Quite mediocre actors earn in San Francisco five hundred dollars a month or more. The wandering pianist, Henri Herz had a full house at eight dollars (forty francs) a ticket. The worst violin scraper is paid for playing in theaters and at dances, fifteen and twenty thousand francs a year. [225] The girls singing in *cafés* are less in need of a voice than of a pretty face to be rolling in gold. So much for the liberal and artistic professions.

Hairdressers and milliners, cooks and laundresses, waiters and maids run no risk of finding themselves out of employment. Domestic service in this atmosphere of equal-

180

ity is freed from the servile dependence which degrades it in its own eyes. You treat with courtesy the man who waits on you at table, for he may be, as I said above, a private secretary, a teacher, a man about town from Broadway, New York, or the boulevards of Paris. The chambermaid who empties your basin and makes your bed expects to be considered a lady, and it depends only on her to become one. If she happens to be of a pleasing appearance and to have a good complexion she is probably hesitating between half a dozen more or less advantageous proposals of marriage.

Eighty to one hundred dollars (four or five hundred francs) a month, such are the wages of servants of both sexes whose work, notwithstanding, is always temporarily undertaken while waiting for something better or possibly something worse.

Laundresses washing shirts at five dollars a dozen soon amass a competency. Recent competition by the Chinese who willingly undertake women's work may, however, bring about a fall in prices. French and Negro cooks, justly reputed the best, earn from one to three hundred dollars a month, depending upon the type of work. Though I am not sure of what milliners earn, judging from their elegant attire at dances, it must be considerably more than their needy sisters in Europe. [226]

Without going any further into this subject merely touched upon above, let it be remembered that in California as long as a woman has not reached forty-five or fifty she has the choice of leading a comfortable or luxurious life. She must choose between wedlock or the "papillonne". She is denied the life of a widow or a vestal.[11] Should she refuse to conform to a tyrannical custom established by great numbers of men united against a handful of women, her position would become unbearable....[232]

At Marysville [Downieville] there lived a young and beautiful Mexican woman. An American attracted to her entered her dwelling at night by force. While calling for help she stabbed her brutal aggressor. It was a case of legitimate defense. A jury selected by the Lynch law declared it a case of murder without extenuating circumstances. Horrible to relate, this heroine whom Rome would have honored

181

as the sister of Lucretia, suffered for her heroic action the punishment due to crime. She was hanged in the public square of Marysville [Downieville] without intervention from the regular court of justice.[12]

It is to be deplored that the great society now developing in California should have some hideous traits. The traveler must be impartial however and point them out just as he would not omit to mention in describing a magnificent tropical forest, the poisonous plants, dangerous reptiles and wild beasts. The mob while exercising the Lynch law is, alas, only too much like a wild beast. Yet the tyranny of the crowd is never as monstrous as that of a single individual who usurps the power that belongs to all and is swayed only by his own cowardliness under the ridiculous pretext of the public welfare; this collective tyranny, even though it has the advantage of being exercised only at rare intervals, is none the less a deplorable anachronism in the nineteenth century and a blot on the escutcheon of American liberty.

For my part, I prefer the transitory aberration of a nation excited by sudden passing rage to the continual disregard of justice usual with kings; but it is unfortunate that the people should through their occasional acts of injustice furnish rulers with sophistical justification of their habitual tyranny. Abuse of power is in glaring contradiction to the principle of democracy, while monarchy has no other principle but this abuse of power. [233] It is the revival of the old monarchical spirit in the midst of republics when the sovereign people, infringing on the rights of individuals, becomes despotic.

Like the botanist who gathers on his way all the plants he deems useful for his collection, I record all thoughts relating to my subject as they happen to flow from my pen. If I am censured for wandering over hill and dale, my excuse is that I attempt nothing more than an informal narrative in which one is permitted to discuss a topic, leave it awhile and return to it again later.

I return then to the glories of California. This land, where the capitalist with even the minimum of ability can in a short time double his fortune, where the liberal professions are generously remunerated, where servile occupations lose

182

their degrading character by reason of the high wages they command, where women enjoy a prestige without compare, this land is the real land of promise for the workman who has but his hands to make a living.[13] The laborer in ancient Europe held in the bonds of slavery, in Europe of the Middle Ages bound as a serf to the soil, and whom modern Europe derisively boasts of having freed while casting him into unending misery, this laborer escapes from slavery only in crossing the Atlantic Ocean. For the institutions of free America as well as the natural resources of its soil emancipate the outcast by pointing out to him beyond the laborious present a future of repose and ease to which all men have a right to aspire. Private property, an essential condition for liberty which otherwise would be enjoyment mingled with bitterness, every man is able to acquire by the labor of his hands in any part of the United States, but especially in California.

I have nothing to add regarding the life of the miners except that it exercises a profound influence on the condition of workers both in the cities and in the country. [234] The miner is practically sure of a minimum profit of five dollars a day (twenty-five francs} and a chance for infinitely more. Now as all men, rightly or wrongly, are affected by the gold fever, the workman will remain at his trade only as long as he earns the equivalent of what he foregoes. Moreover it frequently happens that the discovery of a new mine fascinates the imagination and results in a general exodus as contagious as a stampede of mules or horses in the fields. The artisans then hasten in a body to the designated location, leaving building contractors without masons and merchants without clerks. In this way high wages are maintained.

With cities springing up on all sides and fires destroying them, the workman is never left idle. His pay varies from five to ten dollars a day. Unlike the miner he runs no risks. More people have perhaps made fortunes by the building of houses than by digging for gold. In San Francisco today there are carpenters and joiners who have grown wealthy in a few months. Several occupy elegant homes which they own and which they helped to construct. But cast a glance on the magnificent cities of Europe: there those who erect palaces for the idle rich languish in loathsome hovels [235] What a change there would be in the life of the unfortunate people if they could suddenly find themselves transported to California, their homeland!

Today so many philosophers, that is to say socialists, are seeking with laudable zeal a cure for the disease of poverty. Since each in turn, with the best of intentions, extols a more or less doubtful remedy of his own, so I too who am not ashamed to pass for a philosopher, or a socialist, that is to say for a lover of humanity, offer my humble suggestion. This scheme which has the merit of being not altogether new is emigration, rationally organized emigration.

The habitable portions of the globe I consider to be the common heritage of all mankind. Now, who doubts for a moment that our earth is capable of amply providing for its present population, and for even a far larger one? No one! Who does not know that poverty in some countries is caused by overpopulation while in others wealth lies undeveloped for want of laborers? No one. It is then merely a question of adding here and taking away there. But one may perhaps argue that voluntary emigration and deportation have the same effect. True, but only in an insufficient, unsystematic and irregular way. Among the governments of today some, like England, promote emigration on a small scale; others, like Germany hinder it; others again reject it, as does Russia which would arrive at unheard of prosperity in a few years if only restrictions were removed and freedom of passage in and out of the country granted. [236] As to France, a prey to a fatal hallucination, she persuades herself that brutal, violent and criminal banishment of her best citizens and their confinement in penal colonies is synonymous of emigration. Is that putting into execution the progressive program that was forever to abolish poverty?[14]

That emigration may benefit the country it leaves as well as the country it enters, a change of government is imperative, for it cannot be satisfactorily carried out under the existing system in Europe. The change I suggest as a preliminary is not a Utopia, it is simply a government patterned after that of the United States, nothing more.

Such a system in harmony with the laws dictated by common sense, far from being opposed to the good of the people, as some assert thoughtlessly or maliciously, is on the contrary the only means of rescuing the nations from degradation, corruption, and poverty. As soon as this last ulcer is healed the other two will promptly disappear. Vast sums will fill the treasury wherever there is no royal court of permanent army, or salaried clergy to maintain. Then the first outlay in every republic will be an appropriation for the free transportation of its indigent citizens who wish to leave their country. They will be directed, they and their families, according to their talents, trade—temperament even—to such and such a spot in the world where these talents are most in demand, these trades best paid, these temperaments best adapted to the climate. Artists will not be sent where artisans are needed, nor will men accustomed to the sun be sent to the Polar Regions. France and England will not strive to populate solely their respective colonies.

Egotistic nationalism will disappear in the fusion of the same republican sentiment.[15] Wherever he goes, the emigrant, under the aegis of liberty will consider himself in his fatherland. [237] No more foreign countries, for there will exist but provinces of the great Universal Republic.

A chimera? No, a reality; for the federation of the United States of America, this union of races that has not even a definite name that separates them from their old continent is the gigantic embryo of the Universal Republic simple and multiple, simple through its commerce, currency and intellectual aspirations, multiple through its administration, languages and customs. Let Europe unite with America. Australia and Polynesia will remain united to them. Asia, aroused through the medium of California will seek to join them and Africa will hasten to raise herself in this general amalgamation. There stands the Universal Republic complete: Some refractory nations may attempt to disturb this desirable harmony. Their efforts will be as vain as those of the Iroquois and Hurons against Cromwell's Puritans. These sowed in Massachusetts the first seeds of a constitution brought to light by the act of independence of a few English colonies, extended by successive annexations, and destined, like a tree ever spreading its mighty branches, to shelter the entire human race.

It would take a large volume to explain with necessary details this plan of an emigration that aims to divide up, according to the needs of overcrowded populations and of natural resources, the members of a same family and by this distribution to unite in other ways these severed bonds. It suffices merely to point out this unquestionably practical plan. All that remains to be done is simply to extend and regulate what has been practiced in all ages even as far back as the Phoenicians. [238] It must reconcile private interest with public welfare and settle those disputes which are the principal, if not the only cause of public and private misfortune. It is easy to see what an impetus it will give to agriculture, industry and commerce. Poverty and suffering decreasing, perhaps altogether disappearing, will then have no grievance against civilization. Today already in the United States of America no needy person can rightfully hold the government responsible for the state of destitution in which he vegetates. Why? Because in this country work is ever ready at hand; because labor is regulated without obstacles of any kind and the laborer can hold high his head, having the consciousness of being the son and the champion of liberty.

Let us join the United States! Let us cast aside the fetters with which we wantonly bind ourselves in maintaining throughout Europe (England excepted) the caviling inquisition of the police system that dares to make of traveling a favor dependent on its good pleasure. May then no obstacle hinder the people from moving freely from place to place. Let holy liberty flow in the arteries of the social body like noble blood. Under these circumstances it will be as advantageous as easy to interpret the right to labor, explained so badly by some, misunderstood by others, as a right which arouses neither impossible hopes nor vain fears: *the right to emigrate.*

The right of emigration is nothing more than the right to life. All nations regard it as a mutual benefit among the different groups of human beings. This right comes from the bowels of the earth, it emanates from nature itself, and rea-

186

son sanctions it as a natural law. [239] So long as the egotism of governments and the ignorance of the masses refuse to concede the right to emigrate as a solution of social evils, the present conflicts, civil war between rich and poor, will continue to agitate society and louder and louder will it hear the rumbling of lamentation....[16]

It is inspiring to see, between the apathy of Europe and the somnolence of Asia, the enterprising and resolute attitude of America (apart from her anomalies). It is America and not thou, O misguided France, that holds in her hand the scepter of progress! She promotes humanitarian measures, not by vain and often broken promises, but by actual deeds. Each of these measures consolidates her power and contributes to the general well-being. Thus, through her, California has now become a cosmopolitan country.

This place of refuge which has a population of only two hundred and fifty thousand can shelter ten million more. It still has room for many, many guests. Come then, you who live in tedium and trouble, come and sit at this banquet where you will have joy and abundance. Come all, capitalists and laborers.

Capitalists! Your money will increase.

Workmen! The labor of your hands will provide you with ease or wealth. Whatever may be your native country you will find it here with its customs, its habits, its ideals, its aspirations. [240] All nationalities exist side by side in California marked with their racial characteristics. It is the common fatherland of all the peoples of the earth.

A noble fatherland! For all men who are conscious of their dignity understand that liberty alone constitutes a real patria:

Ubi libertas, ibi patria.

A generous fatherland, where the disinherited of other nations are welcome to share its joy and abundance.

NOTES

TRANSLATOR'S INTRODUCTION

[1]Holinski, *California and the Interoceanic Routes*, 99.
[2]*Ibid.*, 246.
[3]O. Lévy, *Les Français en Californie*, 171. The French population were of very different political views which was the cause of much friction amongst them.
[4]Holinski, *op. cit.*, vi.
[5]*Ibid.*, 129.
[6]*Ibid.*, 295. With America as model.
[7]Holinski, *op. cit.*, 188. "Fear of death as experienced by civilized people is unknown to the savage Indians."
[8]*Ibid.*, 186. At Sutter's Hock Farm.
[9]*Ibid.*, 65, 73, 157.
[10]Holinski, *op. cit.*, 243.
[11]*Ibid.*, ix.
[12]*Ibid.*, vii, viii.

CHAPTER ONE

[1]Holinski, *California and the Interoceanic Routes*, 101. Page reference will be indicated in brackets in the translation.
[2]Several authors have described the bay in terms almost identical with the above. R. C. Cleland, *History of California*, 144. "In his dispatches from Mexico Thompson, U.S. Minister, urged the advisability of securing California...and described the Bay of San Francisco as being 'capacious enough to receive the navies of all the world.'" J. Hittell in his *San Francisco*, 92, 93, 96, quotes similiar passages from Lieutenant Ayala, Ben. Morrell, and Sir George Simpson.
[3]An unusual sight was this "forest of masts" facing a village of shacks and tents! E. Massey, "Diary of a Journey to California," 32. "Usually they [the ships] are unable to leave once they have entered, for the crews as a general

rule desert and no freight is obtainable. As a result San Francisco presents to the eye the appearance of a *magnificent forest of masts*." Dr. Owen C. Coy, in his *Gold Days*, 249, quotes Dr. James Tyson, 50. "What commercial inducement could such a mean and insignificant-looking place as this present, to bring together such a forest of masts as the harbor disclosed?"

[4]Saint-Amant, *Voyages en Californie*, 137. The Customs "is often strict and exacting but then, in details it is accomodating, wonderful even, and at least *does not search the pockets* of the poor traveller." De Massey two years earlier records in his "Journal," 26, "We unpacked our trunks...which had come through the customs who had very considerately passed them without inspection." With the bulk of his merchandise sent as freight "it was another story."

[5]The author gives the name of his ship and date of arrival on p. 99. "I was fairly comfortable on board the *Tennessee*... My voyage from Panama to San Francisco cost me 250 *piastres*, first class; the distance is about 4,000 miles." The ship reached San Francisco on October 1, 1851.

[6]These were well-known hotels; advertisments appeared in the following papers: *The Alta California*, Oct. 19, and Dec. 16, 1851, mention *Jones' Hotel*, *The Oriental*, *Lafayette*, and *Rassett*. F. Soulé in the *Annals*, 639 and 650, gives the location: *The Oriental*, corner of Battery and Bush Streets, *Jones'* (Theama House), Sansome and California, *Rassett*, Bush and Sansome. T. A. Barry, *Men and Memories*, 58. Col. Folsom built the *Theama* or *Jones' Hotel*, the rendezvous of all the army officers of that day.

[7]Further digressions of this nature will be omitted.

[8]Z. S. Eldredge, *The Beginnings of San Francisco*, 511, 514. "Vioget, a Swiss sailor, laid out in 1839 the blocks between Pacific, California, Montgomery, and Dupont Streets." In 1847 "O'Farrell's Swing" changed the direction of the streets. Barry and Patten, *Men and Memories*, 210. "Vioget made the first survey in San Francisco...Had his design been carried into effect, it would as a sanitary proposition have been much better for

the city's inhabitants. Every house would have had an equal share of the sun upon its front and rear during the day. Political scheming, that bane of republics, changed the plan to give one of the party favorites [O'Farrell] a job causing...injury to the health of thousands." Eldredge, 523. Men digging in a street in 1854 found a coffin with the well preserved body of Rae who had been buried in 1846 in what was then the garden of the house used by the Hudson Bay Company.

[9]Soulé's *Annals*, 232. "The *Apollo* was used as a storeship; the *Euphemia* as a prison ship." *Ibid.*, 233. "As the city improvements progressed, lots were piled, capped, and filled in on the flat covered by the waters of the bay far beyond where the *Apollo* lay; and strangers visiting the city were astonished to see the hull of a large ship located in the very heart of the city surrounded on all sides with large blocks of substantial stone and brick edifices."

[10]Hittell, *History of San Francisco*, 216. "The yield of gold was probably larger in 1852 than in any other year, though the exportation as officially reported was largest in 1853, when it reached fifty-seven millions; the next year it fell to fifty-one."

[11]Soulé's *Annals*, 657. The *Jenny Lind* opened next to the City Hall on Oct. 4, 1851—three days after Holinski landed. Its earlier location was "over *Maguire Parker House*, on Kearney St. near Washington."

[12]The following advertisements appeared at this time: In the *Alta California*, Oct. 12, 1849, the "Bella Union." Jan. 14., 1850, "El Dorado"; the *Evening Picayune*, Oct. 14, 1850, the "Polka"; the *California Courier*, Oct. 7, 1851, the "California Exchange"; *The Daily Pacific News*, May 27, 1850, mentions the gambling games. See also Soulé, *Annals*, 645; Barry, *Men and Memories*, 45; Bancroft, *California*, VI, 238-241.

[13]During the early part of the gold rush prices had been exceedingly high. *Star*, Dec. 1848. Eggs sold at twelve dollars a dozen, potatoes, a dollar and a half a pound. Eldredge, 189. Flour, four hundred dollars a barrel, sugar and coffee, four dollars a pound. The *Alta California*, Oct. 12, 1849, fresh Sacramento salmon at one dollar a

pound. "Think of this, ye Eastern epicures, a single fish in California sold for fifty dollars."

[14]*California Pamphlet*, XIX, "Scrap Book" 136: "Ten cent places are patronized by workmen."

[15]The following bookstores are advertised on the Plaza (Holinski uses the word piazza): "Pioneer Book Store," "Wilson and Spaulding" in the *Daily Pacific News*, April 26 and 27, 1850; "The Book Store" on Montgomery St., *ibid.*, April 30, 1850; Soulé, *Annals*, 716. "Medical and Law Library."

[16]Possibly either J. J. Chauviteau's store on Clay Street, or E. de Massey's on Commercial Street.

[17]*Star and California*, Jan. 1849, later *Alta California*; 1850, *Pacific News*, 1851; *Daily Herald*, 1852; *The Golden Era*, the *Journal of Commerce*, *California Courier*, *Evening Picayune*.

[18]The only mention of it is found in the *Alta California*; Oct. 29, 1851: "Agricultural Fair. Exposition of California products by A. Shelton, Esq., held in the 'Verandah', San Francisco, Oct. 25, 1851...In this exhibit was a beet 26 inches long, 26½ inches in circumference and 26½ pounds in weight."

[19]A copy of Wierzbicki's book is to be found in the Bancroft Library at the University of California, Berkeley.

[20]J. Royce, *California*, 393. "The years between 1849-1854 seemed a lifetime." Soulé, *Annals*, 217 and 665. "These things of 1849 seemed to have taken place ages ago... Young men in 1854 already talked of the days of 1849 as they might of a romantic and almost forgotten ancient history."

[21]Rev. A. Williams, a Presbyterian minister.

[22]Massey, 25. "Lawyers, doctors, capitalists...are forced, if they would eat, to black boots...cook, and wash dishes." Lévy, *Les Français en Californie*, 109. "One of them used for this work shoe blacking a golden knife which he constantly made glitter before the eyes of his clients. Another cultivated the muses..." Saint-Amant, *Californie*, 128. "The French undertake menial labor, street sweeping, shoe blacking, dish washing..."

[23]*Alta California*, Dec. 29, 1851, announced a meeting of the "French Benevolent Society." Soulé, *Annals*, 715; Lévy, *Les Français*, 167. Society organized in 1851.

[24]The "Decree" referred to is the G. B. Tingley bill "attempting to introduce the coolie system by an act providing for the enforcement of contracts for foreign labor." Bancroft, *California*, VI, 665.

[25]Soulé, *Annals*, 384. "In 1851 there were only a few Chinese women in the city among whom was the notorious Miss Atoy." News item in *Alta California*, Dec. 11, 1851. "Miss Atoy dashes through the streets after a 'gentleman' guest who took her diamond pin."

[26]Reference is here made to the first "Vigilance Committee," 1851. Royce, *California*, 447. "...many of the committee members were Frenchmen...noteworthy for their fine appearance as soldiers." Saint-Amant, *op. cit.*, 408; Hittell, *op. cit.*, 172; Williams, *Vigilance Committee*, 319. "As the names of the two women arrested by Assing, the Chinese interpreter, were not given in the documents their identity was a matter of conjecture until it was confirmed by a paragraph in Holinski's *California* which narrated the incident and attributed Miss Atoy's arrest to the efforts of the Chinese colony to suppress their notorious country-woman."

[27]Soulé, *Annals*, 384. "It was only in 1851 and 1852 that their rapidly increasing numbers began to attract notice. Considerable apprehension began to be entertained of the supposed bad effect which their presence would have on the white population."

[28]The *Alta California*, Dec. 18, 1850. "Arrival of French Vaudeville Co. consisting of Mesdames Racine, Adelbert, Eleonore, and nine others." This was ten months before Holinski's landing in San Francisco.

[29]*The Picayune*, Dec. 23, 1850. "Pleasing entertainment to a large French audience."

[30]Barry, *Men and Memories*, 138-139. "We remember the day when a woman walking along the streets of San Francisco was more of a sight than an elephant or a giraffe would be today, 1873...We were in Riddle's auction room one day at a crowded sale when in a mo-

mentary pause of the auctioneer's voice, someone shouted, 'Two ladies going along the sidewalk!' Instantly the crowds of purchasers rushed out pell-mell...and in such numbers that the unconscious objects of the commotion were startled with the impression that fire or earthquake had come again."

[31]Hittel, *San Francisco*, 154. "The winter of 1849 and 1850 was very wet. The streets were soon worked into deep mud by the traffic...Two horses sank so deep in the mud in Montgomery St....that they were left there to die." *Ibid.* The rainfall in 1850 was 30 inches; in 1851, 7 inches. *Alta California*, Jan. 14, 1850, reported "heavy and continual rain and big floods." Soulé, *Annals*, 205.

[32]Barry, *Men and Memories*, 205. November 22, 1849 the ship *Oxnard* brought for William D. N. Howard "twenty-five wooden houses, all numbered in sections, and fitted in Boston, for erection in San Francisco."

[33]E. Massey, "Journal d'un Voyage," 30. "Barely are the embers cold before they begin to rebuild."

[34]Eldredge, *San Francisco*, 284. The *Washington House* rented for $1000.00 a month; guests paid $200.00 a month for single rooms. B. Taylor, *Eldorado*, 57, 58. A room at the *Ward House* without board cost $250.00 monthly. A small broker's house, *The Miner's Bank*, for $75,000.00 per annum. Barry, *Men and Memories*, 25. "Sam Gower paid $2500.00 per month for his store, and rented the 'upstairs' to Mr. Crane of the *Courier* for $1000.00 a month."

[35]The seal of the city of San Francisco bears the symbol of the phoenix.

[36]Bancroft, *California*, VI, 223. Many were of the upper classes: "well educated youths from New England." *Ibid.*, 227. Lawyers, doctors, and army officers could be seen toiling for wages...Thus were social grades reversed." Massey, "Journal," 25.

[37]Coy, *Gold Days*, 288. "The census of 1850 indicates that there were only seven women in every hundred of the population." Barry, *Men and Memories*, 129.

[38]Eldredge, *California*, 620. Some of the causes of excesses are said to have been lack of home life, of higher

recreation, influence of climate, strain under which the men labored, and freedom from social restraint.

[39]*Ibid.*, 599. The "Hounds" were formed of disbanded New York soldiers and Australian convicts. They were finally arrested and deported after an attack on the Chilean people on Telegraph Hill, July 15, 1849. Bancroft, *California*, VI, 742. Cleland, *California*, 296. Gleeson, *History of the Catholic Church*, 196.

[40]Reports of pioneers are contradictory. Bancroft, *California*, VI, 228. "In 1848 and '49 locks and watchmen were little thought of"... Saint-Amant, *California*, 402. Eldredge, *San Francsico*, 190. Williams, *Vigilance Committee*, 86. "We read, as it were in parallel columns, of bags of gold dust that lay safe in guarded tents and of merchandise piled up high in the open streets; then of robbery and murder that went unnoticed in a community where a man might drop out of sight without causing a ripple of comment among his self-absorbed neighbors."

[41]J. Royce, *California*, 375. The emigrants acquired practice in self government during the long journey around Cape Horn on overcrowded ships where there was need for strong repressive measures with a rough crowd at close quarters. R. D. Hunt, *Ox Cart to Airplane*, 370. "There were often serious difficulties with crews on long voyages." J. Royce, *California*, 366. Borthwick contrasts finely the organizing power of the American miners with the gregarious habits of the seldom organized French miners, and makes the fact illustrate national peculiarities. Bancroft, *California*, VI, 431. A large proportion of the people had been trained in local political clubs and movements.

[42]*Alta California*, Oct. 31, 1851. An account of the arrival of the *Challenge* and of the attempted lynching of Captain Watterman and his first mate for cruelty to the crew. *Ibid.*, Nov. 4, 1851. Newsboys hang effigy of Captain Watterman in Plaza. Dec. 18, 1851. Captain Ellis is mentioned.

[43]Coy, *Gold Days*, 200. "Corporal punishment was not considered in the same light that it now is and whippings

and more severe punishments were meted out in many states." _Vigilance Committee_, 77.

[44]Bancroft, _California_, VI, 784. The thirty-two congregations of the city embraced eight Protestant, six Catholic, and two Hebrew bodies, besides a convent for the two Sisters of Mercy. Gleeson, _Catholic Church_, 270, 271. The French church on Bush Street was built in 1857. Soulé, _Annals_, 716. San Francisco Orphan Asylum; 717, Sister of Charity Orphanage in 1852.

[45]Engelhardt, _Mission Dolores_, 350. "In 1850 Col. C. L. Wilson conceived a plan of laying a plank-road from Kearney St. to the Mission." He was given a franchise of seven years only, but the road was so greatly needed that it paid for itself in tolls in six months. Bancroft, _California_, VI, 188. For further details concerning the plank-road see _Pacific News, Picayune_, Nov. 4, 20, 1850 _et. seq._; Hittell, _San Francisco_, 151-3. Soulé, _Annals_, 297-8; Barry, _Men and Memories_, 108-9.

[46]Coy, _Gold Days_, 254. "When I had climbed the last sandhill, riding in towards San Francisco...I could scarcely realize the change that had taken place during my absence of three weeks...streets which had been merely laid out were hemmed in with buildings and thronged with people...He walks over an open lot in his before-breakfast stroll—the next morning, a house complete, with a family inside blocks up his way." B. Taylor.

[47]Engelhardt, _op. cit._, 96. Shows the folly of self-government for Indians at that time. Holinski in several passages, here and outside of the portion translated, holds the Franciscans responsible for the backwardness of the Indians. Yet of those with whom Sutter had no better luck the author says, p. 193: "The abject stupidity of those unfortunate creatures was obvious...While education raises the Negro by degrees to the level of the white man, it fails utterly to affect the inert apathy of the Indian...Of the numerous savage tribes I met on my travels, the Californian Indians seemed to me to betray by their appearance an incurable 'dégradation bestiale.'" Revere, _A Tour of Duty_, 124. "These missions would

have been productive of great good if they had been preserved."

[48]Some reasons given for secularization of the missions. Lévy, *Les Français*, 9. The Mexican Government wished to divide up the land and attract white Mexican population to California to keep out the English, French, and Americans. Mr. Forbes, M. Duflot de Mofras, and Frémont were in California in the interests of their respective governments. B. Taylor, *Eldorado*, 181. The government was jealous of the wealth and power of the missions.

[49]All travelers did not share Holinski's opinion. B. Taylor, *Eldorado*, 50. "Lovely as the Mediterranean Coasts are in my memory, they seem cold and pale when I think of the splendor of that scene of the Bay of San Francisco." Tyson, *Diary*, 49. "The morning opened beautifully over the California hills. There were several vessels in sight and the land looked most inviting. The effect on the landscape was very beautiful...all description fails to convey to the mind an adequate impression of its beauty and magnificence."

CHAPTER TWO

[1]Buffum, *Six Months in the Gold Mines*, 109. "Throughout the range of the western slope of the Sierra Nevada and in every little hill that branchos from it runs a formation of quartz rock, found sometimes at a few feet below the earth's surface and sometimes rising above it in large solid masses...Mr. Wright has in his possession a specimen of this quartz weighing twelve pounds, and more than one fourth its weight in pure gold."

[2]Sacramento was a convenient point of departure for the northern mines. Williams, *Vigilance Committee*, 101; Bancroft, *California*, VI, 455; Coy, *Gold Days*, 91, 221.

[3]State Census Report, 1852, p. 972. San Francisco, pop. 36, 154; Sacramento, 12, 418.

[4]Tyson, *op. cit.*, 62, Exaggerated advertisements drew many who found themselves "in a distant land away from

friends and home, and among many who were umprincipled, where their cases were truly pitiable:

> *Through me one goes into the city of sorrow*
> *Through me one goes into deep grief,*
> *Through me one goes among the lost.*"

[5]The San Joaquín was navigable as far as the Tuolumne. Hittell, *op. cit.*, 150. The *McKim* was the first steamboat to run regularly between San Francisco and Sacramento. Buffum *op. cit.*, 110. "The city of San Francisco had assumed a very different aspect at the time I reached it on my return from the northern mines. Where the old store-ship used to be...tall masted ships were moored and the extensive plain was dotted with houses."

[6]For descriptions of mining cities see Bancroft, *California*, VI, 387; Coy, *Gold Days*, 234.

[7]*Ante*, n. 44, p.32.

[8]Holinski is fond of using this English expression, "go ahead" in his French book. As it is of frequent occurrence in contemporary English works, it was probably a popular expression which caught his fancy. Williams, *Vigilance Committee of 1851*, 179. The slogan of the city of San Francisco was said to be: "Go ahead, Young California!"

[9]They are not always so symmetrical in the oldest parts of town.

[10]Not a pheasant, probably a *paisano*, the local term for a species of quail.

[11]Coy, *Gold Days*, 274. Laundry work was sent to Canton and the Hawaiian Isles. In California shirts were laundered at six to eight dollars a dozen, while new ones cost but ten dollars a dozen.

[12]Buffum, *op. cit.*, 105. "Over this immense territory where the smiling earth covered and concealed the vast treasures, the pick and the shovel have created canals, gorges and pits that resemble the labours of giants."

[13]Coy, *Gold Days*, 64. See Luis Peralta's statement: "My sons, God has given this gold to the Americans. Had He

desired us to have it, He would have given it to us ere now..."

[14]Coy, *Pictorial History of California*, 101. Sutter purchased the equipment of Fort Ross in 1841.

[15]This seems to be a mistaken notion of the author. *Encyclopedia Americana*, under "Wrangel." "Ferdinand P. Wrangel was from 1829-34 Governor General of Russian America; 1840-49, Director of same; 1855-58 acting Minister of Marine. He was *opposed* to the sale of Russian America." For other stories regarding the Russian government in California before 1848 see Coy, *Gold Days*, Chapter I.

[16]Bryant, *What I Saw in California*, 450. "In regard to the minerals much is not yet known...From good authority I learned the existence of gold and copper mines, the metals being combined." Dana, *Geology of Exploring Expedition*, "The talcose and allied rocks of Umpqua and Shasta districts resemble in many parts the gold bearing rocks of other regions; but gold if any there be, remains to be discovered." (Mentioned in Sutter's *Statement*, November 1857. Coy, *Gold Days*, Appendix.)

[17]Coy, *Great Trek*, 76. The governments "looked on with dismay as increased immigration decreased their population." Bancroft, *California*, 124. Europe feared a financial crisis.

[18]In Paris the "February Revolution," 1848, overthrew Louis-Philippe and established the Second Republic.

[19]Coy, *Gold Days*, 43. The first piece of gold found weighed fifty cents.

[20]Bancroft, *California*, VI, 116. The report of Mason is given in U.S. Gov. Docs., 30th Cong., 2nd sess., H. Ex. Doc. 1, no. 37, 56-64; Coy, *Gold Days*, 324-334.

[22]E. G. Buffum, *Six Months in the Gold Mines*, 81.

[23]Bancroft, *California*, VI, 94, 231. "The result was widespread sickness, notably fevers, dysentery, and also scurvy owing to lack of vegetables...Buffum was also attacked..." Coy, *Gold Days*, 157-160.

[24]Hittell, *History of San Francisco*, 128-131, 210-215. Spectacular failure of four firms importing flour from Chile. The streets were filled with useless merchandise.

Buffum, *Six Months*, 121-2. *Alta California*, Oct. 12, 1849.

[25]Bancroft, *California*, VI, 89. Note 12. "John Sullivan, an Irish teamster, took out twenty-six thousand dollars from the diggings named after him on Stanislaus..." Soulé, *Annals*, 210. Buffum, *Six Months*, 109.

[26]Hittell, *San Francisco*, 138, 139. An account of miners arriving in 1848. By sea, thirty-five thousand; overland forty-two thousand. Bancroft, *California*, VI, 124, 125. Coy, *Great Trek*, 76.

[27]de Massey, "Journal," 25. "Out here no one is ashamed of what he is doing, no matter how humble it may be... blacking boots, cooking, washing dishes." Coy, *Gold Days*, 144-146. Saint-Amant, *La Californie*, 453. The French undertake menial labor.

[28]Coy, *Gold Days*, 270, 272. "Lots of land which sold for one thousand five hundred dollars six months before have been sold lately for fifteen to twenty thousand dollars." B. Taylor, *Eldorado*, 58. The *Parker House* rented for one hundred and fifty thousand dollars a year. Hittell, *San Francisco*, 150.

[29]Tyson, *Diary*, 57. "As in San Francisco, lots were selling in Sacramento at enormous rates and rapidly changing hands at a daily advance."

[30]Coy, *Gold Days*, 115.

[31]*Ibid.*, 118.

[32]Bancroft, *California*, VI, 397-417. European methods were adopted to some extent.

[33]Tyson, *Diary*, 71. "We approached the brow of a long almost perpendicular hill...attesting to the terrible throes of nature which in former ages had reared these mighty masses from the earth and placed them in their present position." Coy, *Gold Days*, 99.

[34]Colton, *Three Years in California*, 404. "Like a tear that has lost its way among the dimples of a lady's cheek."

[35]Coy, *Gold Days*, 105, 106.

[36]Bancroft, *California*, VI, 91, 409, 423-425. "The increase of production from forty thousand dollars in 1849 by ordinary digging process to sixty thousand dollars in 1852...was at first due to the extension of the field over

much new ground and then to the gradual improvement in methods."

[37]Colton, *Three Years*, 403. "California will prove no exception to other sections of the globe where surface gold has been found." Coy, *Gold Days*, 312. "Eighty years after the discovery, California still leads in gold."

[38]Tyson, *Diary*, 61. "The sun pours its scorching rays on his devoted head...None but a laboring man is fit for the business. He must have been inured to the most trying hardships incident to this work from infancy and have a frame and constitution of iron to endure it for any length of time."

[39]Tyson, *Diary*, 58. "Those who cannot put up with privations and hardships had better stay at home. The mines of California are no place for them."

[40]B. Taylor, *Eldorado*, 243. Bryant suggests taxing all miners sixteen dollars per annum "to build roads, bridges, and facilitate communication to and through the mining districts and reduce the cost of living at the mines." Coy, *Gold Days*, 178-80. "To establish a claim to a piece of ground all that was requisite was to leave upon it a pick or a shovel."

[41]Royce, *California*, 483. The Land Act of 1851 was unfair to the California born. *San Francisco Herald*, May 29, 1852. Massey, "Journal," 32. "Gold Mining" of the lawyers. "They were always successful, charging enormous fees for settling land disputes. They usually got half the value of the land." Cleland, *California*, 304.

[42]Royce, *California*, 400. It was common to hear exaggerations of vice boastfully told. Taylor was told by a passenger in 1849 that he knew of only one preacher of recent standing in San Francisco; but that one "was now a gambler."

[43]Coy, *Gold Days*, 192-194. Not all laws were so drastic. Royce, *California*, 247. The influx of population necessitated a provisional government in 1849. Anarchy threatened.

[44]Eldredge, *History of California*, III, 408; Saint-Amant, *La Californie*, 406; Holinski's account of the Hangtown incident is not an exact translation of Buffum's, 81-85.

200

[45]Bancroft, *California*, VI, 409. "A tax of twenty dollars a month was imposed on foreigners." *Ibid.*, 469, "Although bloodshed was avoided many of them were driven out to swell the robber hordes which subsequently gave so much trouble to the Vigilance Committee and authorities."

[46]Auger, *Voyage en Californie*, 106. "The French work spasmodically and fail to agree among themselves." Bancroft, *California*, VI, 223. The French did not get along with the overbearing Anglo-Saxons. *California Courier*, Nov. 28, 1850. California will never open her arms to better citizens than the *émigrés* of the great European republic. *Evening Picayune*, Nov. 27, 1850.

[47]*Alta California*, Feb. 10, 1852. The *Société du Lingot d'Or* held a lottery in Paris on Nov. 16, 1851, and sent out five thousand emigrants. Lévy, *Les Français*, 72.

[48]Bancroft, *California*, VI, 197. "As life in California is shaping itself we could not get along without the qualities supplied only by the mercurial Gaul."

[49]Reference to the unsuccessful attempt made in 1850 by the Poles to free themselves from the yoke of Russia. Many of the insurgents were executed, many were sent to Siberia.

[50]C. Chapman, *History of California, Spanish Period*, II. "It is generally agreed that...the Indians of this hemisphere came either from Asia or the Pacific Islands, whether by way of Alaska or across some prehistoric Pacific continent has not been definitely determined."

[51]Holinski, *California*, III, 188. Sutter tells the author that his Indians are dying rapidly since they have been paid in currency. They eat and drink too much.

[52]Holinski is enthusiastic over the "universal fraternity" at the mines, but Gerstacher reports that foreigners could not get justice in the remote regions. Williams, *Vigilance Committee*, 126.

CHAPTER THREE

[1]This is Chapter V in Holinski's volume.

[2]Soulé, *Annals*, 143. "The temperature is never too high to prevent active exercise out of doors, nor so low as to need

fires in the houses." This would indicate either a changed climate or a more luxury-loving population in San Francisco today.

[3]Hittell, *San Francisco*, 133. The first great fire in San Francisco occurred December 24, 1849; the sixth, June 22, 1851.

[4]Hittell, *San Francisco*, 157. "The ground burned over was in a few months covered with better buildings than before; and the growth and business of the city appeared to be rather stimulated than checked by the disaster." E. Massey, "Journal," 30.

[5]Which may account for the difficulties of "Prohibition" in California.

[6]B. Taylor, *Eldorado*, 64. "A reckless daring spirit would come over the new arrivals immediately." Bancroft, *California*, VI, 225. "A marked trait of the Californian was exuberance in work and play, in enterprise or pastime...To reach this country was in itself a task." Auger, *Voyage en Californie*, 131. The Californians were the most idle and most dissipated people in the world.

[7]Soulé, *Annals*, 143. "As if to heap upon this happy land all natural blessings, the fecundity of its living creatures— human as well as lower animals—far exceeds what generally occurs elsewhere."

[8]Probably the author had Napoléon's statement in mind: "The English are a nation of shopkeepers."

[9]Dr. James L. Tyson, no doubt. See the following note.

[10]Tyson, *Diary*, 63. "They were walking shadows for months, with impaired intellects...I never saw more broken down constitutions than I witnessed in my stay in California." He found some "wandering about like ghosts of the departed."

[11]*Ibid*, 51. Tyson holds a contrary opinion. He says: "The climate of San Francisco we found anything but agreeable...Upon the whole, in a medical point of view I would not regard San Francisco as a most desirable locality for a large commercial city." Saint-Amant, 129.

[12]See page 15.

[13]B. Taylor, *Eldorado*, II, 221-224. Enumeration of these same products. There is security for all crops, they are

not "spoiled by rain." *Annals*, 143. The grape, the fig, the orange, the olive grow luxuriously in these regions, so do also all sorts of semi-tropical produce. All varieties of European fruits thrive in great plenty. Cleland, *California*, 309. In 1860 a million pounds of grapes were shipped from San Pedro.

[14]Swasey, *Early Days*, 385. "Mr. Briggs, as the oldest dealer in tobacco here, says he expects to see California one of the largest tobacco producers of the Union."

[15]Cleland, *California*, 303. "In 1854 the Los Angeles ranges supported over a hundred thousand cattle." *Ibid.*, 308, "It is said that thirty thousand head of cattle died on the Stearn's Ranchos alone. The great drought of 1863-64 put an end to cattle raising as a distinctive industry of Southern California."

[16]Duflot de Mofras, *Exploration* I, 49. Mentions also Rothschild's monopoly of quicksilver in Almaden in connection with discovery of it in California in 1843.

CHAPTER FOUR

[1]This is Chapter VI in Holinski's volume.

[2]The failure of the revolutions of 1848 is mentioned further on. The *coup d'état* of Napoléon III occurred on December 2, 1851, a month before Holinski left California.

[3]Not so easily as Holinski imagined. He probably had in mind the California conditions of '49. Human frailty, according to him, disappears in a republic.

[4]The author has reference to the socialists Louis Blanc, Considerant, Cabet, Proudhon.

[5]On the title page Holinski styles himself "*citoyen américain*," however.

[6]The industrial revolution brought the need of large capital.

[7]Hittell, *San Francisco*, 208. After the golden era that Holinski witnessed there followed a depression from 1854-61. J. Royce, *California*, 424. "The law of the almost universal failure of the pioneer of a new country was well exemplified in San Francisco... A shrewd newcomer will then buy at low prices ...."

[8]Saint-Amant, *La Californie*, 444. Seventeen ships from French ports brought four thousand individuals sent by the lottery in 1852 and 1853. "None of these succeeded, the investors lost their money and the emigrants failed." "Only those already abroad and used to conditions succeeded."

[9]De Massey, "Journal," 47. In 1850 "as a rule the current rate of interest is ten per cent per month."

[10]The American drug store is to this day a puzzle to Europeans.

[11]Holinski appears to give his attention to topics of this nature regarding women.

[12]Coy, *Gold Days*, 204-205. Holinski's story of Juanita's crime and execution differs slightly from the account usually given by other authors.

[13]Saint-Amant, *Journal*, 127. "For workmen, servants of both sexes, it is the land of promise."

[14]The deportation of the insurgents after the fighting during the "June Days" when the national workshops were closed in Paris in 1848.

[15]Holinski would have revised that statement today.

[16]It is interesting to note here the unsuccessful attempts at organized colonization that have been made by European countries to relieve unemployment since the World War.

BIBLIOGRAPHY: PRIMARY SOURCES

Alta California. San Francisco: 1849, 1850.

Auger, E. *Voyage en Californie.* Paris: 1854.

Barry, T. A., and B. A. Patten. *Men and Memories of San Francisco in the '50.* San Francisco: 1873.

Bancroft, H. H. *History of California.* Vol. VI. San Francisco: 1888.

Borthwick, John David. *Three Years in California.* Edinburgh: 1857.

Bryant, Edwin. *What I Saw in California.* New York: 1848.

Buffum, E. Gould. *Six Months in the Gold Mines.* Philadelphia: 1850.

California Courier. San Francisco: 1851.

Colton, Walter. *Three Years in California.* New York: 1850.

Daily Pacific News. San Francisco: 1850.

Denis, F. *Les Californies, l'Orégon, et l'Amérique Russe.* Paris: Bibliothéque Sainte Geneviève, 1849.

Dwinelle, John V. *Colonial History of the City of San Francisco.* San Francisco: 1863.

Evening Picayune. San Francisco: 1850.

Frémont, Capt. J. C. *Report of the Exploring Expedition to the Rocky Mountains.* Washington: 1845.

Frignet, Ernest. *La Californie.* Paris: 1866.

Gleeson, Rev. William. *History of the Catholic Church in California*, Vol. II. San Francisco: 1872.

Hittell, John S. *A History of the City of San Francisco.* San Francisco: 1878.

Holinski, Alexandre J. J. *La Californie et les routes inter-océaniques.* Second edition. Bruxelles: 1853.

Lévy, O. *Les Français en Californie.* San Francisco: 1884.

Los Ángeles Public Library. California Pamphlets, XIX, *Scrap Book*, 1887.

Massey, Ernest de. "Journal, translated by M. E. Wilbur," in *California Historical Society Quarterly*, Vol. V (1926).

Mofras, M. Duflot de. *Exploration du territoire de l'Orégon, des Californies, et de la mer vermeille*, vol. II. Paris: 1844.

Revere, J. W. *A Tour of Duty in California.* New York: 1849.

Royce, Josiah. *California.* Boston: 1886.

Saint-Amant, M. de. *Voyages en Californie et dans l'Orégon.* Paris: 1854.

Soulé, Frank, J. H. Gihon, and L. Nesbit. *Annals of San Francisco.* New York: 1854.

Swasey, W. F. *Early Days and Men in California.* Oakland: 1891.

Taylor, Bayard. *Eldorado; or, Adventures in the Path of Empire.* New York: 1858.

Taylor, William. *California Life.* New York: 1858.

Tyson, James L. *Diary of a Physician in California.* New York: 1850.

Wierzbicki, F. P. *California As It Is, and As It May Be; or, A Guide to the Gold Region.* San Francisco: 1849.

Wilkes, Charles N. S. *Exploring Expedition.* 1838-1842.

BIBLIOGRAPHY: SECONDARY WORKS

Chapman, Charles E. *A History of California: The Spanish Period.* New York: 1921.

Cleland, R. C. *A History Of California: The American Period.* New York; 1922.

Coy, Owen C. *Gold Days.* Los Ángeles: 1929.

Coy, Owen C. *Great Trek.* Los Ángeles: 1930.

Coy, Owen C. *Pictorial History of California.* Berkeley: California Historical Survey Commission, 1923.

Denis, Alberta J. *Spanish Alta California.* New York: 1927.

Eldredge, Zoeth S. *The Beginnings of San Francisco.* San Francisco: 1912.

Eldredge, Zoeth S. *History of California.* Vol. III. New York: [n.d.].

Engelhardt. *San Francisco and Dolores Mission.* San Francisco: 1924.

Forbes, A. S. C. *California Missions and Landmarks.* Los Ángeles: 1925.

Hunt, R. D., and S. W. Ament. *Ox Cart to Airplane.* Los Ángeles: 1929.

Williams, Mary Floyd. *History of the San Francisco Committee of Vigilance of 1851.* Berkeley: University of California Press, 1921.

IV.

THE AUTOBIOGRAPHY OF MARK LAFAYETTE LANDRUM

INTRODUCTION

All my life I have desired to know as much as possible about my ancestry. I have often felt that it would afford me a great satisfaction to read the story of my Father's life from his earliest recollections, through his school days and early manhood to his declining years. Unfortunately it appears no such memoirs were ever written. I have no doubt that my children in later years will have the same craving for a more intimate knowledge of their Father's life. These, and other considerations, have prompted me to lay before them a brief sketch of my humble career.

My life has not been an eventful one. I have not been in public life to any great extent, and therefore have contributed nothing to history, but I indulge in the vanity of taking credit for having been a useful citizen in my circumscribed sphere of action.

Many of the incidents and circumstances which I shall relate will be of little or no interest to any but my children and their descendants, yet there have been many trials, struggles and triumphs strewn along my pathway from which a profitable lesson might be derived, and, if turned to account, might aid in surmounting difficulties that may arise in the life of anyone.

1.

MY CHILDHOOD DAYS IN GEORGIA

The earliest account of the Landrum family I have been able to get was when two brothers, John and James Landrum, immigrated from Wales or the North of Ireland to the United States and settled in Virginia, in Colonial days. Later, James moved South, and his Son, or Grandson, who was my Great-Grandfather, settled in Tennessee where my Grandfather and Father, James Harvey Landrum, were born, the latter on December 10th, 1810. My Father's oldest brother John left Tennessee before he was grown and went to South Carolina where his education was finished through the aid of a relative, and where he took up the Ministry while yet a very young man, and where he, in after years, became very prominent, not only as a Baptist Minister, but in Civic matters as well. He had three other brothers and several sisters about whom I am not well informed.

My Father went from Tennessee to Georgia before he was grown, and at the age of seventeen years, married Catsy Castleberry who was then sixteen and one-half years old. They were both strong and industrious and intelligent, and managed to raise a family of eleven children in respectability until they were grown, except one son who died at the age of eighteen years. Their names, in the order of their births, were: William Mcrimon, Mcredith Castlcberry, John Merril, Nancy Elizabeth, James Franklin, Mary Ann Delilah, Sarah Jane, Joseph McKindry, Mark Lafayette, Noah Davis, and Benjamin Clement.

In a little log cabin situated on a low ridge between two ravines about one-fourth mile from a public road and seven miles from Cumming, the County-seat of Forsythe

County, Georgia at about eight o'clock on Monday morning, May 17th, 1847, I first saw the light of day.

This cabin was about twenty-two feet long and eighteen feet wide, with an extension on the North side twelve feet wide and with a shed roof. This cabin was all built of hewn pine logs except the roof, which was covered with oak shakes, and the floor, which was split out of pine logs and hewn smooth on the top surface. The rafters were also split out. The West end of the main building was used for a sitting-room and had a large fireplace; the other end was partitioned off for a bedroom. It contained two wide beds and a trundle-bed for small children which stood out in the open at night when occupied and was shoved under one of the big beds in the daytime. There were only two windows in this house, one in each end, with wooden shutters and curtains on the inside. The extension had a fireplace in one end and was used for cooking. The other end was partitioned off for a bedroom. There were three doors all in line, one on the South side of the living-room, one between it and the kitchen, and the other leading out on the North side of the kitchen. The kitchen had one window and the bedroom behind it had one. There were very few houses with glass windows in this part of Georgia in those days, glass being too expensive.

My Father settled on this place, consisting of forty acres of land, about one year before my birth, when he returned from Tennessee with his family, where they had lived the past three years.

If it were possible for my memory to carry me back so far, the first person I would remember having seen would be Mrs. Charlot Vickory, a quarter-breed Indian, but a very intelligent old midwife.

My Grandmother, *i.e.*, my Mother's Mother, seemed to take great interest in me and gave me the name Mark in honor of her departed husband, Mark Castleberry. My Father being an admirer of General Lafayette supplied my middle name in his honor.

I remember several incidents that took place before I was three years old, according to what my Mother has since told me about the time of the occurrence. The occurrence

210

which made the deepest impression on my mind took place in March next preceding the May when I become three years old. A lady cousin came to visit us and brought for me a large red apple, she had saved through the winter. My Mother divided it between my youngest sister, my next older brother, Joseph, and myself. I was eating my part with a table knife, shaving off a little at a time to make it last as long as possible, when Joseph, after finishing his piece, came near me, snatched my little piece, and put it in his mouth. To lose this cherished remnant aroused my resentment so suddenly that I jumped at him, grabbed him by the hair and commenced to saw on his neck with the table knife. This, I remember vividly, was in the yard at the East end of the house where my Father sat talking with a gentleman visitor. He quickly interfered, pulled a switch from a brush broom that lay in the yard, and nettled me while I was trying to crawl under the house to escape the switch. Another circumstance quite clear in my memory is when I got a good spanking for filling myself on peanuts, or "goobers" as they were then called, that were being saved for seed.

In this section of the country both boys and girls wore woolen dresses in winter and long shirts in summer until they were four, five, and some of them six years old. One or two months before I was four years old I begged to go to school. My Mother yielded to my coaxing and allowed me to go, perhaps more to get rid of my constant pleading than for any good it would do me. My brothers and sisters have always accused me of being very persistent and never willing to take "No" for an answer. I have no doubt that it is due to this trait in my character that at the age of thirty-nine years I won the affections of a handsome and accomplished young lady of twenty-five.

My teacher was a young lady whose name was Caroline Bryson. She would take me on her knee to teach me the alphabet and to spell. In the afternoon she would fold her shawl on a bench and place me on it for a nap. I learned to love her almost as a mother. I never heard it intimated that I was a precocious child, but I was told later that I learned the alphabet perfectly in three and one-half days, and by the end of the three months' term of school I could spell all the words in two letters.

The occurrences that impressed me most during those early school days are perfectly clear in my memory today. Some large girl would take me in her arms, some other girl would attempt to catch me. My protectress would swing me from right to left to keep me out of reach of the other girl. This was the greatest fun I can remember ever having had in my life. If by any accident I got hurt on the playground, some large girl would appear to console me. Those school days are among my fondest recollections.

I clearly remember my fourth birthday. Sister Jane and Brother Joseph were going to Grandmother's. I wanted to go with them but Mother would not allow me to go. With my usual persistence, I begged and cried. Mother told me that I was too big to cry, that I was four years old that day. The scene is yet clear to me. My Mother was reeling cotton thread off the "broach" onto the "Swifts" to make "hanks." The ends of the Swifts" were resting on the backs of two chairs and Brother Davis, who was then nearly two years old, was standing in one of the chairs.

During those early years of my life all the everyday or working clothes of the family were carded, spun, woven and made at home. My Mother was skilled in the manufacture of cotton and woolen goods for both men's and women's wear. She was especially proficient in designing and "putting" the warp through the harness of the looms. Many of the neighboring women came to her for aid in this line of work.

Georgia at this time had no public school system or any public money for schools. Usually some public-spirited citizen would go among the neighbors and have each family subscribe one or more pupils at a given price per pupil for a term of three or four months. When a sufficient number of pupils were subscribed to warrant a sufficient salary, a teacher was sought. Any gentleman or lady with a fair knowledge of the three R's—"reading, 'riting and 'rithmetic"—was satisfactory for a teacher.

In the Spring of 1852, when I was nearly five years old, as related by my Mother, I coaxed her to send brother

212

Meredith to get Miss Bryson to come and "teach up" another school. Meredith was sent and Miss Bryson came and taught another term. During this term I made good progress in spelling and began to read. I was fond of school and would cry if anything happened to keep me at home a day. I remember how Sister Mary Ann would see that my clothes were proper and comb my hair nicely, and how I carried my hat in my hand nearly to the schoolhouse so as not to spoil the arrangement of my hair. But I was not so enthusiastic over my teacher this term as before, because she did not take me on her knee to recite and tuck me away so tenderly for my afternoon nap. School life then was somewhat different from what it is today. The adage, "Spare the rod and spoil the child" was religiously observed in those days by the teachers, and their apparent solicitude for the welfare of the child made it quite interesting for the incautious youths. I came in for my share of the rod, and I could not see then, nor can I now, the justice of those beatings.

In my youth I was overstocked with energy and inquisitiveness, and the working off of this surplus was responsible for all my troubles with the teacher, who never lost an opportunity to use his prerogative of applying the rod.

Mr. Buchannon, my last teacher but one, whose school I attended only three weeks, had oral spelling every Friday afternoon. How well I remember on one occasion he called the first class to take their places for spelling. I can almost feel the smarting of the lash now when I think of it. They stood in line and the foot of the class reached just to where I sat. I might mention that we had all been given fifteen minutes to study our spelling lessons, and were then told to close our books. We all spelled out of Townsend's "Speller and Definer," and I was in the second class. The word was given out first to the one at the head of the class, and, if this one failed to spell it correctly, it was passed on down the line until someone did spell it correctly. This one moved up the class and took the place of the one who first missed it. The pupil occupying the position at the head at the end of the lesson was given a Certificate, and at the end of the school term the one having the greatest number of Certificates was given a prize. As soon as the spelling got under way on the occasion referred to, I became interested and opened my book to watch the progress. Kalendar Chatman, who seemed to have a patent on the position at the foot of the class, could look down into my book from where she stood. In the course of the lesson, a very hard word was given to the one at or near the head and was missed. The word passed all the way down the line until it reached Miss Chatman at the foot. She quickly spelled it right out of my book, and was so elated over her triumph that she could not wait for the teacher to say "Correct," but went like a shot to the head. This very unusual and unexpected occurrence seemed to give a shock to both teacher and class. The teacher arose to his feet and demanded, "Mark, did you close your book when I called the class?"

"Yes, Sir."

"Did you not open it again?"

"Yes, Sir."

"Come up here."

On my approach he opened his desk and took from it a hickory switch, the slim end of which he had worn off on Will Kemp and "Bud" Castleberry, and gave me an unmerciful beating. This is only one of a goodly number of beatings I received from this old cousin of the President of the United States.

I will mention one other circumstance that the reader may judge of the kind of bad boy that I was, and to give him an idea of the schools of that day. We were all required to speak pieces on Friday afternoons. One Friday a number of my class was without their pieces. They were told that any of them who did not have their pieces the next Friday would have to sing a song. I thought I saw a chance for a little fun. I usually had my piece, but concluded to neglect it on the next Friday. When the time came, several of the class had spoken their pieces when I was called on. I answered that I had no piece. I was then told to sing a song, whereupon I marched out bravely as ever I had, made my bow and commenced:

I will sing a little song;

It isn't very long,
Teedle-um-a-too—it's out!

The school cackled and tittered as I had expected, and I got the rod as in the other case related. Well, really, it took me some time to regain my interest in speaking, to say nothing of singing, in public.

This was the method of dealing with infractions, no matter how innocently they may have been committed.

Brother Joseph was a good, quiet boy at school and was very rarely chastised. I seemed to get enough for both of us, and still I did not grow very big.

I attended school from time to time for a brief spell until I was twelve years old, and I have heard my Mother say that I attended school thirteen months, altogether, in Georgia. Those school days were full of incidents as bright in my mental vision today as when they occurred.

About the first of April, 1850, my Father and Brother William M. left the family and journeyed to California to seek their fortunes in the gold fields. Brother Meredith, John and James worked the farm at home. In the Summer of 1852, my next oldest Brother, Meredith, left for California to join Father and Brother William.

My Father, who had only partial success in the mines of California, returned to his family in the Summer of 1853, and soon after, purchased an adjoining farm with a fairly good house and other improvements. He moved his family to this place. In the year 1855 he rented one field to a neighbor. This man hired me to pile and burn corn stalks and other rubbish to clear the land before plowing. He paid me ten cents every night for my work. I worked twelve days and received one dollar and twenty cents for it. This was the first money I ever earned. I was about eight and one-half years old. The following Spring Father took Mother, Benny, who was then a babe, Davis and I in an ox wagon down to West Georgia and Alabama to visit relatives. On this trip I saw my old Grandmother who gave me the name "Mark." She still called me her boy and, when I showed her about one dollar of the money I had earned and had not yet spent, she told me I would be a rich man. It is needless to say her prophecy never came true.

In the Fall of 1856, Father sold both farms, rented a house and a small quantity of land, moved the family onto it and again took his departure for California, taking with him my third brother John, who, a few days after their arrival in California, was stricken with Smallpox and died. His object in making this trip was to prepare a home for the family in California.

During Father's absence we small boys cultivated the small farm we were left on, and did what we could towards the support of the family during the three years we were left here. Mother, being anxious to give Father a chance to build the new home, would not complain to him, and concealed the fact that at times we were in want. I remember one of these years when I was eleven years old. We had neither meat nor any money with which to buy it. I coaxed Mother to let me go and earn money. She said I was too little, but that I might try. So I started out one morning and, after calling on several neighbors, I went to a Mr. Ezzard who had a large farm, and asked him for work. He said he would give me four dollars per month to burn corn stalks and clean ground for plowing. The following morning I went to work. When I had cleaned one field, I feared that my job would not last long and so I asked him to let me plow. He said I could try, and gave me a gentle old mare that knew more about plowing than I did. I will state here that nearly all the plowing was done with one horse and a little "bull-tongue" plow. Mr. Ezzard had a grandson and a Negro slave, both large boys, plowing for him. I was put in the field with them. The old man came around in the afternoon to see how I was getting on, and told me that I was doing fine. I plowed with these boys ten or twelve days until, one afternoon when we were finishing up a small piece, the old man came again and told the other boys they could go to another field. He told me to lay this piece off for cotton, if I thought I could do it, and added that it did not make much difference if it were not done well as there was not much of it. Faith being well developed in me, I assured him I could do it. I took great pains to lay the rows off straight, and to have them of equal dis-

216

tance apart. Tommy Ezzard, his grown son, came to me when I was about done with it and told me the job could not be beaten. This made me feel good, but I gave the old mare credit for knowing just where to walk. After this I was kept at laying off corn and cotton ground until my month was up.

Mr. Ezzard's family consisted of three bachelor sons and three old maid daughters. They had two houses. One was called the Boy's House. It had a fireplace and a large sitting room. The old maids often spent their evenings in this house with their brothers. They all petted me and made me feel quite at home. I remember one evening in particular when I had a good time, and they had a lot of fun with me. On this evening the school teacher, a young man, and another gentleman friend came to spend the evening. They all retired to the boy's house. I was taken in as one of the crowd and drawn in to all their sports. Many games were played. The teacher being a jolly fellow made a mark on the wall and proposed that each one, after being blindfolded, should walk across the room and see how near he could place his finger to this mark. Several of them tried it and then I was told to try it. They blindfolded me hard and fast. The teacher got in front of the mark on the wall and let me put my finger in his mouth and then closed his teeth on it. In my excitement it took me some time to get the blind off, to see what had my finger. Later on, another game was proposed wherein one at a time were to be blindfolded and led over a stack of chairs on all fours to see who could perform with the greatest agility. They started with me. After being well blindfolded, they led me over stacks of chairs, up and then down; finally I felt the ground with my hands. I drew my feet down and commenced to get my blind off. When I succeeded, I found everything dark. I could only see a little light shining through the cracks in the floor. I was under the house, and I saw no way to get out. They had shut the floor down where they had put me through. Everything was still. I could not hear a sound. The situation was dreary. After pondering for two or three minutes I saw the joke and sung out for relief. They opened the floor and let me out. The old maids put their arms around me and told me they would not let the boys play any more tricks on me.

217

When the old gentleman came to settle with me I asked him to sell me a piece of bacon, which he did, and gave me the balance in money. It was now after sundown and I had three miles to go. They insisted on my staying till morning, but I was anxious to see home and Mother and take this piece of bacon to her. When I reached home and placed my burden before her, she praised her little man as but few Mothers could do.

I was home but a few days when I asked her to let me go and earn more money. She consented, and on Monday morning I started out again. In the afternoon I passed through a cornfield of James Thompson's. I found his son Joe and daughter Jane hoeing corn leisurely. After talking to them awhile I went on to the house and found Mr. Thompson at home. I asked for work and was told that he did not want to hire. I told him that I came through his field and saw that it was very foul, and I thought the grass and weeds were growing faster than Joe and Jane were cutting them. He replied that he had no money to pay for help. I asked him if he had bacon. He replied that he had plenty of it. I told him that bacon was as good as money to me. "All right," said he. "You can go to work tomorrow morning." I slept with Joe, and the next morning I picked out a hoe that suited me and Joe, Jane and I went out to the field. Each of us took a row side by side, and in a short time we were racing. We kept up this racing all the week so that by Saturday evening we had the field nearly finished. After supper, at my request, Mr. Thompson weighed out for me a good piece of bacon, allowing me twenty-five cents per day for my work. I took the bacon on my shoulder and hurried home as fast as I could go. I had only two miles to travel and was not long on the road. When I arrived at home the family was still in the kitchen where they had just finished supper. When they saw the bacon, not only my Mother, but my Sisters as well, made me feel that I was of some importance to the family.

The manners and customs in Georgia at that time were somewhat different from those now prevalent in California. Traveling was pretty much all done on horseback. When the family went, it was in a two-horse or two-ox wagon. A young man took his sweetheart on the horse behind him and rode to church. Buggies were a scarce article. I remember how Father laughed when Mr. Bacon, a well-to-do farmer, who had bought a new buggy, his first one, and on his way home from church had called at the gate to speak to Father, when old Andy, Grandmother's Negro man, who was allowed more privileges than most Negroes, called out, "Mars' Bacon, Don' it make yo' head swim to ride in a buggy?" This was the first buggy I remember seeing, and it was about the year 1855.

Pianos and organs were an unknown quantity. Violins, banjos and flutes were the only musical instruments I can remember, in the neighborhood. The violin or fiddle, as it was called, was not popular as a society instrument, and was not allowed in every family. The Church people—and nearly everybody belonged to some Christian Church—did not like it because its music incited the young to dance. Singing was very popular, though cultivation in this line was not carried to a very high standard. Playing cards were taboo; the Devil was in cards, and they were not allowed in the house. Dancing was frowned upon, but parties where the young folks played games which inflicted much kissing as a punishment on the girls and boys for their many intentional mistakes, were common.

There were no theatres in our part of the country, or any public entertainments except some traveling Punch-and-Judy shows that might come through the country once in a year or two. I remember that Robinson's Circus came through the country once and showed at Cumming, our county seat, when I was about seven years old. We were all taken to the show, and I can remember many of the performances as well as if I had seen them a year ago.

Religious camp meetings were the great events looked forward to by the community. A large brush arbor was constructed at some convenient place where there was a good spring of water. A pulpit was built and benches placed for a large congregation. One section was set apart for the Negroes.

Families would go in wagons drawn by horses, mules or oxen, pitch their tents, and stay for several days until the meeting was over. All classes seemed to enjoy these meetings. The young men would promenade about the grounds with their sweethearts. The small boys would play about their camps and ramble around from place to place throwing rocks at birds, jumping and wrestling, etc., and I have seen some of the older people, during their revivals, prance up and down before the altar wringing their hands and shouting until they were exhausted.

The custom was, when the white folks were through with their services, the Negro minister delivered his sermon and his dusky flock would have their revival. The Negroes are a very enthusiastic people, and during their revivals they would pound each other on the back shouting "Praise the Lord," "God bless you," and other loving short sentences, until they were tired out. During some of these evening revivals, which were in semi-darkness, some of the rude young white men would get in among the Negroes, join in the shouting and, feigning unbounded joy, and happiness, beat some of the bucks half to death.

One evening while the Negroes were singing, working up a revival, a young Negro man was standing in the edge of the crowd with his arms folded, yelling at the top of his voice, "Bow, wow, wow. Bow, wow, wow," when Pope Allen stepped up to him and demanded, "Al, what are you standing here barking like a damned dog for?"

"Mars' Pope, it don' make no diffense 'bout de words so long as yo' keep de chune."

I remember another very amusing circumstance that occurred among the boys at the spring where we went to get a drink of water. Wilson Harris, an awkward, long-legged boy, had on a pair of linen breeches that he had outgrown and which were several inches too short for him. To remedy the defect and to keep the legs of his breeches from crawling up to his knees, he sewed straps on the bottoms of the legs and brought them across under his feet to hold the legs down. There was only one gourd at the spring and only one could drink at a time. Wilson became impatient waiting for the gourd to come to him, and concluded to drink out of the spring. He got down on his knees on a flat rock at the approach to the spring and about six inches above the water. When Wilson bent over towards the water, the straps were drawn very tight, so that when his lips were about to touch the water, pop! went the straps, and head first went Wilson into the spring.

These incidents are mentioned simply to carry the reader back to my young days, when everything was different from now.

On leaving this particular camp-meeting I have had in mind, I was the last of the family getting into our ox-wagon to start home. As I was just straddling the hind end of the wagon someone said "All ready," whereupon the driver struck the oxen and caused them to start with a jerk which threw me back onto the ground behind the wagon. I was helped into the wagon, and I suffered great pain all the way home. On examination it was found that my collarbone was broken.

This part of Georgia in those days furnished fine sport for boys, differing in many respects from the sports practiced by boys in California today. We gathered wild nuts, fruits and berries of different kinds, went fishing, hunted coons, rabbits and opossums, trapped quail and other birds, sleighed down steep hillsides, jumped, ran foot-races and wrestled. We sometimes went in the river bathing and swimming, but my Mother was a very good disciplinarian and kept her boys out of the water except when there was a man present to see that they did not get drowned. We never dared disobey her even if it might seem impossible for her to find it out.

My surplus energy kept me alive to all the sports. At running, I was below the average; at jumping I was above, and at wrestling I rarely if ever found a boy of my own age who could put my back to the ground more often than I could put him. This was one of my most enjoyable sports.

Our sports at school were chiefly with marbles or balls. I was never very good at either—my school days were too limited.

At home in winter, we children enjoyed the evenings in a manner never to be forgotten. Our living room had a large fireplace which kept the house warm. We played all sorts of children's games, including Hide-and-go-seek. We cracked nuts on the hearth, and parched corn in a Dutch oven. My Mother's teeth were too poor to grind the grains, so we vied with each other in grinding a portion for her in the coffee mill.

2.

WE LEAVE FOR CALIFORNIA

Having been three years preparing a home for us in California, Father sent Brother William back to Georgia for the family in the spring of 1860. It was William's intention to have us come by land with ox-teams, but when we reached St. Louis he found that the train which he expected to travel with had started many days ahead of us. It was not safe to travel so far alone, and there was no prospect of catching up with the train; besides, he was anxious to take out to California with him a pair of Angora goats, so he concluded to stay over in St. Louis until the following spring, allowing due time to go back to Georgia and get the goats in time to join an early emigrant train next spring. He rented a house on the corner of Seventh Street and Allen Avenue, where the family spent a monotonous eight months.

William, being a good, all-around mechanic, secured employment with a large firm to set up mowers and other farm implements. There being nine of us in the family, it took quite a sum of money to keep us. Brother Joseph and I got employment part of the time, which helped somewhat. I worked in a glass factory awhile, for a mattress maker awhile, and set up ten-pins in a bowling alley at another time.

We got along pretty well until late in the summer, when our finances ran down to zero, only having William's earnings to live on at one time. I will never forget one occasion when William went to work one Saturday morning leaving not a cent of money in the house nor even a bit to eat except flour. Mother told us we would have to get along somehow until evening when William would get his week's pay. We all cared more about Mother than we did about ourselves, so I conceived an idea but said nothing about it for fear it might fail. About nine o'clock I went out to Yager's gardens and stopped outside the gate where the hitching posts were. Several horses were hitched there then, but I waited for others to come. In a short time a couple of well-dressed Germans drove up with a fancy buggy and a stylish horse. As soon as they had stopped I stepped up and asked them if I could take care of their horse. One of them said "Yes," and handed me a thin halter. They passed on into the garden, took seats at a table, and drank beer. When they had chatted over their beer for awhile they came out, handed me a dime, took their horse and drove away. I did not tarry there but put off for the public market place on Corrandulet Avenue. When I reached the place I went into a grocery store and bought a dime's worth of bacon. Bacon was not so high then as it is now, and I got a fine juicy piece for my dime. I then went across the street to the market. Each farmer had a stall where he sold vegetables. I saw a large pile of turnip tops that had been thrown back when the turnips were sold. I asked for some of them, and was told to help myself. I picked out a good mess of the tenderest and set out for home.

On reaching the house, I saw no one about the kitchen. I deposited the greens and the bacon on the kitchen table, went to the living room and beckoned out Sister Nancy, who was chief cook, and could always be depended on to keep an honest secret. I showed her the greens and the bacon, and told her to put them on to cook, but not to say anything about it until dinner was ready.

About one o'clock Nancy came into the room where Mother and the other girls were and announced dinner. I was hanging around to see the effect. The other girls, not being let into the secret, laughed at the farce of going to dinner on bread and water or, perhaps, coffee. Mother looked up with a humorous smile and said, "It is poorly worth while, but we will go as a matter of form." When all reached the dining room and saw the big dish of turnip greens and a big chunk of boiled bacon, the girls threw up their hands and shouted, "Where did you get it?" Mother stood dumbfounded. When Nancy explained the surprise, Mother put her arm around my neck and said, "My little man will never let me starve." If there ever was a Mother who could inspire her child to his best efforts, it was my Mother.

Brother Davis and I were generally together in our rambles about the city, and we were many times forced into altercations with the city boys, who called us "Hoosiers." The most noteworthy incident that occurred in my career at St. Louis took place at the dry docks at the river. Several boys, including Davis and myself, were at the docks gathering chips to cook with. While we were playing around, I walked out on a narrow footing against a wall seven or eight feet beyond the floor of the docks. I had to keep my body perfectly straight or fall off. When I was out to the end, someone called my attention to a gull that had taken up a fish from the water. I looked up, and when I looked back at my feet I lost my balance, and pitched forward. As I went, I saw a log moored to the docks and, by reaching out as far as I could, I caught my hand over it as I went into the water. Without making any cry for help as I should have done, I climbed onto the log, and, by the rope it was tied with, pulled the log up to the place from which I fell, and climbed onto this narrow board again, soon working my way back to the docks, and safety. When I looked back and realized the danger I had been in, I began to get frightened and became so weak I could hardly walk. The water was very deep at this place and there was a strong current, so that if I had not caught this log I might have been carried under the dock and drowned. How I accomplished this difficult feat has always been a mystery to me.

My Father, in California, became impatient over our delay in coming to him, and got together a sufficient amount of money to bring us out by water. He reached St. Louis during the latter part of October, but my three sisters, at the solicitation of Brother William, concluded to stay over till spring and come with him across the plains.

After having our pictures taken and making the other necessary arrangements for the journey, Father, Mother, and we four boys took the train for New York. We stayed over one day in the city, visited Barnum's Museum and saw the Prince of Wales dressed in his knee breeches in a carriage on the street. Then we boarded the ship for Aspinwall. Father

224

wanted Mother to go in the cabin and the rest of us to go in the steerage, but she refused to fare better than the balance, and so we all went in the steerage. We had not proceeded far when we encountered very rough seas. Nearly everybody got seasick. One incident occurred during this trying time that amused my Mother so much that she never forgot it. This was when a little girl was very sick—was vomiting and crying. Her Mother told her not to cry, that the ship might go down. She replied, crying all the while, "I don't care whether her goes up or her goes down."

After we were a day or two out to sea, and had recovered from our sickness, I got around to the ship's kitchen, made the acquaintance of the cooks and porters, and, without bargaining with anyone, I engaged myself peeling potatoes and doing other odd jobs. The cooks were very friendly with me, and gave me everything I wanted to eat. I told them I wanted to take some food to my Mother in the steerage and so they gave me roast beef, chicken, cake, pie and such other food as the cabin passengers got, and told me not to let the other passengers see what I had. So I would hide the things under my coat and take them down to Mother's stateroom. In this way I supplied her with cabin fare all the way to Aspinwall.

After we crossed the isthmus and boarded the old *Cortes* on this side, I lost no time in getting acquainted with her cooks and, as before, I furnished my Mother with the best the ship afforded until we reached San Francisco. Again my Mother praised me for my thrift.

There were but few happenings on this voyage worth mentioning. Somewhere about the Gulf of California, the ship took fire in the hold, and Father told us it burned two days before the ship's crew could subdue it. Very few passengers knew anything about it, until charred lumber was brought on deck.

3.

WE ARE SETTLED IN CALIFORNIA

We reached San Francisco on the Thirtieth day of November, 1860. Here we boarded a river boat for Stockton. We spent our first night on land in California at the old _Weber House_ at the corner of Main and Center Streets in Stockton. We were met here by Brother Meredith and taken to Brother William's place on the Stanislaus River where we were to remain one year, or until his return home.

The first winter after our arrival, Brother Davis and I both being active, were given five yokes of oxen and a gang plow and set to plowing on the sand plains for a barley crop. There was very little for us to do but follow the cattle as they were yoked up in the morning by the men. We were venturesome lads and broke in all these steers to ride while pulling the plow. Getting thrown off did not daunt us, and we rode them to and from the field in spite of them.

Brother William, who had spent the winter in St. Louis, went back to Georgia about the first of March and purchased a pair of Angora buck goats of J. D. Peters, brought them to St. Louis, purchased his outfit and joined an emigrant train for California. He reached his home on the Stanislaus River in September, 1861.

A short time after his arrival, Father moved his family to his own place twelve miles higher up the river, and, in furtherance of the object of bringing the Angoras to California, Father and Brother William being partners in the goats, bought a flock of Common or California goats and commenced crossing them with the Angora bucks. Brother Davis and I were given the care of these goats, and we soon became adepts in goat raising. As soon as the crossbreeds were old enough, they were sold to men in different parts of the State who wished to grade up a flock of Angoras by crossing with the common goat.

The high price of the fleece made the Angora a desirable property, but the scarcity of these animals, there being only two small flocks in the United States at this time, one at Atlanta, Georgia, and the other in Kentucky, and the great cost of importing them from Asia or Africa, made it beyond a common man's reach to get a flock of fleece-bearing goats, except by crossings. Father and Brother being the first importers to this Coast, it gave them the lead in the goat business. As a consequence, a large number of flocks were started from the Landrum flock, not only in California, but in several other States. Later importations have been brought out from Asia and Africa by different parties to different states, until now the goat business is one of the staple industries of the country.

During the first several years we were in California, there was no school nearer to our place than Knight's Ferry, a distance of eight miles, in consequence of which I had no opportunity for further education except two or three weeks at a time on two or three occasions. When I could be spared from home I chose to earn money. Before I was fifteen years old, I hired to a neighbor to herd ewes and lambs. After spring opened bringing on pleasant weather and good grass, the sheep fed quietly and I found time to read and write. The only books I found at camp were three or four of Charles Dickens's novels. I read these and also newspapers, when I could get them. I had a pencil and a good sized memorandum or day book, and I filled it with verse. I wrote in it a story of "One Day of a Shepherd's Life," in verse and rhyme. My spelling was bad and my English poor. I wrote several little would-be poems. I found the book among my old keepsakes a few years ago, and after reading all that was legible, I decided that it could have been worse, coming as it did from a boy with very little learning. Some of the verses are too blurred to be read. The following are the verses that are yet legible:

One Day of a Shepherd's Life

*While comfortably dreaming the clock broke
    the charm,
By fearfully screaming its dreadful alarm.
Accordingly as I set it to strike at just five,
When every good shepherd from his bed
    ought to rise.*

I would spring from my bed and through the
    window peep,
Not daring to lie longer lest I should fall
    asleep.
When an hour was passed and my breakfast
    was eat
Yet it seemed early to go on my beat.

A few words to my dog and loosed her from
    the chain,
Now we are off rosey for a day on the plain.
I stalked to the pen where the sheep were all
    waiting
To greet me with white faces and cheer me
    with bleating.

When I opened the gate,for a moment they'd
    hush,
Then bolt for the plains with a terrible rush.
Not stopping or halting but marching in rows,
Until checked in front by Shepherdess Rose.

They would turn with a murmur—this restless
    mass,
As though they were complaining about the
    poor grass.

After ascending the highest hill, I stood
With proud survey o'er the pershing brood,
While instinct taught the hungry band
That they were under my command.
               Beautiful Spring

Gloomy Winter has slowly passed;
Bright Summer is on her way.
Beautiful Spring is here at last.
Oh, could she but only stay.

    'Tis joy to see the verdant hill
Adorned with varied colors, rare.

228

For beauty, taste, order and skill,
Oh, none with nature can compare.

'Tis joy to see the grum old trees
with smiling blooms their branches hide,
Welcoming back the little bees
To feast in pleasure, joy and pride.

'Tis joy to see the jubilee,
While cheerful voices ring,
Of feathered songsters in their glee,
Shouting praise to merry Spring.

Alas, how soon shall Summer's heat
Confuse this glorious scene.
Arrest the songster on his beat—
Make dust where flowers have been.

Before I gave up this job of herding sheep, spring shearing came on and I utilized every moment of my spare time learning to shear. My shearing furnished merriment for the crowd. The boss said the sheep was bigger than I was, but that ever present persistency brought success and the following Spring I joined a crowd of shearers and earned from one dollar and a half to two dollars and a half per day during the season, although I only weighed ninety-five pounds. The following five years I sheared sheep without missing a season. I have sheared several disconnected seasons since, and became one of the fastest shearers among those with whom I came in contact. Though the best whole day's work I ever did was one hundred and one two-year-old wethers, yet I have shorn sixty-six of the same kind of sheep in one forenoon.

After I became a good shearer, when shearing season was near at hand I went out over the country and engaged sheep to shear, and arranged the time to commence on each flock so that there would be no lost time between flocks. I then organized a crowd of about six good shearers, and managed the work through the season. My time and expenses in arranging our season's work was paid by the other boys.

The last season I sheared in the San Joaquín Valley, Pope Allen, whom I have before mentioned, a man of unusual wit and humor, with Brother Joseph and myself, left the other boys at the close of the season to shear a little job by ourselves. Late in the afternoon we reached the camp on the bank of the Mariposa creek, where we were to shear. There was no one there, and no preparations had been made for shearing. There was no place to sleep but on the bare ground without any protection from the wind. It was late in the season and the nights were cold and we had only one pair of blankets each. Brother Joe and I put our blankets down and slept together. Allen, with his one blanket, coiled up a short distance from us.

About one or two o'clock a strong and very cold wind arose. Some little time afterwards I was awakened by Allen's voice calling my name. I looked out and saw him standing with his blankets in one hand and his pants in the other while his linen was fluttering in the wind. He was shivering and he called to me in a very tremulous voice, "Here, take these blankets if they will do you any good. They are not doing me a damned bit. It is better to save some of you." His ludicrous appearance, made vivid by his wit, convulsed me in laughter, but as soon as I could speak I invited him to spread his blankets on our bed and get in with us. He, of course, knew that I would invite him to share our bed with us, but he could not lose the opportunity to make a witty pass, although he froze to death while doing it. Allen cut his own throat some years later in a spell of Delirium Tremens, and I feel sure that, if anyone had been present, he would have said something witty before he drew the fatal knife across his throat.

Father had his family in their new home on the Stanislaus River about two years when he learned that the land was claimed by a Mexican land grant. This almost broke his heart and ambition, and consequently no further effort at improvement of this place was made. After this he engaged in the Hog business with Brother Meredith for a few years, and later moved up on the San Joaquín River and located another claim on government land, where he remained until a short time before his death in 1872.

I worked at home when Father had work for me to do, and at other times I worked away from home until I was twenty-two years old and all the money I earned, except what it took to buy my inexpensive clothes and pay my incidental expenses, I turned over to my Mother.

4.

I START OUT FOR MYSELF

My three sisters were now married, and, there being no especial demand for me at home, besides being in poor health, I borrowed one hundred and fifty dollars from Robert Ramsbottom, bought a horse and saddle for seventy-five dollars, a pair of saddlebags for six dollars, took an agency from H. H. Bancroft & Company and went to Sacramento County to sell books by subscription. My principal object in this move was to bring myself in contact with strangers and learn to do business with the public. I succeeded pretty well in effecting sales and would have cleared some money had not the issue of the second volume of Alexander H. Stephen's *History of the Rebellion* been delayed. I delivered the first volume and had to wait at Sacramento city on expenses, for the second volume.

During my wait in Sacramento, the celebration of the completion of the Central Pacific first trans-continental railroad took place there, on the ninth day of May, 1869.

I finally had to leave Sacramento and lose my profits on the sale of the second volume. I went from there to Santa Clara County and worked two or three weeks with some other books. Then Brother William engaged me to go out to Peachtree Valley, in Monterey County, to superintend his sheep and goat business. I worked for him fifteen months. I now had money enough to pay off the one hundred and fifty dollars Ramsbottom debt with his high rate of interest, and have one hundred dollars left. When I came to work for William I located a government claim on unsurveyed land in Peachtree Valley. This claim commanded a considerable amount of grass or range land in the hills.

The San Lorenzo Creek ran down through the Valley, but the water was strongly impregnated with sulphurate of magnesia and was unfit for drinking purposes for man, though animals did very well upon it. I had to carry my cooking and drinking water on horseback from a spring two miles away in the hills. I being the first settler in this locality, no prospecting had been done for good water in the Valley. I dug two or three wells but got the same kind of water as that in the Creek. Finally I observed on the corner of my claim a bench of land which jutted out into the Valley and appeared to be of a different formation and of a different soil from the balance of the country around it. The peculiarity of this spot led me to dig a well here with the hope of getting good water. This was in the spring of 1871, about eighteen months after I came into the Valley. At a depth of twenty-two feet, my hopes were realized. During the summer, two families came in, settled near me and got water at my well, and for several years all the incoming settlers got water at my well until they were able to make cisterns to catch rain water.

Mr. W. H. Stone, whose acquaintance I had enjoyed ever since I came to the Valley, offered to buy a flock of sheep for me to take on shares, and during the latter part of October I went with him to hunt a flock that was for sale. We found only one flock that could be bought and these were fresh shorn and very thin. I told Mr. Stone that if we should have an early storm, which sometimes occurs, and the weather should turn very cold, there would probably be a great loss in this flock. He thought not, but I declined to take the flock at the time. However, on the way home, he urged me and agreed to bear one-half the loss the first year. I accepted this proposal and received the sheep on a three years' lease for one-half of the wool and one-half of the increase of the flock. I was to make the old stock good out of my half of the increase, except that the first year's loss was to be born by each of us equally.

This flock was near Pleyto, about forty miles from my place in Peachtree, and on the opposite side of the Salinas River. I concluded to keep the sheep where they were as the grass was better than on my range. After the first rains when the new grass started, I intended to take them home.

Sometime in November a storm came on lasting four or five days, and was very cold. I soon saw that my fears were going to be realized. The oldest and poorest ewes were humping their backs and stopping wherever they could get any shelter whatever, and some were freezing to death before the storm was half over. It was impossible to keep them together, and by the time the storm was over the flock was scattered all over the range. I gathered them in as soon as practicable, and out of a flock of twelve hundred I left four hundred and fifty dead on the range.

My first effort in business for myself, meeting with such discouragement in the very beginning was a great shock to me, and as a consequence I was very disconsolate. A whole year's work was lost in the first three weeks, not only the loss of the sheep but the loss of the mothers, from which I was to get my increase. It was a hard situation to face.

The man I had helping me through the storm volunteered a solution of the difficulty. He advised me to write to Mr. Stone to come and get his sheep. I was out only a few dollars so far, and this would leave me free to go at something else. But I told him I was not built that way; that I would not shift my misfortunes on to anyone else, that I had taken the sheep for three years and would stay with my agreement regardless of the outcome.

This heavy storm raised the Salinas River, and this precluded a possibility of crossing it with the sheep before spring. I kept the sheep through winter where they were. In April the water was down so that I crossed the river with my sheep and moved them to Peachtree.

On reaching home I found a man with his family on my place with lumber ready to build a house. I learned that his name was Gabler. I informed him that he was on my claim, but he refused to go. I undertook to pass my flock over the claim. He turned them back, and being much larger and stronger than I, it was apparent to me that I could not cope with him without weapons. So I went to a friend some miles away and borrowed a Colt's revolver. It was loaded for me and I supposed it was all right and therefore did not examine it. The following morning I again attempted to pass my sheep over the claim, and again my claim-jumper emerged from his camp, this time with a large rifle, and started to turn the sheep back as he had the day before. He was some distance away and I knew that a rifle was more accurate than a pistol except at short range, so preferred not to open the fight just yet. I pressed the sheep ahead and was gaining on him, when his Wife and Sister-in-law came out with their shepherd dog to help drive the sheep off of the claim. The dog was very excitable and ran around to where I was. I, having had much experience with sheep dogs, took advantage of this, and urged the dog with great effect making good headway. I thought it possible that when Gabler saw that I was gaining my point he would fire at me, but a short distance ahead was a deep gulch which most of the sheep had already crossed. He was on the opposite side near the gulch, and the only scheme which seemed at all plausible for me to stand any show to win the contest was to get into this gulch, draw and cock my pistol, run along in the gulch and suddenly come up the bank near him, where I might get a short range shot at him. On reaching the bottom of the gulch I drew the pistol from the holster, and attempted to cock it, but to my great surprise and bewildering chagrin, the hammer would raise only half way. There was no time to see what the matter was with the pistol. I was now helpless and at his mercy. What could I do? Time was the essence of the situation. Thoughts revolved rapidly through my mind. I could not entertain the thought of surrender. No, I would go ahead until I fell, so I ran up the bank where I was. By this time I had their dog under good control and the work he was doing for me was equal to that of half a dozen people, and with his aid I passed my flock by and on all sides of my adversaries, passing, myself, within a few feet of my antagonist, he with his rifle at half aim and I with my pistol pointed to the ground. We looked at each other squarely in the eye as I passed, but neither of us spoke. When I had passed to the hills where I wanted to go, they went back to their camp.

When the heat of the day came on, the sheep went under trees to camp, and I came back to my cabin. After my lunch, I went over to the camp of my adversary. We talked

234

the matter over, and to avoid a possible calamity to one of us, agreed upon terms for a temporary purpose. We staked off a portion of the claim which I was to respect, and he was to respect my rights on the remainder, until such time as our rights could be amicably or legally settled.

Mr. Gabler forthwith brought suit against me in the nearest Justice Court for trespass. In the settlement of this suit my right to the possession of this claim was upheld. I bought his lumber. He vacated the claim and thus the controversy was ended. Mr. Gabler remained in the neighborhood for many years, and we maintained a cordial friendship.

For the past two years Brother Joseph had been in Texas. I wrote to him and induced him to come to me. He arrived in Peachtree during the summer of this year 1872. I took him in as a partner in all that I had without the investment by him of one cent. We thenceforth lived together, worked together, and owned everything together, and no account was ever kept between us.

5.

EARLY DAYS IN PEACHTREE

During the years 1872, 1873, and 1874 the Valley was pretty well filled up with new settlers, and the lack of many of the conveniences incident to a well-civilized community, such as a Post Office, a School, improved roads, etc., began to be felt. Someone must lead in the acquisition of these, and I, being a young man unencumbered with a family, was sought and urged by the neighbors to move in the matter. So far as schooling and experience was concerned, I was poorly equipped for the task, but, acting on the theory that where there is a will there is a way, I betook myself to Salinas, the County seat, and consulted professional men and enlisted their sympathy and aid.

One lawyer gave me an old set of *California Codes* so that I could study the procedure in forming a school district, getting a school-house built, etc., and drew for me a petition to be presented to the Board of Supervisors and also a petition to the Post Office Department for the establishment of a Post Office and a postal route. After gaining all the information my untrained mind would hold on these lines, I came home and pushed forward the work. In due course I was elected Assessor and Collector for the purpose of collecting money to build a school-house. I was also elected Clerk of the Board of School Trustees, and in a few months we had a good school-house, a teacher, and a small attendance of children. A Post Office was established with a weekly mail. A road district was formed and a road master appointed. With these steps of progress Peachtree began to take the form and practice of a well-regulated community.

These years were fraught with hardship and self-denial, but we were not without sources of amusement and we spent many happy moments together. Perfect harmony prevailed in the neighborhood, because up to this time we had nothing to quarrel about, and because it took all of us to do anything. We had many evening parties, some picnics, and an occasional dance in the school-house, where almost every member of the community attended. The women folk, mostly wives and mothers, brought to all our gatherings an abundance of good things to eat.

There were quite a number of bachelors in the neighborhood and among them were some very fair musicians. Brother Joseph was a good violinist, and George Engel was considered especially good, and also played the flute; George Parker was very good on the guitar; Dan Morton played the banjo; Louis Engel played on the bones and danced clogs and jigs; Henry Mosely played the tambourine and danced the Highland Fling and other fancy dances. These and several other boys in the neighborhood frequently met at some of the bachelor cabins and spent the evening with music, dancing and minstrel performances. I could never forget those evenings of hilarity.

During the winter of 1877-1878, we bachelors organized an amateur Negro-minstrel troupe, and gave two performances, one at home and one in a distant neighborhood, with great success. Louis Engel and Henry Mosely acted as end men and I as Interlocutor.

In the latter part of October, 1874, my lease on the sheep from Mr. Stone expired. After dividing with him,

236

we—for Joseph and I were together now—had about four hundred young sheep. About one-half of these were ewes—a number too small for a profitable flock alone. So we took another flock of twelve hundred ewes on shares from another party during the fall of 1876. Very little rain fell the following winter. However, we got along pretty well until April, when the grass was exhausted all over the county. All who were financially able were moving their stock to the Sierra Nevada Mountains, but we were without money and were helpless to save our sheep.

To give the owner of the sheep which we had on shares, a chance to save as many as possible out of the flock, we surrendered our lease, including the fine crop of lambs we had raised. The small flock that belonged to us we let on shares to a man who was prepared to keep them through the season, and allowed him all our lambs and one-half of the old sheep for returning to us the other half when new grass came. Grass started early the following season, and our sheep were returned. By this time incoming settlers had so encroached upon our holdings that we concluded not to take other sheep on shares, but sold our sheep and went out of the sheep business.

During these years—from 1872 to 1878—that Brother Joseph and I were together in the sheep business, we did our own herding most of the time, especially in winter. In rainy weather the corrals would get very muddy and the young lambs would get down in the mud and freeze to death. To save our lambs, we frequently camped the sheep out in some sheltered place where the ground was hard and clear, and to prevent their scattering over the hills and being killed by coyotes, we would put a blanket around us and stay with the flock. When a tree was in the neighborhood of the flock, we would squat down with our backs against the tree and get a little sleep. Sometimes the flock would move off until the mothers would awaken us by calling to their lambs. We would then hurry off as fast as we could go to bring them back to camp. If the night was rainy and very dark, we had to go more by sound than by sight. We kept going as long as we could hear a sheep ahead of us. Stumbling over something here and into a hole there, until we had them turned back, would keep our feet wet, cold and muddy all night, and when morning came one of us at a time would go to the cabin and get our breakfast and the other remain with the sheep. This is a sample of the hardships I have undergone to get a start to build a home.

Under the adverse circumstances as related above, we had accumulated but little property. Our assets consisted of our possessary claims—a comfortable little four-room house, a pair of small horses, a "two-gang" plow, some poultry and a cow. The only thing we saw to do now was to farm and try to accumulate more horses, cows and hogs.

About this time our Mother, who had been living with our Sister, Mary Williams, came to live with us, and remained with us until November, 1880, when she passed away at the age of sixty-nine years and seven months. A few days before her death, I was stricken with pneumonia while at Soledad and was too sick to be brought home until afterwards. On this account I was not at home when she died; neither was Brother Joseph at home, as he was taking care of me at Soledad. Brother Benjamin was the only person with Mother when she died. He told me that she got up one morning with a severe cold, and the following night, quietly breathed her last. Her Father, Mark Castleberry, was of English and German extraction. Her Mother's maiden name was Bragdon and was said to be of Scotch and Welsh blood. Her Grandmother—that is to say, my Great-Grandmother—before marriage bore the family name of Redfern. My Mother's Grandfather Castleberry was killed by the "Tories" in his own home during the Revolutionary War. I have the vest worn by him before his death, which was of cotton, carded, spun, woven and made by his Wife. I leave his vest, together with these memories, with you, my children. These, and all my other ancestors, after their arrival into the United States, have lived in some of the Southern States.

During the year 1876, settlers were beginning to crowd each other in Peachtree and were quarreling over boundary lines, and other disputes were becoming quite common, many of them requiring judicial adjustment and hence a Justice Court in the community became necessary. I was put forward as a Candidate for Justice of the Peace and,

238

without opposition, I was elected and I assumed my duties on the first day of January, 1877.

Up to this time my learning was so meager, and my experience in business affairs had been so limited, that I now wonder how I mustered courage to undertake anything that required knowledge to perform. I had read comparatively little, and my associations had been with people with moderate learning. The only books that I had read that were of any value were two volumes of Dr. Dick's works; One on *A General Diffusion of Useful Knowledge* and another, *An Essay on Education*; Rawlen's *Ancient History*, Green's *History of England*, Josephus's *History of the Jews* and two or three of Charles Dickens's novels. There was another book I must not neglect to mention. My Sister Mrs. Williams sent me a Bible which I read from beginning to end, and I frankly confess that this reading made an Infidel of me. It abounded with statements that impressed my unprejudiced mind as being purely mythical.

Realizing that, to render valuable service to the community through the office to which they had elected me it would be necessary for me to study the elementary principles of law and that it would involve much time and labor familiarizing myself with the Codes and Statutes of California, in order to mete out substantial justice to those who might seek relief at the bar of my Court, I accepted the office with due appreciation of the responsibility resting upon me.

In setting out upon the arduous task of self-education, I accepted help wherever it was available. The lawyers at Salinas were very kind to me. Some of them loaned books to me and took great pains in counseling me when called upon. To improve myself in language and composition I corresponded with newspapers and had my manuscript corrected by our school teacher. I also associated with cultivated men and women as much as possible, and thus, by persistent study, I acquired a sufficient knowledge and use of the English language to make myself fairly well understood. In later years, I remember seeing one of my articles written for the *San Francisco Call* republished in the *Los Angeles Times*.

My strong desire to become a useful citizen kindled in me a desire to speak in public, and for cultivation in this line I participated in debates at every opportunity, and later, after the Farmers' Alliance was organized in Monterey County, I lectured in the alliance (See Appendix), and, as an active worker in the "Peoples' Party," I was afforded further practice by addressing Conventions and the people on the hustings, until at length I acquired comparative ease in expressing my thoughts to an audience.

During my incumbency as Justice of the Peace, I had all classes of litigation within the jurisdiction of a Justice Court come before me, and out of about seventy-five civil cases tried before me only three juries were ever called for, nor an appeal taken from any of my decisions. I attributed this to my known habit of painstaking in all my work.

It fell to my lot to solemnize the marriages of seven couples and as *ex-officio* coroner I held inquests over dead bodies.

After thus serving six years on the bench, I concluded to turn my attention to the practice of law before the Justice Courts in the southern end of the county where I lived.

In connection with my Court practice, I performed legal services in many ways, such as drawing agreements, leases, conveyances and other legal documents, and to facilitate this work I secured the appointment of "Notary Public" which increased my business materially, as it often saved people a long trip to Salinas. I held this appointment four terms, or sixteen years. The office of Notary Public required a bond with two or more sufficient sureties to qualify in the sum of Ten Thousand Dollars, and Mr. Stone, who let me have sheep on shares and knew the manner of man that I was, voluntarily went on this bond for one-half the amount.

It was not uncommon for men who had very little knowledge of legal proceedings to represent their friends who knew less, in these Justice Courts, and it was a common characteristic in these amateur lawyers to take up the time of the Court in objecting and contending in matters when they had no legal grounds, to the great annoyance of the opposing counsel, and sometimes of the Court. During my practice in these Courts, I frequently met and tried cases with lawyers from Salinas and Hollister, and found it much more agreeable to have a professional lawyer for my opponent than a

240

layman who was not acquainted with the rules of practice in the Courts. Through being very careful and painstaking in the preparation of a case, I rarely went into Court with an action that could not be won on its merits. My familiarity with the facts which I expected to prove, and the law involved in the case, enabled me to present it before the Court and jury with sufficient clearness to make my practice very successful.

Brother Joseph and I also bought an anvil, a bellows and a partial set of blacksmith tools with which, he being mechanical and handy with tools, we did all our repairing and what job work he could get from the neighbors. He and I were both sheep-shearers and during the shearing season we sheared in our neighborhood, earning handsome wages during the time employed.

During all these years we farmed all we were able to, also kept a roadside hotel, and from all these various sources of income—the farm, blacksmith shop, sheep shearing, Justice Court fees, Notary and Attorney services and the Hotel—we equipped our farm with implements and improvements, acquired title to our lands and gradually increased our possessions until we had fourteen hundred acres of land stocked with horses, cattle and hogs, but these achievements were accomplished through the most rigid economy and careful management, being attended as they were by many drawbacks. In 1875, Brother Joseph had an abscess just above the knee that disabled him several months and caused considerable expense. Two or three years later he had an ulcerated tooth which caused necrosis of the jawbone. This trouble cost a considerable amount in time and money. In November, 1880, I was stricken with pneumonia which cost us time and money. In 1885, Brother Joseph was stricken with Sciatica, which rendered him helpless for two years, during which time he went to Texas hoping to improve his health thereby. In 1892, my whole family, including Brother Joseph had La Grippe, and his sickness was so severe he went to the French Hospital in San Francisco and was treated there about three months. From this time on he was subject to Asthma which rendered him unable to work for many days, weeks and months at a time. About 1895 he had a severe attack of pneumonia which confined him to his bed and the house for several months. Again, during the winters of 1902-1903, he was attacked with Inflammatory Rheumatism, which confined him to his bed between three and four months, and disabled him from work the balance of his life. During all of these afflictions each of us was constant in our attention to the other in all his needs and wants, and all that we both had was drawn upon to defray the expenses of the sickness of either or us without any account being taken of it.

Peachtree, prior to 1885, was thirty miles from any church and it was very rare that a Preacher had come into our neighborhood. There were, however, two or three ladies in the Valley who had been church members, and they asked me at one time to go among the neighbors and make up a fund to bring a Preacher into the neighborhood. I told them to send someone else; that I could not make up anything for a Preacher—not even my own mind. On one occasion when one did come into the Valley and hold services in the school-house, one lady came to me again and asked me to join the church. When I begged off, she told me she had told the preacher that I was a good, moral man and she thought he could get me to join, and the preacher replied that good, moral men were the hardest to get into the church. Later, someone sent him to me, and he told me that I should join the church to be acceptable with God. I replied with this question, "If there is a personal God who foreknows all things and is all-powerful, and if that God made me, ought he not to be satisfied with his own work?" The preacher went away without answering my question.

In this nonprofessional community, I was frequently called upon to perform the functions of Doctor and several times, Preacher also in the case of funerals. I was always active in helping to organize literary societies, debating clubs, plays and other entertainments for the improvement of our society, and we enjoyed many such social affairs in Peachtree.

6.

I MARRY

During the summer of 1883, I made the acquaintance of Miss Mary E. King, an accomplished young lady, while teaching her first school. I cherished and cultivated this acquaintance until January the Twenty-sixth, 1887 when we were married at the home of her parents in San Francisco. On my return home to Peachtree with my bride, my old neighbors welcomed us with a splendid banquet concluding with a dance. (See Appendix.) Young and old participated, although some of them had not danced for twenty years. Our first child was born on the first day of December following our marriage in January. This happy event seemed to double my interest in life. Our other children followed in rapid succession until, at the end of nine years from our marriage, we had three boys and two girls. The all-absorbing question that now engaged my attention was the education and development of these children and the preservation of their Mother.

I had so keenly felt the want of proper schooling in my young days while I was qualifying myself for professional work, and when I was in company with educated men and women I had felt the sting of not being able to entertain them as well as they had entertained me, that I now looked upon it as the highest duty of parents to see that their children were given an education suitable to their tastes and natural endowments, and commensurate with the needs and wants of the times. My Wife, who had enjoyed the benefits of a liberal education, and whose heart and soul was wrapped up in the welfare of her children, took the same view of the subject of education that I did. Although born, raised and educated in the large city of San Francisco, she lived contented in her country home, the environment of which she constantly labored to improve. Her untiring zeal, coupled with her rare ability as a teacher of children, and her tact in building within them good sturdy characters, caused me to regard her services as invaluable, if not indispensable, to our children's highest development. The mutual interest in our family predominating, nothing ever transpired during our married life to mar the pleasures of a happy union. Brother Joseph, who was a member of the same household, lived a true brother to her and she a true sister to him, and

243

hence our days were laden with the richest joys of a married life.

During the spring of 1898, Mrs. Landrum was called to the funeral of her Father, who had lived to the age of seventy-eight years. One year later she was summoned to the bedside of her dying Mother, then sixty-six years old. William King, my Wife's Father, was born in Brixam, England, and her Mother, Catherine Kelly, was born in County Mayo, Ireland. A few months after she buried her Mother, my Wife underwent an operation for an intrauterine tumor, from which, a few days later, she was attacked with septicemia, which caused her death on the twenty-second day of December, 1899, just thirty days after the operation.

This circumstance left me stranded, as it were, and feeling helpless to carry out the plans we had made for the rearing and education of our children. By summoning all the fortitude I could command, I struggled against adversity, there being a series of dry seasons then upon us, until I got a new hold upon life, and by doing the cooking, washing and mending myself, I was able to keep the children in constant attendance at school.

Our farm did not yield more than one-fourth of an average yield for the season of 1897. 1898 was a total failure of both grain and hay; 1899 and 1900 yielded no grain and very little hay; 1901 was a good year, and we harvested a big crop, but the three years following this was but little better than the three years preceding it. 1905 was a good year for crops, and the return from this crop enabled us to pay all the debts we had incurred during the previous crop failures, and we had a few dollars left.

During the summer of 1904, my Wife's Sister, Miss Matilda King, the only living member of the King family, while visiting my children at Peachtree, had the misfortune to be burned to death. She was boiling clothes in a cauldron, and while leaning forward over it her dress caught fire and when she discovered the blaze she ran with fright. Before help could extinguish the flame, she was burned so seriously that she died a few days later. My children, being her only heirs, inherited her estate, amounting to Fourteen Hundred and Fifty Dollars, net, which sum was applied towards their education. When the three oldest had been graduated from the Grammar School in Peachtree, Brother Joseph and I leased our farm and I moved my family to Santa Clara, where the older children entered High School and the others continued in the Grammar School.

We were now offering our place for sale, and during the month of October, 1907, an Agent of the Standard Oil Company offered us Fourteen Thousand Dollars for twelve hundred acres, the price we had set upon it. We accepted the offer and the sale was consummated. The following year in July, I moved my family to Stockton and purchased a home there.

I had two hundred acres near Peachtree which belonged to me individually, that I sold after I came to Stockton.

7.

I ENTER THE POLITICAL FIELD

I desire now to take the reader back again to the years when I led an active life; when my public spirit was given sway and my political ambitions went unbridled.

In the year 1879, a Constitutional Convention was held in Sacramento for the purpose of framing a new Constitution for the State of California. The following year this new instrument was submitted to the people of the state for their adoption or rejection. The Railroads, Banks, and all the capitalistic interests in the State were arrayed against it. All the leading newspapers except the *San Francisco Chronicle* opposed it. Both political parties, so far as they exercised any influence, were against it. Copies of this new fundamental law were sent to every voter in the State, with the result that the people became very much interested in it. It soon developed that a majority of the common people, and especially the farmers, favored its adoption. Many good and able men took the stump in its favor, and many of humbler station worked in their immediate localities for its adoption. I made a careful study of its provisions and was converted to its support, and made several public speeches in its favor in my home district. On one occasion Hon. E. C. Tully, Hon. J. H. Matthews, and myself went out together and filled several appointments, endeavoring to show its advantages over the old Constitution. Its friends had no money with which to disseminate literature, or hire speakers to explain its provisions to the people, while the powers that opposed it flooded the country with literature and sent out able speakers to accomplish its defeat. But when the election came on and the votes were counted, it was found that the New Constitution was adopted by a majority of over fifteen thousand votes. I look back upon this circumstance as indicating that when the people believe that there is a substantial benefit to be gained, they can not be bought nor driven from their position.

The autumn following this election, the general election came on. Legislators were to be elected, and many of those who supported the new instrument thought it was safer to trust its friends to make laws to put it into force than its enemies, who had told the people that its enforcement would ruin the country and bring all manner of trouble to our people. In consequence of this view, a "New Constitution Party" was organized and the party nominated a full State ticket, and in many of the counties a full county ticket was nominated. The new party nominated a ticket in Monterey County. Judge Gregory was named for Superior Judge and I for Assessor. He and I made the canvass together in my buggy. But it is needless to say that the ticket was defeated all over the State with but few exceptions, as independent movements usually are. (See Appendix.)

Early in the spring of 1891, the "Farmer's Alliance and Industrial Union" having originated in Arkansas and Texas reached across the continent and effected an organization in California. Soon after, an organizer came into Monterey County and organized a number of sub-alliances. One of these was organized at Peachtree and I was chosen as its President. During the first year of its existence I initiated into the order a large majority of the residents of Peachtree. All farmers and their families over sixteen years old, were eligible to become members. All subjects pertaining to the general welfare of the community were discussed at the Alliance Meetings. Literature along industrial lines was distrib-

246

uted. New sources of enjoyment were created and social relations improved, resulting in much benefit to the community.

Two or three months later, a County Alliance, composed of delegates from the sub-alliances, was organized at King City to meet quarterly. I was chosen as County Lecturer. (See Appendix.)

About the month of August of this year, a mass meeting of Alliance men was called to meet at San Miguel for the purpose of devising ways and means to build a Farmer's Alliance grist mill for the joint benefit of the Alliances of Monterey and San Luis Obispo Counties. An organization was effected and steps taken for the construction of the mill at San Miguel. I was chosen as one of its Directors and repeatedly elected, until I had served on the Board for six years.

In due course the mill was completed, but not until the Board of Directors had borrowed Five Thousand Dollars on their personal note to finish its construction. The necessity for this arose from the fact that the past season had been very unfavorable to the farmers, a large number of whom were new settlers and were unprepared to take up the stock of the mill and pay cash for it. The duty fell upon me to make a report to the stockholders at their first meeting after its completion, of the costs and disbursements of the construction of the plant. Through the lack of systematic bookkeeping by those in control, it took me eight days of arduous labor. The Directors carried this note along for two or three years, hoping that the farmers would become able to buy up the stock and clear up the debt, but short crops followed, one after another, until the Bank wanted its money. The Board temporized as long as they could until it seemed inevitable that we would have to pay the note. Looking over the situation carefully, it appeared to me that the debt would fall on two of us, and possibly on me alone. This would break me up and leave my family to suffer. It was agonizing to me. I could not entertain the thought of causing my Wife to worry by telling her about it, so long as there was any hope of extricating myself from the difficulty. The question of what to do to free myself from this impending danger had weighed upon my mind until I was sick so that I could not digest any-

247

thing I ate. When I had almost despaired of finding any means of escape, I met Mr. Henry Tollett of Salinas at the depot at San Miguel. He was just ready to board the train for Salinas. We shook hands and I held onto his hand until the train pulled out, at the same time telling him that I must have a talk with him. As a result of our talk, I prevailed upon him to take up this note and relieve us directors from our personal obligations to the Bank. I then brought him back before the Board of Directors, who were now about to meet. The arrangement was consummated and the mill was made to stand good for the debt, and we were relieved from our obligation. I went home happy and I resolved never again to obligate myself personally for an indifferent public.

During October, 1891, the State Alliance, composed of delegates from the County Alliances, met at Los Ángeles. I was chosen as one of the delegates from Monterey County. This convention of men was for the greater part selected for their superior intelligence in the locality from whence they came, and it proved to be a very interesting meeting.

We had a distinguished guest at this meeting, in the person of L. L. Polk, President of the national "Farmer's Alliance and Industrial Union." While a guest of ours, Mr. Polk delivered an address to over five thousand people in "Hazzard's Pavilion." At the close of his address, I heard an old man, who had known James K. Polk personally, say that L. L. Polk was an abler speaker than his Uncle, the President of the United States.

During this session of the State Alliance, a mass meeting was held in Hazzard's Pavilion, at which the People's Party had its birth in the State of California. The party having now been launched, its organization extended from one county to another until every county in the State was represented in the People's Party.

This session of the State Alliance closed just as the Railroad from Los Ángeles to Long Beach was completed, and the Railroad Company invited the Alliance delegates in a body to be their guests on the road's initial trip to Long Beach, October the twenty-third, 1891.

During the following year, 1892, a People's Party ticket was named in several counties and two assemblymen

248

to the legislature were elected. In 1894 a full State ticket was nominated by the People's Party with Hon. J. V. Webster at the head, for Governor, Hon. Thomas V. Cator was named as the Party's choice for United States Senator. County nominations were made in all or nearly all of the counties. Monterey County honored me with the nomination for the Assembly. (See Appendix.) The Democratic County Convention met soon after ours, but no one could be found to accept its nomination for the Assembly. For some time afterwards, it was generally thought I would be elected, but the Republican leaders always alert, conspired with the Democratic County committee to hire a Democrat to accept the nomination and it was an open secret that the Republican managers paid this irresponsible Democrat five hundred dollars to accept the Democratic nomination for the Assembly, and the Democratic County central committee put his name on the ticket in the interest of the Republican nominee. Straight Democrats, who knew nothing of the conspiracy, felt bound to support the nominee of their party, and the County being strongly Republican, in a three-handed contest the Republican Candidate was elected.

W. C. Bowman was our Nominee for Congress in my district. He and I made the canvass of Monterey County together. Many of the measures we advocated, then looked upon by many as visionary, have lately been enacted into law with great satisfaction to the people. Direct Legislation, was my slogan, and I had it printed on my cards. I devoted a portion of my public addresses to an explanation of the provisions, operation and effects, of the "Initiative, Referendum and Recall." (See Appendix.)

Mr. Bowman was an orator of rare ability and he received a large vote in the district.

Our Candidate for Governor, Mr. Webster, received fifty-one thousand votes in the State, and I received more votes in the Southern end of the county where I lived than both the old party candidates combined, and two hundred more votes in the County than any other candidate on our ticket, our candidate for Governor included.

From 1872 to 1891 I had attended many Democratic conventions. I had been a member of that memorable Democratic State Convention of 1884 held at Stockton. Thus, when I helped to organize the People's Party in 1891, I left the Democratic Party and cut all the bridges behind me.

From 1891 to 1898 I attended many People's Party conventions and conferences. I was a member of the last People's Party convention held in California, which met at Sacramento in July, 1898. This convention was infested with Democrats who had worked their way in as delegates from certain districts through political trade arrangements with office-seekers of both parties. Certain of our party leaders who were willing to sacrifice principles, party and all for the sake of office, had connived with Democratic managers prior to this convention.

The work of the first day of the convention made it clear to my mind that the fusion element with their Democratic allies had control of the convention. (See Appendix.) I was opposed to fusion and held that a Party that was good enough to fuse with was good enough to support altogether. My contention was that the ultimate triumph of the People's Party depended upon its steadfastness of purpose. That to win and hold on to the confidence of the people it must keep itself free from all entangling alliances with other political parties. All those opposed to fusion were called "Middle-of-the-Road Populists" and the others were called "Fusionists." Fusion resolutions had been adopted before Noon the second day, and a recess taken for lunch. After lunch I returned to the Capitol building, where the convention was held, alone. I halted at the front steps, ruminating over the deplorable situation the People's Party had fallen into. Presently Hon. J. V. Webster came along and suggested that we go into the convention hall. I replied that I had had all I wanted of that convention. After talking a few minutes, he agreed with me that we could do no good by working with those fusionists. Mr. Gilstrap, of Tulare, was the next who came and readily agreed with us and others came in rapid succession until there were a dozen or more in the crowd, including Hon. Thomas V. Cator, the Party's candidate for United States Senator.

It was finally determined by those present to call a caucus meeting of the Middle-of-the-Roaders to meet in the

Supreme Court chamber that evening to consider what measures, if any, should be taken by the Middle-of-the-Road wing of the Party. The caucus met. I was called to the chair. The deliberations of the meeting resulted in the calling of a nominating convention on the following day in the same place. The convention met and placed Prof. D. T. Fowler in the chair, after which a full State ticket was named with Prof. Shanahan at the head. Hon. T. V. Cator was again endorsed for United States Senator. I was named for Congress from my district. (See Appendix.)

The convention being over, the question arose as to which of the two tickets was entitled to the People's Party designation. Mr. Cator, before mentioned, tendered his legal services to the Party free of charge, and, he being an attorney of high repute, was given charge of the case. The matter was taken before the proper authorities and Mr. Cator got a decision in our favor. The Fusionists appealed to the Supreme Court and won the Party designation. This put an end to the Middle-of-the-Road movement and the fusion deal with the Democratic Party put an end to the People's Party in the State of California. (See Appendix.)

From that day to this I might have been called a politician without a party. My course has been entirely independent, invariably supporting men and measures regardless of Party organization.

My views on political issues have changed materially since I was a young man, mainly through observation and a partial study of Political Economy. I was taught to believe from a boy that the tariff was responsible for all the political ills that man is heir to. As I now see it, Finance and Transportation are the paramount issues before the American people. The volume of the currency, I think, should be controlled by the Government and be made flexible so as to guarantee the equilibrium of business. A leading economist has said: "He who controls the currency of a country controls every industry in it."

The United States covers such a vast territory and has such a variety of climates, soils and products, that an exchange of commodities between localities widely separated becomes a very important factor in the livelihood of the people, and, hence, to permit private individuals to control the means of transportation, an industry indispensable to the life of the nation, is on its face ridiculous. My opinion is that all such public utilities that cannot be dispensed with, even for a brief season, should be owned or absolutely controlled by the general Government.

—Mark L. Landrum

RECORD OF BIRTHS

MARK LAFAYETTE LANDRUM, Son of James Harvey Landrum, was born Monday Morning, May 17th, 1847.

MARY ELIZABETH LANDRUM, daughter of William King and Kathron King, and wife of Mark Lafayette Landrum, was born at 8 o'clock A.M. on the 31st of October, 1861.

MARK LAFAYETTE LANDRUM AND MARY ELIZABETH KING were married at 11 A.M. on Wednesday, January 26th, 1887.

The children of this union were born in the order as shown in the following:

> JOHN SYDNEY LANDRUM, 1 o'clock P.M. Wednesday, December 1st, 1887.

> WILLIAM KING LANDRUM, March 27th, 1889.

> MATILDA DOROTHY LANDRUM, January 11th, 1891.

> CATSEY KATHRON LANDRUM, January 16th, 1893.

MARK LAFAYETTE LANDRUM, JR., October 13th, 1895.

[EDITOR'S NOTE: The following dates have been extracted from the Social Security Death Index and California Death Index]

MARK LAFAYETTE LANDRUM died on 10 February 1922 in San Joaquin Co., CA; MARK LAFAYETTE LANDRUM JR. died 25 May 1967 in Long Beach, California; JOHN SYDNEY LANDRUM died 29 October 1943 in San Joaquin Co., CA; WILLIAM KING LANDRUM died 23 August 1970 in Seattle, Washington.

APPENDICES

Edited By
John S. Landrum, Berkeley, California
May, 1913

The foregoing Autobiography was written by my Father in this, the sixty-sixth year of his life; and in view of the fact that it was so lately written, a few extracts taken from his effects—speeches delivered by himself, and newspaper clippings written for publication by himself and by others—will serve to amplify this slender sketch of his life. The best of his speeches were never written, and my selection here is in consequence scarcely typical.

The first article is one written by Hon. E. C. Tulley and printed by the *San Miguel Courier* in 1894. It is self-explanatory, the event of which it makes mention being also spoken of in the foregoing autobiography.

* * * * * * *

A TRIBUTE TO MARK L. LANDRUM

I have just learned with much pleasure that the People's Party convention has nominated for Assemblyman of Monterey County my old friend and neighbor (for twenty-five years) Judge M. L. Landrum of Peach Tree; and, though myself an outsider only, I beg to say, through your valuable journal, a word to the voters of Monterey County.

I have known Mr. Landrum intimately and well for many years. He was born in the State of Georgia forty-seven years ago, left there in 1860 (before the war) and came West to a home previously prepared by his Father in Stanislaus county, California, where he remained until 1869, when he settled in Peach Tree Valley, being the pioneer settler in that valley, where he has resided ever since, engaged, originally, in the sheep business, subsequently in farming and stock-raising, generally. Peach Tree Valley, at the time of his settlement, was almost a *terra incognita.* Neighbors were, like Angel's visits, few and far between. Schools, post offices, courthouses, churches and jails were an unknown quantity. Grizzlies and coyotes, interspersed occasionally with a Mason, a Harvey, or a Vasquez, were rather more frequent than agreeable, and served to give zest to an otherwise monotonous Arcadian life. But in the natural course of events there came a change. There came a higher civilization, and with it came new conditions, new requirements, new wants. The valley was settled up. The grizzlies, coyotes, Masons, Henrys, and Vasquezes gave way to the "honest squatter" or home seeker. Neighbors became plentiful and the usual differences, difficulties and conflicts of interest, consequent upon the advent of the higher civilization, begat the necessity for law and courts of justice, and Mr. Landrum was, without regard to party, unanimously chosen first Justice of the Peace and served as such for six years, when he declined further honors in that line. It was my privilege to practice before him during his entire term of office, and of more than one hundred cases, civil and criminal, tried before him, I believe there was never an appeal taken from his decisions, and never during the six years (such being the confidence of the people in his honesty and accurate perceptions of the principles of justice and right) was there to exceed three or four juries empanelled to try cases. This, of itself alone, speaks

254

volumes for his judgment and integrity. After he retired from the bench, there being few professional lawyers nearer than Salinas City, he having meanwhile qualified himself for the profession, practiced law, more in the interest of peace and harmony than for pecuniary advantages, preferring his more homely farm duties, to which he is thoroughly devoted. He is now, and has been for several years past, notary public and postmaster, the duties of which offices he has satisfactorily discharged to date.

As before intimated Mr. Landrum is now forty-seven years old, was married in the early part of 1887, resides at Peach Tree where he has a comfortable home of his own creation, in company with his wife and four children, and though not a bloated bond holder or millionaire, enjoys the comforts, if not the luxuries, of a happy life. He is physically and mentally in the fullness of mature manhood—a good specimen of America's "self-made" men. Having entered into the battle of life with very little education, obtained at an early age in our common schools, he has found time and opportunity to acquire a reasonably fair education, and, which is better, a thorough knowledge of men and things; of his surroundings; of this country and its people; of the political, social and especially its industrial and economic conditions—is, in short, a thoroughly posted and practical man. He is fully abreast of the times, takes an active interest in everything affecting the welfare of the country generally, and especially in what affects the farmer, laborer and producer. Was among the first to organize F.A.& I.U.'s; took an active interest in the Alliance Mill at San Miguel— was one of its Directors; and, or course, an earnest and enthusiastic Populist, endorsing and earnestly advocating all the reforms set forth in the Ocala and subsequent Alliance and People's Party platforms.

If the people of Monterey shall do themselves the honor to elect Mr. Landrum to the Assembly, they will have in him an intelligent, broadminded, unbiased, able representative, who will labor conscientiously for the good of the whole people, and reflect honor, not only upon himself, but upon those whom he will represent as well. That they may do so, is the sincere wish of

—E. C. Tully

* * * * * * *

The article following is a bit of an editorial note from the *Salinas Democrat* on the event of my Father's nomination by the People's Party for Congressman.

The Middle-of-the-Road Populists at Sacramento on Thursday nominated M. L. Landrum of Peach Tree for Congress in this (Sixth) district. Mr. Landrum is well known in this county as a most trustworthy and upright citizen, a man of strong convictions and a People's Party man from principle. He accepted the nomination simply as a matter of conviction that it is best for his Party to stand up for its principles and not be swallowed up by any other Party organization. If his election were within the range of possibility, the district would be well and honestly served with him in congress.

* * * * * * *

This next is a newspaper sketch of my Father's welcome home after his wedding.

Among the many happy and pleasant events that occur in one's lifetime is that of a marriage for love. Such a marriage, we believe, recently occurred between one of our well known and worthy citizens and a young lady in the city. On the 26th day of January, 1857, at the residence of the bride's parents, Mark L. Landrum of Peach Tree was married to Miss Mary E. King of San Francisco who formerly had been a teacher in the Monterey County schools, and bore a most enviable reputation. Then it was that Mark laid his plans for the capture of the maiden's heart and succeeded. The wedding breakfast at the parents' house was a sumptuous affair and largely attended by friends. After that they started upon their honeymoon, and visited at Stockton the sisters of the Groom. Their visit was extremely pleasant and on the 2nd day of February they returned to their really comfortable home at Peach Tree, accompanied by a Miss King, an accomplished sister of the bride. But they were not to be let alone. The whole country was astir to give them a grand housewarming. The reception, and in fact the whole plan of the ceremony, was under the auspices of Simeon Goldwater and wife. All were alike splendid. The supper (grand indeed) was given at Mr. Simeon Goldwater's residence. From supper until the appearance of morn, dancing was all the go, and Tully's band played splendidly. Everything was done by Simeon Goldwater and wife and James W. Church, to make everyone more than happy. The grand party broke up at daylight.

Among the many present at this fine entertainment were: Mr. and Mrs. M . L. Landrum, Mr. and Mrs. Judge Wm. Griswold, Mr. and Mrs. Simeon Goldwater, Mr. and Mrs. Dan Monroe, Mr. and Mrs. A. J. Myers, Mr. and Mrs. John Reynolds, Mr. and Mrs. Frank Palmer, Mr. and Mrs. Geo. E. Pullen, Mr. and Mrs. Dr. Livingston, Mr. and Mrs. Natrass, Mr. and Mrs. A. J. Copley, Mr. and Mrs. B. F. Hames, Mr. and Mrs. Thos. Lynn, Mr. and Mrs. H. Tompkin, Mr. and Mrs. Jas. Bengard, Mr. and Mrs. H. Rist, Mr. and Mrs. William Smith, Mr. and Mrs. John Bray, Mr. and Mrs. Jas. Baley.

—J.W.C.

* * * * * * *

Of my Father's speeches, as I have said, there remains but few in writing. This first is a clipping from a newspaper account of a speech delivered by him at Salinas and describes his delivery as viewed by a newspaper correspondent.

M. L. Landrum was the first speaker and in a plain, business-like way and without attempt at oratory explained the distinctive doctrines of the People's Party, explaining with some degree of minuteness what is meant by the initiative and the referendum arguing that their adoption would take the bitterness of partisanship, that binds voters now, out of law-making, would speedily work the abolishment of un-satisfactory or bad laws, and allow each good proposition that is now buried in a party platform to be taken out of it, voted on separately on its own merits, and be adopted if it met the approbation of the people instead of the bosses and the lobby. Mr. Landrum combated Mr. Estee's assertion that the proposed system of legislating would be a reversal of business methods.

* * * * * * *

The following is the earliest speech I have been able to find. It was delivered in 1879 before a Popular gathering in honor of the anniversary of Washington's birth.

Members of the Shakespearean Literary Society

Revolving time has brought about another anniver-sary of the birth of the great chieftain of our liberties and fa-ther of our country, George Washington.

We are all taught that it is largely due to the energy, wisdom and patriotism of Washington that we are now per-mitted to live in peace and prosperity, enjoying the fruits of our Labor and protected in our lives, liberty and property under a free and independent Government.

As a mark of our high appreciation of the valuable services and incalculable benefits conferred upon us by this great man, it becomes our most pleasant duty to celebrate in our way the anniversary of his birth, and to refresh in our memory the true greatness of our illustrious father I had in-tended to read his Farewell address of 1796, but it is too lengthy for this occasion.

I will only read a few extracts from it to illustrate his penetrating wisdom and deep concern for the welfare of pos-terity.

Comprehending the many dangers attending our form of Government, Washington warned in his farewell address those entrusted with the control of national affairs in the most solemn manner against the baneful effects of party spirit, in the following language: [Reading the extract]

258

He also warned them against the tendency of our proud nation to foster prejudices for or against other nations in equally strong terms, as follows: [Reading the extract]

A more elaborate delineation of the immortal character of Geo. Washington I will leave to the Orator of the day.

* * * * * * *

The next two articles are addresses delivered by my Father in his capacity as county lecturer for the "Farmers' Alliance" in 1891. As such, it was his duty to advertize the purpose and so increase the membership of the organization. The first is a mere introduction, the body to which has been lost:

Brothers and Sisters: Having been chosen as your Lecturer, I suppose I am expected to suggest something as food for reflection; something to stimulate our brothers and sisters to energetic action in our worthy cause; something to encourage them in the good work of the Order; and like most farmers, I have had but little leisure to prepare for this occasion.

Fraternal feeling, harmony and unanimity of action are the crowning features of success in our worthy cause, and to promote these it is not only necessary that every member should understand the general objects and purposes of the "Farmer's Alliance" but should be familiar with its history and the cause which led to its organization. The present name dates back to but one year, but the "Agricultural Wheel," the name first given to this Order, according to the historian: "was born on the 15th of February, 1882, in an old log schoolhouse near the town of Des Arc. in Prairie County, Arkansas. Its parents were monopoly and oppression. A monopoly that wants to buy the earth and with it the souls and bodies of the people who inhabit it. A spirit instigated by Satan, the head of the firm and proprietor-in-chief of the entire concern who has inaugurated the infamous system, sent forth to reduce the world to hellish slavery. It demands everything God has made for its own use. It would absorb Europe, Asia, Africa, America, Australia and the Islands of the sea, with the cattle on a thousand hills, and everything given mankind for his use and comfort. Monopoly aspires to make the people its servants, politically, financially and socially, and demands that we offer on its golden altar all that we are and have—souls, bodies, lives, liberty and common country, unreservedly and without complaint. it recognizes no rights, makes no compromises. Like other sins, it comes to us draped in broadcloth and silk, with a smile of seeming innocence playing over its countenance as bright as the sunshine after an April shower, but inwardly it is as black as midnight, the home of the Devil himself.

* * * * * * *

This next is a complete speech delivered a little later at another place:

Ladies, Gentlemen, Friends and Citizens: I have not come among you as an Orator or politician, but simply as a humble citizen of your county, a farmer, a neighbor, to reason with you on matters that seem of great importance at this time.

It is a hopeful sign to see such large numbers of the common plain people interesting themselves in the vital public questions of the day. I am more than pleased at the good attendance here this evening.

The present depressed condition of the country, of commerce and business generally and especially of agriculture, demands the most serious attention of every citizen in the land.

It is somewhat a query to a great many people how such stagnation, in business and consequent suffering among the people can exist while every force of production is at its climax; while we are blessed with the most bounteous yields of all kinds of agricultural products; while the earth is giving forth an unlimited supply of raw material for the factories and while the advance in science has enabled us to produce almost everything necessary to the wants and comforts of man. Yes, I say that it seems strange to many that while we are favored with all these blessings of divine providence that every industry should be languishing, that farmers should be

260

losing their homes, that workshops and factories should be closing down throwing out of employment hundreds of thousands of laboring men and women, that want and destitution should stalk unbridled through the land. But such are the present sad conditions that surround us and when we look around us and realize the truth of this picture, it cannot but arouse a suspicion in the mind of every intelligent man that there is something wrong somewhere. To bend his every energy to ascertain the cause of this distress and determine upon a remedy for these evils is one of the highest duties every American citizen owes to himself, to his family and to his country. Many of our wisest and most patriotic citizens have for many years seen this crisis coming on. They have given us their warnings but we have not heeded them, and even had we all been aware of the coming disastrous results of our vicious financial system, we were powerless to avert it without some concert of action.

Before all the industrial forces can be brought together for the common good of all, the masses must be educated on the science of Government. They must be made to understand their business and social interests and be taught through the principles of cooperation and fraternity to defend those interests.

"From the time to which the memory of man runneth not to the contrary" the money changers of the world have cooperated in the matter of controlling legislation for the purpose of controlling every industry and for the further purpose of absorbing to themselves all the profits of the labor of the industrial masses. Hence; we now find ourselves under the necessity of offering an organized resistance to the merciless aggressions of these money mongers.

This is one of the grand purposes for which the Farmers Alliance was organized. Its mission was to furnish a school for the study of economic questions. A school to teach farmers, mechanics and laborers how to cooperate for their mutual protection. A school wherein the spirit of fraternity is ever-present pleading with the individual to sink prejudice in the grand object of securing the general good of all.

For the past quarter of a century or more the daily press of the country has been controlled by subsidy, or other influence, in the interest of the money brokers, or so much so that not a daily newspaper in all this broad land can be found advocating the cause of the people, but to the contrary they all seem to be vying with each other in advocating measures calculated to foster the interests of these moneyed lords. From this abandonment of patriotism by the public press, the masses have been unable to glean any correct knowledge of the inner working of our Government or to form any correct idea of the effect of governmental policy upon the industries of the country. For these many years the venal press have been educating the masses to believe that they are incapable of grasping or understanding the vital questions that most concern them—that they must leave all the vexed questions of finance to the politicians—that they must bend their backs in endless toil and be content with the results.

They tell us—and have crammed their fallacious argument down the throats of many intelligent people—that hard times and money panics come on as a matter of course, periodically, as winter, summer, eclipses of the sun and moon, etc., and that it is beyond the power of man to avert them. They thus seek to keep the people quiet while the vultures and hyenas of society are devouring the vitals of commerce and business.

There is probably not a man within the hearing of my voice who is not intellectually capable of understanding all financial questions with sufficient clearness to enable him to defend his interests at the ballot box.

From just a little bit of study and research he will find that all economic writers agree upon the most vital points in Government finance. They all agree that a certain volume of money is necessary to balance a certain volume of business done in a country; that to contract the volume of money below the necessary amount tends to lower prices of all products—that is, to decrease the amount of currency of a country increases the demand for it, and by reason of its scarcity makes it harder to obtain and, consequently, requires more of the products of labor to buy a dollar than when the volume of money and the volume of business is equal.

262

The consequence of this lowering of prices is to depress business, shut up workshops, close factories and spread distress through the land. They all agree that to maintain a good and sufficient volume of currency keeps in operation factories and all machinery of commerce; stimulates all the forces of production, and keeps up a healthy development of the country's industries thus promoting comfort and happiness among the people.

The principal points of difference between writers on Government finance, arises from the difference in the standpoint from which they view the subject.

The National Banker or money brokers' interest is diagonally opposed to that of the industrial classes. The man whose stock in trade is dollars is interested in making a dollar worth as much as possible. This man would favor contracting the currency for the purpose of increasing the power of his capital and the value of his income.

The man whose stock in trade is labor or the products of labor, as the farmer, mechanic, merchant, etc., would favor a sufficient volume of currency to sustain the equilibrium of commerce and business. He does not want a dollar to buy too much of his products. He wants there to be sufficient money in the country to make it easily obtainable when needed in business without having to sacrifice his property to get it. He wants a volume of money beyond the power of the money brokers to control, so that business progress cannot be blocked at their sweet will.

Both of these classes are right from their respective standpoints. The financial system that is advantageous to one is disadvantageous to the other, and, hence, the struggle.

It will require but a little insight into our present financial system to enable any one to observe the cause of these hard times and money panics, and to observe also that these money kings are reaping a harvest off of our losses.

There have been nearly five times as many business failures during the past year as any year in the history of the country, but has the national banker lost anything? Oh no. The papers tell us that the national banker has a greater surplus on hand now than ever before.

263

The truth is that our present financial system dictated by these bankers, is making the rich richer and the poor poorer. I have not the time this evening to discuss at length our monetary system, but I assert that our present laws give the national banker the control of the currency of the country, and some of our wisest statesmen have said that "he who controls the currency of a country controls every industry in it." Congress has stricken down one-half of the metal currency of the country when it was already too small by half, thus leaving us to struggle with the question whether we will do business on the primitive plan, by barter and trade, or pay a ruinous rate of interest to the bankers for gold. Most of this metal is owned by them.

Either course will almost block the wheels of commerce and ultimately divide us into two classes, aristocracy and slaves.

Now, my friends, are you satisfied with these conditions? Are you willing to uphold this system with the hope that someday you may be a millionaire and in a position to take advantage of it? Or do you believe you are incapable of self-government and that you must content yourself with just such crumbs as the rich see fit to drop for you? If not, then strike for liberty. Organize yourselves for the conflict, for without organization you can do nothing.

By organization you can maintain a bureau of information that will give you the truth on all matters of interest.

By organization you can maintain a press that will afford you an opportunity to discuss all important questions from your own standpoint and from an aggregation of thought, knowledge and experience. You can arrive at correct conclusions and through organization you can secure a concert of action and bring the full force of your numbers to bear upon a course of action in defense of your rights.

Without organization you cannot get a fair hearing before our national council on any proposition. If you make a truthful and manly presentation of your grievances, applying the lash where it is deserved, the old party will not publish it. My friends, let me admonish you to organize, educate and agitate, and when you are satisfied of the justness and necessity of a measure, support it with dignity and courage.

264

The Farmers Alliance has done more to enlighten the masses on national affairs than all the partisan newspapers in the land. By cooperation they have been able to do this. Its journals and periodicals are subsidized by the people instead of the money brokers and railroads, and their columns are filled with discussions of all important questions from our own standpoint.

The Alliance papers are published to enlighten the public. The daily press, subsidized by the banks, is published to mislead the public. Join the Alliance, my friends, and if you are willing to use your heads to think with, I assure you that it will not take you long to find out how panics and consequent hard times can exist in a land of plenty, nor will you be long in doubt as to the remedy for them.

* * * * * * *

In connection with this I wish to publish resolutions drafted by my Father for the People's Party Convention. This party in his section of the country at least, was an outgrowth of the older Farmers Alliance, and these resolutions were simply statements of his conception of the purposes of both.

MONTEREY COUNTY RESOLUTIONS

The People's Party of Monterey County represented in convention assembled at King City this 30th of June, 1896, puts forth the following declarations:

FIRST: The People's Party is here to stay and with the help of God we will defend its life against all enemies, including fusion.

SECOND: We cherish an abiding faith in the principles of the Omaha and St. Louis platforms.

THIRD: We declare as a paramount principle of our party for direct legislation by means of the initiative and referendum, a system by which the people may protect themselves against dishonest legislators.

FOURTH: We believe in the strictest economy in the handling of the people's tax money.

FIFTH: We are emphatically opposed to party bosses, ring rule and machine politics in general, believing that in this evil may be traced the cause of a large share of official corruption.

SIXTH: We are strenuously opposed to the discontinuance by the state of the publication of our school text books.

SEVENTH: We vow our unfaltering opposition to fusion upon any terms with either old party.

EIGHTH: We oppose fusion because it is inconsistent, illogical, impracticable and calculated to destroy the People's party without leaving its adherents one consoling hope of obtaining any substantial reforms from any other source.

NINTH: We oppose the action of our state executive committee in inviting fusion with the Democratic Party, and hereby instruct our delegates to the People's Party state convention to be held at Sacramento, July 12, 1890, to oppose with voice and vote every proposition for fusion coming before said convention, and that in case said convention should take action looking to fusion with either old party that said delegates shall withdraw from the convention and refuse to act further with it.

TENTH: We have implicit faith in the wisdom and justice of our demands and rely upon the merits of our platform and the good sense of the voters for support.

ELEVENTH: Feeling that the People's Party is entitled to recognition, we invite all good citizens of this county to unite with us in our endeavor to correct, so far as it is possible, all abuses of public trust.

TWELFTH: We sympathize with the struggling patriots of Cuba and believe that they should have the right to govern themselves.

—Mark L. Landrum
D. N. Lander
D. W. Potter

[Drafted by M.L.L.]   Committee

* * * * * * *

There remains but one of my Father's many political speeches. It was delivered in 1880 during the campaign to elect a legislature to enact laws to put the New Constitution which had been adopted into force, as the speech will explain.

Speech at Slack's Canyon
For the New Constitution Party

Mr. Chairman and Fellow Citizens: you have met here today, as I understand it, not as Republicans, Democrats or "Working Men," but as the honest citizens of Slack's Canyon, having in your minds the common interests of your country.

The question before you now is, are each and every one of you willing to perform your duty by lending your individual efforts towards putting into office this Fall men of known integrity and who will stand by the rights of the people and carry out their will as expressed on the 7th of May, *i.e.*, that the New Constitution may prove, not as its enemies construe it, an instrument for the oppression of the poor, but a law in the hands of the people and for the people.

Or will you, by your dereliction allow the money kings and corporations who are always on the alert to take advantage of the people's lukewarmness, to fill the Legislature and Supreme bench with men to do their bidding, to construe its provisions in their interest and enact laws to enforce them.

This, Gentlemen, is the question for your consideration, and it is a question which rises far above party consideration.

Just think for a moment what would be the consequence if the people should feel unconcerned about the election this fall, as is generally the case with the common people who are not politicians, at the time when tickets are being made up. The money kings and corporations would be industriously at work with all sorts of scheming and chicanery, getting men on all tickets that have been their tools, or that they know can be used as such, to do their dirty work.

Mr. Chairman, it has been the negligence and manifest indifference on the part of the producing classes that has brought our country to its present deplorable condition. Why, Sir, these men would, if permitted to interpret the New Constitution, twist it into such a hideous form as would bring our people to ridicule.

They have told us it would, if carried out and enforced, create double and treble taxation. They have told us that it will tax the poor man more than ever he was in this country and that his burdens will be much greater than before its adoption. They have told us that they will buy the Railroad Commission, and many other things.

Now, Gentlemen, could you suppose for a moment that they would not, if vested with the power, make their words good in this particular—not on account of their integrity to keep their word, but because it would be to their interest to so do in this case? And, Gentlemen, they certainly would have the power to do great mischief if allowed to control the legislative, judiciary and executive departments of Government, and, instead of construing it in the interest of the people to equalize the public burdens and mete out substantial justice to all men, would make it an instrument of mischief and oppression.

This could easily be done. All laws are like fishermen's nets—full of loop holes to crawl in and out at. It is said that the great lawgiver, Dan O'Connell, told the English House of Parliament that they had never enacted a law that he could not drive a coach and four through.

Fellow Citizens, we cannot afford by any neglect of ours, to allow the enemies of the New Constitution to construe and enforce it. It would prove ruinous to our common interest.

It is a true maxim that "Negligence is the price of liberty." This is a time when it behooves us all to be vigilant and see that none but good and true men who are willing to stand by and vindicate the peoples' rights are elected to office this fall.

If the new Constitution is properly put into operation in the beginning, we will not have so much trouble to guard against corrupt influences hereafter.

There are no very important questions of party politics before us this fall, and the best thing that we can do is to meet each other on the half-way ground without any regard to former party predilections and unite our efforts in one common interest to carry out our new organic law as it was intended by those who framed it. If we do this and do not suffer any division of the votes of those who were friendly to it, we are sure of success. Otherwise all our efforts toward reform may be defeated.

We did so when we voted upon its adoption and who not do so now? It is not necessary to yield up any of our party principles, but simply to lay them down until we finish this fight for reform, which is only half done.

Fellow Citizens, I can see no other way of accomplishing this union of effort, except through the organization of the New Constitution Party, and when we accomplish our object in the fall election, we will not owe any allegiance to the new Party, as such, but will be free to pick up our party banners and fight under them as before, whether we be Democrats, Republicans, or Working Men.

This is the only unselfish plan that could be suggested as the success of this plan will not give prestige to any party.

Fellow Citizens, now is the time when your most earnest consideration is called upon and my advice, if it is to be considered, would be to organize a New Constitution Club here today so as to cooperate with other clubs and see that a reliable and trustworthy delegate is sent from here to the county convention and do not leave your work until the sun goes down on election day.

* * * * * * *

My Father's newspaper correspondence is better represented. This one was written early in 1894, during the campaign to elect Mr. Bowman to Congress.

Our Political Parties

History teaches that not more than two political parties can exist permanently in any country; that no matter how
many parties may exist at some given time, they will all,
sooner or later, simmer down to two, one representing the
wealth or vested interests of the country, and the other the
industrial masses; and when existing parties cease to represent the masses, a new party is inevitably organized for that
purpose. For many years the Republican and Democratic
Parties have been vying with each other for first place in the
confidence of the wealth owners of this country, and in their
zealous scramble to see which could best serve the railroads,
banks, oil kings and other moneyed corporations the people
were lost sight of. This made a new party necessary to give
the people representation, and hence the People's Party was
organized. Just how long the three parties will all survive
can not be foreseen, but it is morally certain that one of the
three will vanish after the next presidential campaign. Now
the question is, which one?

Neither the Republican nor Democratic Parties, as
national parties, are showing any disposition to espouse the
cause of the people; and there is no probability that either
will, because their whole fabric rests on the support of the
corporations and monopolies and for either party to turn its
back on the corporations would be self-destruction. So we
must conclude that one of the old parties must go.

Since both the old parties depend for their existence
on money to run their campaigns, and since corporations are
in the habit of putting their money into the strongest party,
where it will do the most good, and since the Democratic
Party is clearly on the wane, it seems clear that she can make
only one more presidential campaign, if that. The party is so
old (which is nothing in its favor) that many old Democrats
have a superstitious notion that, though she may stand in the
minority for years, she will yet come to the front again, and
for this reason, while they acknowledge that the party no
longer represents their interests, they do not want to cut
loose from it, for if it should rise again they would have the
honor of having been faithful to their first love. Fidelity is a
valuable trait in man, but in this progressive age fidelity to a

political party after it has ceased to represent you is a false conception of duty.

Within the last year scores of the ablest statesmen and patriots in this country have turned their backs on the old parties because they recognize the impossibility of rescuing them from under the control of the corporations, and they recognize also the fact that the changed conditions of this country requires a change in the policy of government. Only a few days ago Judge Trumbull, an able statesman, and patriot, once a United States Senator, spoke at a Populist mass meeting in Music Hall at Chicago. He advocated radical changes and went even farther towards Socialism than the Populist platform.

Men of this character are coming to the People's Party every week and almost every day. They see that there is a new problem to be solved, and, as Mr. Bowman said at Central Hall, new problems must be solved by new forces. Necessity appeals to you, citizens, to not let fidelity to party interfere with your fidelity to yourselves, your family and your country.

The People's Party is the only party that is unfettered by obligations to corporations and monopolies, and, consequently the only party in a position to save the country.

Z.A.Z.—M.L.L.

* * * * * * *

This next article was printed by the *Tulare County News* during the campaign of 1898. The Editor's note explains the circumstances under which it was written.

Never So Completely Upset

Many of our readers will remember W. C. Bowman, who delivered several speeches in this county in behalf of the People's Party during the campaign of 1894. No more eloquent appeals were ever uttered in behalf of the cause of humanity, yet he was carried away from his moorings by the Bryan fad which swept over the country and deceived so many Populists who should have known better than to have believed that the leopard could change its spots, or the Democratic politicians become patriotic reformers. The following reply to Rev. Mr. Bowman, by the present nominee of the People's Party for Congressman, from the sixth district, was published several weeks ago, and, although we are since informed that Mr. Bowman has announced his allegiance to Populism, will be of interest to those of our readers who can appreciate the sentiments of loyalty to principle expressed therein:

Editor, *Civic Review*: Will you allow me a little of your valuable space to address a few words to my old friend W. C. Bowman?

I am always very much pleased to read anything from your lucid, logical mind, Brother Bowman, but never was I so completely upset as when I read your communication in the *Civic Review* of February 5th.

In 1894 I stumped Monterey County with you, I was in your company for eleven days continuously. I was eloquently entertained for several hours each day by your logical discourses as we traveled along the road, and during this time I listened to fourteen or fifteen of your splendid public addresses, about which I heard much favorable comment. Your speeches were particularly logical and argumentative. You are still argumentative, but your old argument seems to be turned wrong side out. You told the people then that no organization, whether religious or political, after it had once become corrupt, had ever been reformed; that the solving of new problems required new forces; that the cleansing power, the correcting influence, must come from without; that a man in a strong current cannot save himself, that if saved at all it must be from some power on the bank, out of the influence of the current; this outside force might arrest his downward course and haul him ashore, and hence the necessity for a third party. You laid down many valuable propositions, among which was to avoid all association with corrupt bodies lest we become contaminated. Now the thing that is puzzling my mind is, what could have caused this somersault in your fruitful mind.

272

You say now that you want the People's Party to combine with the Democratic Party; that you believe that the Bryan movement is in the right direction. This is an admission that the Democratic Party has not been reformed but that it is making an effort to reform.

Now, do you believe it will succeed in reforming itself? Do you believe that natural laws have been changed for the accommodation of the Democratic Party? Do you believe the man will seize himself by the nape of the neck and drag himself out of the stream? Was there anything in the last campaign to warrant such belief? Was Bryan's monkeying with old Ben Hill and "Goldbug" Gorman and refusing to accept the nomination of the People's Party strengthening to such conclusions? Was the abuse the Democratic Party heaped upon our nominee for vice president, together with their retaining old Misfit Sewall on their national ticket, calculated to restore your lost confidence?

If I remember aright I read an interview in the *Examiner* with many of the California delegates to the Chicago convention just before they started east as to their choice of President of the United States, in which W. W. Foote was represented to have stated that his first choice was William C. Whitney of New York, and second, Judge Patterson of Pennsylvania. Everybody knows that both of these men are the most pronounced gold men, but when they came back nobody in the country could beat Billy Foote yelling "free silver," and if I am correctly informed, that combination was made up largely of this class of adventurous politicians.

Do such accessions to the silver cause prove to your mind the sincerity of the so-called Bryan movement, or does the refusal of the Democratic Party during the last few months to treat with the People's party in any of the states where they could get along without them, satisfy your mind that they are honestly in favor of reform? Very few Populists are so credulous as to believe they are.

Old "Goldbug" Gorman was National Chairman Jones's chief adviser in the Bryan campaign, and through our combining with such a misfit party our grand organization was almost destroyed, and now you want us to join ourselves again to this fraudulent movement, the chief aim of which is

273

to get rid of the People's Party, and upon this accomplishment of which they will drift back into the old gold channel. [*Editor's note: The Wilson-Gorman Act of 1894, supported by the Democratic Party, contained provisions for the first United States income tax; the Act was struck down by the Supreme Court in 1895 (Pollock v. Farmers' Loan & Trust Co.), but ratification of the 16th Amendment to the Constitution in 1913 confirmed a national income tax.*]

You speak of the numerical strength of the Democratic Party as a reason for joining ours to it. Don't you know that if a small man yokes himself to a large ox that the ox will wallop him around wherever he please and kill the man if he likes? Well, everybody can see that nothing would please the Democratic Party better than to kill the People's Party. I am opposed to giving them the opportunity. Let us go it alone, and rely upon the merits of our platform and the good sense of the people for success.

In my humble opinion there is no use trying to rally the People's party again in this state except on independent lines. Brother Bowman my intercourse with you was very profitable for me. You may, but I never shall depart from the lessons taught by those grand truths so ably expounded by you in private and on the rostrum.

—Mark L. Landrum
Peachtree, February 10, 1898

* * * * * * *

The following is a communication printed by the *San Francisco Call* in 1898, after the fusion of the Democratic and Popular Parties.

Thinks His Party Was Betrayed

The manner in which the conscientious Populists of the state look upon the fusion arrangement by which their party was sold out to the Democrats through the manipulations of a few men who were seeking office and were determined to have it at any price, is illustrated by the following statement from one of the most prominent and most respected Populists in the state:

Editor *Call*: I have been asked by some of the friends of Hon. A. C. Barlow why I cast my lot with the middle-of-the-road or straight Populists at Sacramento, and why I accepted their nomination for Congress in the Sixth District against the said C. A. Barlow, the incumbent, who was elected as a Populist two years ago. As there may be others who would like to know, a few of my reasons will be given in the following article:

It is deemed a sacred right belonging to every man, no matter to what political party he belongs, to oppose by every honorable means at his command every other political party, and it is the duty of every party to sustain its members in the exercise of this right.

No action had by any convention or party trenching upon this right can bind its individual members without their consent, even though such action be sanctified by a majority of such convention or party.

This right from the very nature of things is inherent in the individual, and is not subject to majority rules. It is so sacred that any infringement upon it by any party convention, no matter by what majority thereof, is in derogation of the spirit and policy of our Government and subversive of every principle of political ethics and public morals.

The convention held at Los Angeles Oct. 22, 1891, which first organized the People's Party in California, and in which I participated guaranteed to every man who should become a member a free and unencumbered political home, free from the domination or influence of the old parties, both of which were by this as well as by all subsequent People's Party conventions, most vehemently denounced as being antagonistic to the best interests of the common people of this commonwealth and unworthy of public confidence. The People's Party was built up under their guarantee, and under this opposition to the dishonored old parties. Any disregard or sacrifice of this principle by any faction of the People's Party should be considered by its loyal members as an abandonment of its organization and a sacrifice of its principles—a bolt—and I believe any court of justice would so hold.

Fusion as consummated at Sacramento by a domineering faction of the People's Party was theoretically, practically and of all intents and purposes a surrender of the party and its principles to the Democratic Party, and I, a Populist, could not and would not become a party to such action, preferring to stand with my own party and nominate a regular, straight, middle-of-the-road People's party ticket, as distinguished from the fusion ticket.

This convention was pleased to tender me the nomination for Congress for the Sixth District. I accepted. I would have declined and gladly have presented the name of Hon. C. A. Barlow had he remained loyal to the People's Party and its principles, but it was my understanding then, and still is, that he had measurably abandoned both party and principles.

It is a principle of Populism incorporated in both of our National and State platforms, that office holders shall not participate in making such platforms, in shaping our party policy nor in any way manipulating nominating conventions.

Mr. Barlow unquestionably used, actively, his personal and official influence to bring about a fusion between the Populist and Democratic parties, thereby denying to every conscientious Populist his guaranteed right to oppose the Democratic Party or brand him as a bolter for so doing.

Mr. Barlow accepted an appointment as a member of the National Congressional Committee for the State of California.

Mr. Barlow participated in holding conferences with the officers of other political parties while in Congress.

Mr. Barlow has been publicly charged, and it has not been denied, so far as I know, with having participated with others in issuing an address advising Populists to unite with the Democrats on a platform other than any heretofore adopted by any National or State People's Party Convention.

Mr. Barlow participated in the meeting of the National Committee of the People's Party at Omaha in June of this year, all of which is in flagrant violation of the principles

276

of the party that honored him with a seat in Congress. By these acts the servant has sought to become the master.

I do not impugn Mr. Barlow's honesty, his intentions may have been good all through, but no amount of good intentions will suffice to cover up or counteract the injurious effects of his abandonment of principle.

Mr. Barlow cannot plead in extenuation a lack of knowledge on the subject, for such ignorance would be fatal, nor is the fact that others have been guilty of the same errors any defense in his case.

The fundamental principles relative to the inherent and guaranteed rights of members of the People's Party are of vital importance and are necessarily involved in the question of fusion, some little skimming editors, who never get below the surface of any subject they aspire to treat, to the contrary notwithstanding.

If a political party desires to disband, it has the unquestioned right to do so, but no party has the right or the power to commit its members to the support of any other party. Such right belongs to the individual member and to him alone and cannot be honestly delegated or surrendered.

I say to my People's Party brethren of this state, if you would have People's Party principles prevail, you must stand firmly by the party and jealously guard the principles upon which it is founded, until they triumph throughout the land.

Keep forever in your mind these facts and axioms: The solving of new problems requires new forces; no party having once become corrupt can ever become a true reform party—it has not the power, if it would, to purify itself; reforms must come, if at all, from a new organization—free from such dominant and corrupting influences as now handicap both the old parties.

For the People's Party to fuse with an old party at this time is destructive to its existence. Every Populist leader, including my friend, Mr. Barlow, has all along said that the Democratic Party is a party of pledge breakers and spoilsmen, corrupt to the core. For us Populists now to combine or fuse with it for the purposes of reform, would be stultifying ourselves and placing our party in the same category with the disreputable old parties.

The world would say, and justly, too, that we were insincere, that we were frauds, that our pretensions of reform were deceptions, our opposition to the old parties and their practices is a sham, a delusion and a snare, that we were false to our own teaching and were after office and pelf only.

It must be apparent to all observing men that fusion is based solely upon local and individual selfishness—a basis upon which no party can stand or ought to long survive.

—Mark L. Landrum
Peachtree, Monterey County
August 8, 1898

* * * * * * *

Here is another article on "Fusion" by my Father, taken from the *Reasoner*, the People's Party organ.

Editor *Reasoner*: We learn through the press that the People's Party Senators and Representatives at Washington have been holding conferences with the leaders of the Democratic Party and Silver Republican party. As a result of said conference the said Senators and Representatives have issued an address to the people laying down the gold conspiracy as the issue of the coming campaign, virtually declaring that there are no other issues to be fought, and for the triumph of this issue, they say: "Then let us, maintaining at all times party integrity, incite the harmonious cooperation of all seeking the same ends." One of the tenets of the People's Party is that office holders shall have no part in shaping the policy of the party or making its platform, but even we should concede to these self-constituted leaders the rights they have assumed: what are we to understand they mean by inviting the harmonious cooperation of all seeking the same ends. If they mean that we should invite all individuals who believe as we do, to come into our councils and help us to choose candidates and elect men to take charge of State affairs, and to break down the tyranny that oppresses this

278

country, then I am with them heart and soul, and I am satisfied that such an invitation will be unanimously supported by
the members of the People's Party. But if they mean that the
People's party should invite the Democratic Party and the
silver Republican party to fuse with it, by dividing the offices and supporting each other's candidate, then I object, on
these and other grounds as follows, to wit:

FIRST: We cannot maintain our party's integrity
without maintaining its principles, and we cannot maintain
the principles of two other parties, and ours at the same time,
unless they were all agreed; and if they were the three should
merge into one. There is no need of more than one party to
one platform; if we support their nominees, we support their
principles. But it is well-known that the Democratic Party
does not accept but a portion of our platform and the so-
called Silver Republicans are only looked upon as a piece
club. Then what folly it would be to join ours with the Democratic Party on the basis of our numerical strength at the
last election. Now, admitting that the fusion would succeed
and would wipe up the earth with the Republican Party, it
would be a complete surrender of our platform, because the
Democrats would be in the majority and would make all the
laws. The only figure we would cut would be as aids to the
Democratic Party. If we have no higher aims than this let us
disband. It is true we would be helping individual members
into lucrative positions but the People's Party care nothing
about individuals except where by helping an individual we
help the cause of the masses.

SECOND: It destroys our party's identity and record
of voting strengths. No man knows or ever will know the
number of votes cast by the People's Party men at the last
general election. The identical same group of men constitut-
ing both the Democratic and People's Party tickets, it was
only strong partisans who took any notice as to which ticket
they placed their cross upon.

THIRD: The Democratic Party has refused to treat
with the People's Party in any of the states where the Populist vote was not essential to Democratic issues. This should
be convincing proof that the Democratic Party's supreme
desire is to get rid of the People's Party, which gives us just

279

cause to doubt their sincerity in adopting a portion of our platform at Chicago.

FOURTH: The People's Party believes that the great mass of voters in both the Democratic and Republican Parties, are honestly in favor of the best government obtainable under our system, and when once convinced as to the measures necessary for the accomplishment of this and they will join us in the support of such measures, and we believe that the time is near at hand when the correctness of the principles of the People's Party and the justness of its demands will be recognized by the yeomanry and organized labor everywhere. Hence, I say that the People's Party should by all means keep itself free from all entangling alliances with other political parties. By acting on strictly independent lines it has all to gain and nothing to lose. It certainly cannot gain anything by combining with an unfriendly party.

—Mark L. Landrum
Peachtree, February 25, 1898

* * * * * * *

This is a clipping from the *Salinas Journal* and is an answer to that paper's own adoption of Cleveland's policy on finance.

Monetary Discussion

Our Peach Tree correspondent denounces the Baltimore Bankers' plan.

Dear Editor: We notice in the *Journal* of the 5th your comment on Cleveland's message to Congress in which you say: "We believe with Mr. Cleveland that, 'the absolute divorcement of government from the business of banking is the ideal relation of the government to the monetary circulation of the country.'"

In the same message Cleveland recommended a plan by which the National bankers will have complete control of the volume of circulating currency of the country. The government is to print, sign and stamp in blank the notes that are to be issued as money. Whenever the Banker feels like issuing more money, he calls for those notes, puts his fist to them, and loans them out to business men for all the traffic will bear. All it costs him is one percent for cost of printing, but he must lock up in his safe 30 cents for every dollar, not in gold, silver or bonds, but in the despised greenbacks that the banker says is dishonest money and what Cleveland says was the weak point in our present financial system. The government stands good for the whole thing and all the security it has is this 30 percent in greenbacks.

This is equivalent to the Government loaning its credit free of charge and without security to the amount of 70 cents on every dollar these bankers may see fit to issue, not exceeding the amount the basis will permit—say about $1,500,000,000 as a special favor to these fellows.

This will retire the greenbacks and treasury notes of 1890. Government will coin no more silver, issue no more treasury notes nor make any more money of any kind except gold money, and most of this will be tied up by reserves so that but little of it can enter into general circulation. Thus you see that this diabolical scheme, which had its birth in the banker's convention at Baltimore, will give to the bankers a complete monopoly on making money, and in direct violation of the Constitution which says that Congress shall have the sole power to coin money and regulate the value thereof. It not only gives them the monopoly in making our money, but gives them the power to regulate its value. The law of supply and demand regulates the value of money. The banker will have control of the supply, and nothing but his modesty will check his power to rob production and commerce of its profits. Where will the people get money to carry on business? They can do nothing in the wide world but go to these fellows and get their money on just such terms as they may see fit to exact; either this or shut up shop.

There is not a voter in the country of ordinary intelligence that can't see the working of this plan if he will take the trouble to study it for one hour. It permits these foreign money mongers to pile up their millions off the honest sweat of our toiling masses; and it is but little worse than our pre-

281

sent system. A man must be very much in love with his party who will support its plans to give the Rothschilds and other shylocks complete control of his country and of every industry in it, thereby entailing slavery upon his children to gratify a foolish prejudice.

Under this system the bankers can bring on a full grown money panic by calling in their loans whenever it suits their purpose to do so.

Mr. Editor, is this what you call absolute divorcement of government from the business of banking? Mr. Cleveland impliedly admits the marital relation of our government to the banks, and instead of issuing a decree of dissolution, as he pretends, he announces the golden wedding.

Full, fair and honest discussion of our monetary system seems peculiarly appropriate at this particular stage of the nation's progress. Please give us your ideas more fully, Mr. Editor. The subject ought to be interesting to all your readers.

—Z.A.Z.
M.L.L.
Peachtree, Dec. 19, 1894

* * * * * * *

Nor was my Father's time entirely occupied with matters of strictly party issues. Here is an article which he contributed on a local bond issue in 1897.

The Bond Question

The question of refunding the county's bonded indebtedness is, to my mind, a very important matter, and notwithstanding the fact that we are to vote upon it the 30th of this month, very little interest, it seems, is being taken in the subject. I have neither heard nor read any comment or discussion of the question. I expected that when the board of supervisors sent out their proclamation or notice of special election, they would fully explain the situation so that all voters could determine for themselves how they should vote, but I was disappointed. The statement contained in the said notice is partial and quite misleading.

I cannot expect enough of your valuable space to more than call public attention to the subject, and suggest careful investigation which, in my opinion will richly reward any freeholder for his pains. It will be observed that the notice of election fails to tell us that $78,000 of the county's present outstanding bonds are bearing only 5 percent per annum interest, which is but little more than the proposed 4½ percent per annum interest payable semi-annually, and that this $78,000 may be all paid off within the next ten years. The county has discharged $72,000 of this debt in the past eight years and can continue at the same rate. The notice also failed to tell us that the $60,000, the balance of the county's outstanding bonds, bearing 7 percent per annum interest, can be paid as rapidly as the county sees fit to do it, after the 1st of July, 1898.

My memory does not serve me as to the exact amount of the assessed valuation of all property in Monterey County, but I feel warranted in saying that a slight raise of a few cents on the $100 in the tax rate would liquidate the whole outstanding debt before the first installment of the refunded debt would become due, and thus leave to the taxpayers of the county a large share of the $95,000 interest, compounding, that will accrue on the refunded bonds before the first payment of principle is made, to say nothing of the enormous amount of interest that will afterwards accrue before the whole debt is wiped out.

The refunding at a lower rate of interest sounds well on first thought, but it will not bear the light of investigation. I will not attempt to account for the favorable view the board of supervisors takes of the refunding scheme, but I do say that I can see no excuse whatever on the part of the taxpayers for refunding at this time. Let us pay the debt as contracted by us, with the least possible interest, and not shuffle it off onto our children, who will, in all probability, be worse crushed by the gold standard than we are. It is a bad business proposition to defer paying a debt longer than necessary, or to borrow money when we do not need it. The credit system has lured many a man to his ruin, and interest grows equally as hard upon the vitals of a county as upon an individual.

Some man will rise to say "Put the paying of our debts off as long as possible. I may be dead or may have left the county before payday comes around if refunding carries." This is childish talk. It must be borne in mind that every dollar of this debt must be paid by someone, and that every dollar of it stands as a mortgage upon every foot of land owned in this county. Hence, just so long as this debt rests upon our lands, just so long will the price of real estate in this county be reduced in proportion to the amount of the debt. The debt cannot be dodged even by death. Our property will have to pay it, even in the hands of our heirs, and hence I say that Monterey County cannot afford to enter upon such a system of prodigality as this refunding system offers. Just think of it: the refunding system will require the payment of more interest than the principal before we are done with it, and needlessly, too. I, myself, and I believe a large majority of the taxpayers of this county, ought to know by sad experience the cancerous effects of usury, and being guided by the light of experience, they should vote solidly against this un-business-like proposition.

—Mark L. Landrum
Peachtree, Nov. 1, 1897

* * * * * * *

During his later years spirited campaigns revived my Father's interest in politics. The first of the next two is an answer to Bell in the Gubernatorial election of 1910. The latter is my Father's view of Roosevelt's "bolt" in the Republican Convention of 1912.

Old Populist Wallops Bell

Editor *Record*: My interest in the present political situation is my apology for making space for these thoughts and observations.

It is certainly amusing to an old Populist like myself to read of some of the utterances of one of our candidates for Governor.

Mr. Bell accuses Mr. Johnson and the Republican party of stealing a portion of the Democratic platform. As a matter of fact, all the best features of the Democratic platform are copied almost bodily from the People's Party platform adopted at Los Ángeles October 21, 1891, and reiterated at many subsequent Populist conventions. In those days the Democratic organs, as well as others, called it visionary and communistic, and its supporters wild-eyed anarchists.

Mr. Bell seems to have forgotten that later on the Democratic Party lured the People's Party into ambush, robbed it of its platform, and left it there to die from the injuries they inflicted.

The People's Party did not seek to have its platform patented or claim any monopoly of its principles, but hoped and believed that all parties would in time adopt its principles. Now comes Mr. Bell, who thinks that he has the exclusive right to use the platform.

Several thousand years ago, Confucius the Chinese philosopher, taught the Golden Rule. Later the great Nazarene philosopher taught the same virtues, but no one ever thought of accusing Him of theft, but He is honored unto this day.

Principles are common property and no one who is sincerely imbued with correct principles can or does find fault with any person who adopts the same or with any party for incorporating them in their platform.

Mr. Bell's platform is typical of the Democrat's party, as at present organized. Politically speaking, it proposes to cure "all the ills that flesh is heir to," but has no particular place to commence. Mr. Johnson proposes to commence on the most glaring and important evil and stay with it until he has completely eradicated it from our body politic. This idea suits me. Do one thing at a time and do it thoroughly and well.

There is one principle in public service, I have observed, that operates uniformly, namely: The successful candidate feels himself under obligations to the powers that placed him in office and the man, if he is a man, will feel like discharging this obligation.

If Mr. Johnson is elected Governor of this state, he will be under obligations to none except those who want clean, honest government. All others are fighting him.

If Mr. Bell is elected—well, it looks today like he will be under heavy obligations to the special interests.

If elected, Mr. Johnson will occupy a more advantageous position than any of the other candidates could occupy, and I think his election will result in much good to this state. We cannot do better than to support him to a man.

—M. L. Landrum
Stockton, October 20th, 1910

* * * * * * *

Editor *Record*: Roosevelt proposes to organize a new party of his own. It will be distinctively a Roosevelt Party.

The new problems which have arisen will require new forces to solve them. When a political party has become corrupt it is powerless to reform itself. The party's machinery is maintained by the powers we wish to dethrone. The members of a party that are corrupt are in the putrid mess and it needs clean hands to cleanse it.

Its members cannot do it, because they are in it. Outside forces must come to the rescue.

I would rejoice to see an independent or outside party formed to defeat the two corrupt old parties. But, to succeed, the new party must be one in which all reformers can participate. If a national mass convention should be called by known progressives, inviting representatives from the reform forces all over the country to meet, formulate a platform and select a standard bearer, it would be distinctively a progressive movement and would draw to it all the reform forces of the country. It would have behind it the patriotic sentiment of the toiling millions who are groaning under the burdens saddled on them through the system of special privilege.

286

I believe the time is ripe for such a movement. But it must be free for all to promise success. A Roosevelt party will go the same road the Hearst Independent League went.

—Mark L. Landrum
Stockton, June 23, 1912

* * * * * * *

In contrast to these abstract political discussions, I wish finally to publish a few verses of rhyme which my Father rather enjoyed composing during idle moments. These were all written on the backs of envelopes, or on bits of scratch paper, as the idea happened to strike him.

Part of a Valentine

May all the good thou knowst of me
Live in thy memory forever,
And all my faults and errors be
Forgiven, forgotten forever.

Let charity be thy constant theme,
Mercy and Truth thy guiding star,
That you may share the high esteem
of all who plead at Cupid's bar.

* * * * * * *

With cords of love our hearts entwining
Smooth the path of life's declining.
Brighten our hopes, dispell our fears,
Solace our souls in the glad New Years.
"And one by one with some treasures won,
They come to our hearts till they all are gone."

Obituary of Mrs. R. J. Rogers

A gentle spirit has flown from earth
To that realm above that gave it birth.

287

The Angel of Death living souls revere
Loosed the chains which bound that spirit here.

A wife so loving and so true and kind,
Gentle in spirit; in thought so refined;
From the path of duty was never beguiled,
She blessed the home of husband and child.

Minister of peace to the troubled heart,
Clears the fountain where human sorrows start,
Her counsel and prayers were given free,
That all weary souls might happy be.

Thoughts on the Earthquake at San Francisco
April 18, 1906

The havoc and destruction so quickly wrought,
And the sorrow and the suffering that it brought,
Were the sad but the true lessons that it taught.

Hope is not gone for even those that it hit,
For surely some good will yet come out of it.

Castle and hut met alike the raging flame,
The high, the low, the rich and poor, hit the same.
The strong, the weak, proud and meek to a level
came.

To vanquished pride a noble spirit was lent
And fellowship reigned ere its fury was spent.

—Mark L. Landrum
Santa Clara, April 26, 1906

V.

THE STATEMENT OF
ALEXANDER H. TODD

I left on the 3^d of January, 1849, on the pilot boat *"Wm. J. H. Hackstaff,"* and came by the way of the Straits of Magellan. In the Gulf Stream we lost our mate, who was washed overboard and drowned, a brother-in-law of Dunbar here. We arrived here on the 23^d of June. Everyone formed the impression then that we had reached a very wild country. There was neither head nor tail to anything at that time; there were a few merchants doing business here. We landed in a small boat at the foot of Washington St. on Montgomery. We left San Francisco on a little Spanish launch for Stockton, paying an ounce for fare each, and proceeded thence to Mokelumne Big Bar to the mines. There was only one wooden building in Stockton at that time, but most of the town was of canvas tents, and every other tent was a gambling house or whisky mill.

In July '49, my health failed, and I started a letter express from San Francisco to the mines. I took the names of the miners, charging them a dollar apiece for recording their names, came down to San Francisco, got the letters from the Post Office, and took them back to the mines, charging an ounce a letter for taking them up. *New York Heralds* were eight dollars apiece at that time. I had at one time over two thousand names in my express list. The Post Master at San Francisco swore me in as a clerk, and I paid him 25 cents bonus for letters, for the privilege of going into the office and getting out my letters quickly, with the assistance of his force. The Post Office was at the corner of Pike St. and Clay at that time, and some ten or twelve men were employed in

290

it. The lines of men waiting for their letters would reach far down the street, and a man would frequently give an ounce to get a place in the line.

When I had collected a long list of names, and was making my arrangements for my first trip to San Francisco, on reaching Stockton some merchants there asked me when I was going to start my express, and I told them the next morning, and they said they had something to send, and I went into Bell's store to see what it was. He had a lot of gold dust in boxes, and he gave it to me to bring down. I put it in a butter keg, in different packages, and I delivered it to the firm of [text missing] here, one of the oldest firms in San Francisco. My express matter was pretty heavy. I suppose I had at least two hundred thousand dollars worth of dust with me. We landed at the corner of Clay and Lausane Sts. where the old "*Niantic*" was lying. There was a wooden staging along the side to walk up from the water, and I had to roll my keg of gold dust, which contained probably a hundred and fifty thousand dollars, along this place, and it cracked and creaked, and I felt uneasy until it was delivered. I charged five percent on the dust for bringing it down.

I got a good quantity of letters for my return trip, the postage on them running into the hundreds of dollars, with the bonus I paid the Post Master. Postage was then 40 and 80 cents, and it was rarely prepaid. After getting my letters, I bought a rowboat to go back to Stockton, and took up sixteen passengers, who paid me an ounce a piece for passage, and "eat themselves." I was the Captain, and though I did not know anything of the river, I sat in the stern and steered, and they rowed. We got there in about twenty-four hours, and that gave me a reputation. I had paid $300 for my boat, and sold her for $500 in Stockton, and had made a handsome turn with the passengers and freight I carried up. I had sometimes from 1500 to 2000 letters to carry up on a trip. A good many I had to return. We numbered then 1, 2, 3 and so on, so as not to take them out a second time. The Post Master did not like to take them back, it was too much work to handle them.

I was in the express business from '49 to '52. When the steamers came in, we used to take a boat and go out to the Head and get aboard, and collect all the New York papers we could from the passengers, paying from $1.00 to $3.00 apiece for them, sometimes getting a thousand in this way, and selling them for eight dollars apiece at first. Our express business extended rapidly from the first. Our main office was in Stockton, and we were taking every camp from Stockton to Jacksonville, and from Jacksonville to the Gold Creeks, taking the whole Southern country at that time. We had an office at every important point. The principal merchants were our agents; every store of any prominence was an agency for the express, and it was a great advantage for them to be so, for it brought everybody there for their letters.

It was not long before the miners came to us to get us to take care of their money for them. It was a very common thing for me to start out from Stockton with two horses, loaded down with letters and papers, and return loaded down with gold dust. The miners had no opportunities for taking care of their dust, and we were obliged to have safes at our different offices, and our express business soon merged into a banking business. We charged them for taking care of their dust one half percent a month, and they gave us the privilege of using it also. That was termed a general deposit. A special deposit was when a miner would bring in his dust, and put his name on it, and put a seal on it, and for keeping such deposits in our safe, we charged them one percent a month. All the security the miner had was our receipt, stating that we had so much of his property on hand. Our business in that way was very large. For months and months there our net earnings were a thousand dollars a day.

After that we met with a great many losses from fires and robberies. An express man on the road was almost exempt from interference, because everybody was interested, and if an express man had been attacked, and his assailant discovered, the punishment would have been very speedy. I don't know that people were any more honest then than now, but property was safe from fear of the immediate punishment which would follow the detection of theft. An express man, though carrying large sums of money, bore almost a charmed life in those days. We were robbed by our clerks. One of our confidential clerks in 1852 robbed us of $70,000 in

Stockton, and then of $50,000 in Mariposa, and another of $40,000 at Mokolumne Hill. In the latter case, the thing came to our knowledge when we came to settle up, and he committed suicide. I have been burned out nine times in different parts of the country since I have been here. In the first days there was no insurance, and the only safety was to jump and run. In the May fire of 1850, I wrote to my partner at another point, after I was burned out, saying how I had escaped and had no clothing, and asked him to send me some money. He wrote back, saying that he could sympathize with me, as the night before he had to jump out of the window to save his life, on account of a fire which burned him out, and he could do nothing for me. As soon as I could get to my safe in the ruins, I got coined up, and was all right.

In 1849 I went to Oregon to arrange for an express throughout that territory, and I was paddled in a canoe with two Indians from Astoria to Oregon City, a distance of about 120 miles. I started the first express that ever ran in Oregon, with offices at Portland and Oregon City. The steamers "*California*," "*Panama*," and "*Oregon*" ran to Oregon in '49. We commenced there in 1850; prices were very much less than they had been in California, but the business there was a success. The Lieut. Governor of Oregon was our agent there, and afterwards Steinberger of the Samoan Islands was our agent there. When we left the business in 1853, prices had materially fallen; the Government had established Post Offices in different parts of the country, and prices had fallen from dollars down to bits, as they have since from bits down to cents.

An express man's occupation in those days was one of risk. I remember on one occasion I came to Knight's Ferry, on the road between Stockton and Sonoma on the Stanislaus River, and Capt. Knight, who kept the ferry, said it was not safe to cross in the boat, the water was so high and swift. Adams's express man was behind on the road, and I could not wait. I was riding a large Mexican stallion, and urged him in and caught his tail, and he took me across, and the Indians caught me on the other side of the river, and prevented me from going over the rapids. It was a great risk to take.

When Adams & Co.'s express commenced here, there was considerable rivalry between them and us. In April 1851 the President's Message came here from the East, and our express determined to get it up to Stockton and other points in the interior in advance of Adams & Co. When the steamer which brought it arrived here it was a Saturday afternoon, and the steamer for Stockton had already left, and there was no other boat going up before Monday. I knew that Adams & Co. would watch my movements, and to throw them off their guard I went into the theatre, while my partners got the message and other papers and exchanges ready and packed them in an Indian rubber waterproof sack. Adams & Co.'s messenger started off as soon as possible to go to Stockton in a rowboat by the regular water route. When all was ready, I got into a boat and went quietly over to Oakland, and took a horse and rode through as fast as possible, swimming streams where it was necessary by catching hold of my horse's tail, as he could not carry me on his back while swimming, and got up to Stockton the next morning about two o'clock, delivered the message to the printer there, and took to my horse again, and went on to all the principal points supplying the message clear over to Mariposa, and then returned, getting back to Stockton in about three days.

Meanwhile, Adams & Co.'s messenger made his way up the river, but not knowing the way very well, when they came to the three creeks which come in this side of Stockton, they went first up one of them, and finding it was the wrong one, went up another, which was also wrong, and finally took the third, which proved to be right, and in this way lost half a day. On Monday they were overtaken by the steamer "*Jenny Lind*," the next one up to Stockton from San Francisco, and they did not get into Stockton until Tuesday, paying the steamer people $50 to put them off at a certain point, so that they might outstrip our messenger, who was also on board, and who they presumed had the message in charge. When they came to deliver the message to the printers, they were astonished to find that they had got it the Sunday before, and asked how such a thing could be. They were told that Todd had brought it, and said that could not be, for they had left him in the theatre on Saturday afternoon. They were nevertheless convinced that Todd had effectively outstripped them that time. I knew every little cut and byway in the country, and therefore had the advantage of them. When I was getting in toward Stockton on my return from Mariposa, about 40 miles out, I met their messenger just going out in the country beyond.

Ralston was certainly one of the most remarkable men that the country has produced. He doubtless had his faults, but he has done a great deal for California. The remark has been made (it is attributed to Sharon, I don't know how correctly) that Ralston robbed the rich to give to the poor, while Flood and O'Brien robbed the rich *and* the poor, and kept all they got for themselves.

VI.

THE ADVENTURES OF
WILLIAM T. BALLOU

From an Interview Conducted in Seattle in 1878

Wm. T. Ballou, of French descent, was in the Mexican War and arrived in San Francisco July 17th 1849. Bought a cargo of beans in connection with J. F. Peale and J. H. Coghill from a Chilano [sic] ship for ¼ of a pound. Took it to Sacramento and sold them at 17 cts. a pound, costing only ¼ a cent for transportation. Then he went to the southern mines of California, and commenced the express business alone. This was the first express in California. Following is the interview conducted with him at the behest of historian H. H. Bancroft.

Interviewer's note: Ballou is noted as a spinner of great yarns. His sober tongue may have vibrated a little over the bounds of truth here.

—A. B.

"Ballou's Express" was the first express started on the Pacific Coast in fact. Our charges for carrying letters were $4 a piece, and for newspapers the same. There was at that time no means of weighing the gold dust; there were no scales to be had, until finally we got a thimble. It would just hold $4 worth of gold dust.

Mr. Upman (?) then came on; he had formerly been messenger for Harden's Express, the oldest express men in the world; and established an express between Sacramento and San Francisco. He came right after me, about December 1849. Then John Freeman took the express from there to

296

New York. He came out to establish Adams & Co.'s Express, and he took the express further to New York; and between them they established Adams Express Co., but did not extend it through California nor through the larger towns. I sold my branch line out to them, to the Adams Co., and I went to the Northern mines. Went in with Sam L. W. Laughton in the "Yuba Express." I sold out to him afterwards.

While on the Marysville and Downieville route once, Dobson and I were on the stage together. Near the "Mountain House" thirteen robbers attacked the two of us. They shot a Negro woman, Mrs. Tilman, in the head, and the driver in the arm. We fought them and whipped them. Neither of us got hurt. We succeeded in keeping our treasure. We had $35,000 in gold dust. I have got my present yet—a gold mounted pistol and pair of gold mounted spurs—amounting to $250 apiece. They met us when we went into Marysville with a band of music. They had heard of it; we had sent ahead a rider to Marysville.

After that I abandoned the express business in California and went into merchandising at Downieville and Forest City.

I omitted to say that while in the express business I arrived in Downieville one day, July 5th 1851, just as the woman was hung there. I had just got to the edge of the town when looking down the grade I saw something on the bridge looking like a piece of calico. When we came down we found it was a Spanish woman that had killed a man. The mob took her out and hung her. It was the first woman I ever saw hung, and it was the most degrading sight I ever saw.

In 1855 I had a fight with robbers.

Remained at merchandising until 1857, when I came up here [Seattle]. I first went into business here in Olympia with Garfield & Williams. During my absence they played off the stock at poker, and "busted" me almost. I got even with them, however.

That winter I heard of the gold on Fraser River; in fact I saw it—some gold from Fraser River. The people at Olympia did not know the value of it. McDonald, the man

297

who brought it, had killed his partner Adams on their way down, at the mouth of Fraser River, and got this gold. I think these two men were the first that found it. The Hudson Bay Co. reported that it had been found by Indians, but I doubt it, or they would have realized more. McDonald brought the gold to Olympia. That first attracted my attention to Fraser River. Went with John Scranton, Gov, McMullen, and several other gentlemen to Victoria. The news was reported there. I went to the Hudson Bay Co. and Gen. Douglas, who was manager, told me the facts. McMullen, Scranton, and Secretary of the Territory Mason, with myself found it was the fact, that gold had been found on the Fraser; that the people were leaving the sawmills on the Sound to go there. Workmen could not be hired for love nor money in Puget Sound.

I then went to San Francisco before starting my express up there and made arrangements with my partners and went up and started an express and store. It was an express from San Francisco clear up. This was the first express in British Columbia, called "Ballou's Express." I sold out to Dietz & Nelson, and they sold to Barnard.

I continued my express there in British Columbia, but not without meeting opposition. Wells Fargo & Co. started an opposition to me first, and then Kent & Smith. I ran them all off. They could not make it pay and hauled off; I connected with them then. I could not make the lower route pay and they could not make the upper route pay; and so we "joined gibbets." First it was Wells & Fargo, then it was Kent & Smith. Then there was Smith, and another Smith. Then there was a fellow of the name of Yale, a Jew. Then there was W. J. Jeffries. I ran them all off. All started in opposition to me. I put down letters to cents and made the custom house business pay me; charging 5 cents commission for passing things through the Custom House made that up. I had plenty of money then to pay for goods and they had not. If anybody wanted anything done I could do it and charge nothing at all for it. If they wanted a hat I would buy it, and charge neither freight nor nothing. It did not last very long. Old Jeffries died very hard, but he died sure. He was kept up by the Scotch, and they were all clannish. He got in debt $6,000 or $7,000 and then "busted out."

I sold out in the winter of 1863 my Express in British Columbia to Dietz & Nelson, who now own the Burrard Inlet Sawmill. I went then to Montana; and then to Idaho. Went all through Montana, and all through Idaho, hunting for fields to operate in. I had money.

Finally in the winter of 1863 I found myself a member of the Council of Idaho Territory, elected without ever knowing that I was running. I thought I would go up to Lewiston and get lousy, and I succeeded. Did not do anything in the Express business there; have done nothing at it since.

In Idaho I sold out 1600 (feet?) of Idaho quartz for $3,200 in greenbacks. J. P. Jordan, after whom Jordan Creek was named, discovered the gold first in Idaho. He was killed by the Indians in 1864. He lived on Owijhee River.

Talk about Indian fighting—I did some of it over there. Twenty-one men went out there once to fight the Indians and just one got back. Jordan was in command of the crowd, and the fellow who got back was shot.

Then we started 150 strong and got them into a *cañón*; we had hand grenades, and one thing and another; and Lord bless your soul if we did not let them have it. We killed everything that looked like an Indian, dog, or anything else; young ones, by George—shot them all. Col. Moore said "Kill them all, little as well as big; knits make lice." That was on one of the forks of the Owijhee. We chased them up to Salmon Falls on Snake River. The place is just about 60 miles from where they are sending troops to now. I have been all over that country alone. The Gambrinas quartz ledge is right in the lava beds. Myself and Billy Clements from Oregon were the discoverers of that.

(I do not know why it is, while I was riding Express I took money and I have been on roads where they have robbed everything of the kind, and through the worst Indian countries alone, or with one man; and I never had any fear, and never had any thought of being interrupted; and I never was interrupted except that time I was on the stage. And if I had been alone I do not believe I would have been interrupted then, although it was Tom Bell's gang of highway robbers that was in the road. I knew Tom Bell in Mexico; he was a doctor there of one of the regiments.)

This last Indian fight was in Idaho. We killed about 125 Indians in the fight. There were about 200 in the band. We captured 300 horses, 120 cattle, and all their stuff that was of any account. The balance we burnt up. That was in the latter part of July 1864. There was no trouble afterwards. The fight was on St. John's Day, July 25th 1864. I knew that because one of the boys called it the Battle of St. John's.

In speaking of the roughs, rowdies, and murderers and one thing and another in countries, Idaho—well take Boise City and the Owijhee mines there, and it beat anything I ever saw for murder. I have seen, in one night, just when a crowd would come in—it was called Bannock then, it is called Idaho City now—and another crowd would come in perhaps from South Boise; they would come together and get gambling and drinking; and then some of those "road agents" would get in too, and would get to drinking. One fellow would sing out "he was Chief," and another would say he was a liar, and the pistols would come out.

I saw 7 men one morning lying dead on the sidewalk—every one dead as a hammer.

I went out to see Capt. Seidenstriker one morning, and in company with him down Boise River to fish. We saw nine men hanging on the two windlasses of the butcher where he strung cattle up; nine men all labeled: Horse-thief, Robber, Murderer, etc. Every one was labeled a different thing. It was done by the Vigilance Committee.

No part of California was ever so bad. The first people who came to California were men—men with souls. It took a man in the first place to get there; he had to be a smart man. They were the best class of people that ever I saw.

But up there they were the rough scourings of creation; all those who had been run off from California, Sydney Ducks and jail birds from all sides; they worked in gradually like a ringworm on a man's face.

There were not many of that class on Fraser River. They soon cleaned them out there. Old Judge Begbie mighty soon made them understand who was boss.

300

I saw a fellow named Gilchrist, who had killed two men in California on trial there. He killed a man also after coming to B.C., one who was gambling with him while setting at the table. A miner came in, threw down his bag of gold dust, bet an ounce, and won. Gilchrist paid; and the man "went another." Gilchrist took his pistol and shot him in the head. He was tried, and the jury brought in a verdict of manslaughter.

Said the Judge: "It is not a pleasant duty to me to only have to sentence you for life to the chain gang or prison. If that jury had done their duty you would have been hung to the first tree that could be found in the neighborhood. And gentlemen of the jury, it would do me pleasure to see you hung, each one of you, after bringing in as guilty of manslaughter, a man as guilty of murder as he is."

That was in Beaver Lake in the Cariboo country. I used to go up there once a week, and to every other point where there were ten men mining together.

While carrying the express on the Lower Fraser I had to run in winter when I could with canoes, and when I could not go by canoe, with snowshoes. It was very seldom you could get ice enough to skate on. There were no steamboats run then for four months in the year.

Capt. J. C. Ainsworth of Portland, Oregon took the steamer *"Umatilla"* up there, the first boat that ever went up the Fraser to the head of navigation. That was in 1857. I was a passenger on board. The first boat that ever went to Fort Hope was the *"Surprise."* This one went to Yale. Then there was no boat that went up to Yale after that, until the summer *"Yale"* was built. She made two or three trips and then blew up.

Then there were two other steamers built that went to Yale without any trouble at all. The boats that first went up the passengers had to pole up, or push, by getting off and going into the water to their waists, the steam going all the time too.

There was an incident that happened on Fraser River in the latter part of July 1858. The Indians became very troublesome from Yale up to Lytton City at the mouth of Thompson River. Under the leadership of Sprinkulum, the

301

head Chief of all those Indians there, they were led on to kill the whites and Chinese, and it was no uncommon occurrence to find a white man, or a Chinaman, or even four or five of them a day, to be seen floating down the river with their heads off. This enraged the people, the miners, until finally a band of New Yorkers from (Hall's?) Bar and others from Yale under the command of Andy McCarty and Jim Nolan, and Martin Gallagher, prospectors all from San Francisco, and a man by the name of Snyder from Yale in charge, went up the river to quiet the troubles. They had a fight at Boston Bar, and killed 18 Indians. They then succeeded in driving the Indians up to Lytton, and from Lytton to Nicola, and from Nicola to Buonaparte [sic] River; and there the Indians got away from them, and they did not chase them any further. That is the only Indian War they ever had there to amount to anything.

In Montana the whites were worse than the Indians. At Bitter Root Valley John Owens, at one time a rich merchant in Missouri, settled in 1848; he went up there then, and he has been there ever since. He has an Indian woman, a large band of cattle, and many horses. The Indians gave him there a grant of land. It is a valley containing 25,000 acres of the prettiest land I ever saw in my life. He stays there perfectly quiet and happy; brings down a hundred head of horses every now and then and loads them up with goods and takes them back. He has kept the Indians down there more than anybody else. In the Southern portion of Montana and on the Yellowstone they have been very bad, and they used to be in early days.

In Montana I prospected around for two or three months. I could see that there was nothing there for me; did not like the looks of things very well; and so I bolted for Idaho.

Saw a big crowd going by way of Fort Lomhi for Idaho, and followed the crowd. There I had success again.

The big claims in Owijhee were the Morning Star, Oro Fino, Poor Man, Blazing Star, Allison Hayes, Ray & Empire. The War Eagle never turned out much.

From there I went to San Francisco. I went to Lewiston in 1864, to the Legislature. From there I came to Walla

302

Walla. Stayed there a couple or three months—all through that country, Lapwai, Coeur d'Alene, Pend d'Oreille, up to Colville, and then back.

During the session of the Legislature, they were trying to get a franchise for Holladay's stage line. That was the second Legislature. I was chairman of the Finance Committee and did not have a cent. That was in the Council. The only thing we did of note was to change the name of the bed bugs in the hotel to lunatics.

[Ballou here narrated how the "it" got inserted between "stallions, running" and "at large," in the territorial laws of Idaho; how he and Mark Twain and Ollendorf the dog traveled to Salt Lake.]

My life here [Seattle] has been "here and away." Although I came first in 1853, making just a flying trip, and then back in 1856. Came in 1856 on the "*Decatur*," and in 1857 again. In 1853 I was here about 2 days.

The first vessel that ever loaded here was old Capt. Plummer's (now of the "*Western Shore*"). That is published in the *Intelligencer*—when there was only one house here, the one Dr. Maynard lived in.

We came here first on the "*Decatur*" and the "*Massachusetts*" followed. She stopped to watch the Northern Indians that were then coming in the straits and committing depredations on the citizens of Whidby Island, San Juan, and the Lower Sound. The "*Decatur*" came in up here in command of Capt. Gauzevoort. We anchored off here. Mr. Yesler and several other citizens came aboard and complained that the Indians were getting very saucy, and wanted the Captain to send some men ashore. So we sent, three or four times, some men ashore, but they could not get any fight. The Indians went back towards Lake Washington. Finally they had made up a plan to kill everybody in town while they were at breakfast, and they told old Dr. Williamson over here, who had a squaw, their plans, his squaw divulging the secret; and I think it was Mr. Yesler that came on board and asked the Captain to send cannon ashore and some men to shell the Indians, that they were gathering in here to kill everybody at 6 o'clock in the morning. At 4 o'clock we were mustered on deck, and we came ashore at 4 ½; and at 5

303

o'clock we commenced shelling the point where Mrs. Plummer's house now stands and over across into this depression that runs down there. The Indians were all camped in there from around the brickyard. We shelled them out of there. It was all an island over there then, southwest of the Occidental Hotel. There was a slough there about 100 yards wide that formed an island where the New England Hotel is—that high ground. There is where we commenced shelling from. Over where the *Intelligencer* office is there was a blockhouse; and where the back end of this house (the Occidental) is, there was a tremendous forest. In here there was a lot of trees, a windfall.

Here (pointing into the street just North of the Occidental) there was a hovel for loggers to keep their cattle in. We managed to get our guns to bear in here, and ran the Indians up the hill here. They killed two whites. Holgate was one, and Simpson was the other. The Indians made an awful noise. I do not know how many were killed, but there were a great many buried on the hill back of Seattle and at Lake Washington, and I presume some of them were killed then. We followed the Indians up the Dwamish and White Rivers. I went with six men to intercept Capt. Hoyt from the Puyallup. We went up to a place called "Slaughter" on Green River, where an Indian killed Slaughter by shooting him through a crack in the log house where he was staying. Met Hoyt, and he continued the pursuit of the Indians while I returned by way of the Puyallup.

In the meantime they had stolen Squire C. C. Lewis's daughter in White River while she was going for a bucket of water. The Indians nabbed her and took her off, and kept her for a long time; but finally she got away and got back to her own people. I think she was bought back by a kind of a compromise. Capt. Hoyt followed them up and affected the arrangement. The family live on White River yet. They treated the girl just like they did the squaws, she says. She afterwards married a man who she says is a great deal worse than the Indians were.

In Idaho in 1855 there was a massacre. Fifty miles from Boise City on the road to Camas Prairie, where the present Indian outbreak is supposed to be, there is a stream

304

called Massacre Creek, which has a deep *cañón* and a small flat in the bottom where the emigrants crossed going to Fort Hall, on what is called the Camas Prairie road to Fort Hall. At the bottom along this creek there was a beautiful valley perhaps 150 yards wide, on both sides of a nice creek, filled with elegant grass. Fifteen wagons, with oxen and mules, and 45 people, men and women and children, who were coming to Washington Territory were camped there. The place being so desirable they concluded to stay a day or two to recruit. The Indians discovered them and massacred the entire party except one girl, Eva Jennings, now the wife of John Ward, on Cottonwood slough on the Boise City and Walla Walla road. She was badly wounded and picked up by an emigrant train that came along a few days afterwards and taken care of until she recovered at Boise City.

The Indians burnt the wagons and everything contained in them. This girl was two days without water or anything to eat. They drove off all the stock. In the massacre they took the children by the heels and mashed out their brains over the wagon tires. They mutilated the men, cut off their limbs, and threw them all around; took the king bolts out of the wagons and heated them and ran them into their behind; cut out their hearts and put them in their mouths. There are twenty living witnesses to these facts, as seen after the massacre. A party of whites pursued the Indians, and at Fort Hall they sued for peace. The commander invited them to take food. They were dressed in fine array. Meantime, while the Indians were strung along with coffee, down the road for half a mile he placed a gun in position behind a screen loaded with log chains, and at the proper time drew the curtain and blazed away. He must have killed 150 of them. He made peace with them. They have never troubled those parts again. Capt. Tom Claybourne was the name of the officer; I saw him at Monterey [Mexico] with his hat and boots off scaling the walls of Moline del Rey—the King's mill. I was in every fight from Vera Cruz to the close of the War with Mexico, and was promoted three times on the battlefield. Have retained a few little tokens of respect from the Mexicans; they meant well enough but they shot carelessly.

I got the massacre from the girl's mouth, and also from Claybourne and Abbott and another person—I used to court his gal but I do not remember his name—Hendershott; he helped to bury the 45.

At Yankee Jim's, California, old Jim Goodland was the old original Yankee Jim. He had a whiskey shop and store, and the boys used to go down there every Sunday to gamble and drink and get their grub.

Hangtown was named so because they hung an Irishman and two Negroes.

Georgetown was settled by old Dutch George Ehrenhaft. He is in San Francisco now. He lives out there close to Wheelans.

Downieville after Wm. Downie the discoverer of gold at the forks of the North Yuba.

Marysville was named after Michael Nyes's daughter Mary—a Pike County Missouri family.

Foster's Bar after old Cut-Eye Foster, one of the biggest rogues that ever lived.

Park's Bar got its name from old Judge Parks, the first owner there. He and the present Chief Justice of the United States, Stephen J. Field, mined there together.

Bidwell's Bar after Capt. John Bidwell.

Greenwood Valley was named after Bill Greenwood from the Rocky Mountains.

Calaveras and Tuolumne are Spanish

Mormon Bar, a settlement of Mormons.

Kanaka Bar, a settlement of Kansans.

I laid out the town of Elko and own the Hot Springs there yet. There is hot water at 112° on the one side, and cold water on the other. This spring is right on the bank of the Humboldt 3/4ths of a mile West of the town of Elko. The people from Elko go there, sit on the bank of the river, and fish, winter and summer, and catch beautiful trout. They can sit on the bank of the Humboldt, catch trout, and without moving from their seat turn around and cook them in the hot water of the spring. I have done it.

The town of Elko was laid out in 1869. It was thought by the Railroad Co. that it would be the nearest point to reach the Owijhee and Boise country on the North, and the diggings that then created such an excitement, White Pine, in the South. There are beautiful valleys extending both North and South in getting to those places; and it was believed that in time a railroad would be built both ways from Elko.

The place was named by Mrs. Chas. Crocker. As the train was first passing by Crocker took his wife out, and they saw a band of Elk crossing the river and going from the LeMoyle and across the Humboldt northwards towards the Coupe country. She sang out "Elk—Oh!" I got that from her and him both.

The White Pine mines were discovered in 1869 by Joe Everhardt, Dutch Bill, and old Negro Blum. In 4 months from the time it was discovered there was a population of 6,000. It is likely there never were any mines discovered where there was so much money lost.

Rich Bar, California was discovered when we were all out prospecting for Gold Lake. An old crazy fool started that; he dreamed that there was a lake shaped like a fiddle and an island like a bridge. We went up Feather river, 150 of us. Found a *cañón* and concluded that must be the place. So we went down there. A fellow named Bill Poole went to get a drink of water and found a nugget as big as a hen's egg. That was Rich Bar.

Mike Redding discovered the mines at Forest City, the richest mines ever found in California. Mike Redding and Tom Taylor started a little store and rum shop. This place and Smith's Bar, six miles apart, turned out millions of money; an ounce and a half, or $25 a day, to the man.

At Park's Bar the principal part of the bar was very rich panning; then they put in sluices and worked down, then wing dams, and finally they dammed the river. Field there made his first start. He then went to Marysville and prac-ticed law.

Smartsville took its name from old James Smart, the first settler.

French Corral took its name from a lot of French packers who had their stock corralled there a whole winter.

Cherokee got its name from Cherokee Smith, the first discoverer of gold there.

Murderer's Bar, his men were killed and found dead there.

I am 48 years of age. Born in Alabama; at least I claim that as my native state.

VII.

THE LETTER OF
AMOS CARPENTER ROGERS

1511-B Fairview Street, South Berkeley   August 7th 1919

My name is Amos C. Rogers. I was born the 16th of January 1828 in the town of Danby, Rutland County, Vermont. When I was 16 years old I used to keep up my row of Holland corn and potatoes and mowing, and milk ten cows every night and morning. I am the oldest of nine children. I taught school when I was 18 yrs old. When I went to school the boys used to wrestle a good deal. I got so I could throw almost any of them. We had great times snowballing.

I worked for Merritt Cook for $10.00 a month. I told him one day I could throw John Bartlett. He set me to working the garden. I got it done and come in. I says to him, "What next?" He says to me, "You can throw John Bartlett?" "Yes," I said, "I can." He said, "Come out... I will try you." His wife and the hired girl come to the door. We took hold. I threw him three times before he would give it up. He told all the neighbors that I was the best hand he ever had. They were good people.

The next year I hired out to David Rogers, second cousin of mine, for $90.00 a year and three months schooling. I helped do the chores. He had 150 cows. I milked my ten cows and worked all kinds of work to be done on a farm.

One night I was driving the cows in the yard. I was coming up through the yard to get my pail. David and the girls and men with their pails came out. David said to me that he never had a man to work for him that he couldn't throw. I told him that I thought he had one this year he couldn't throw. Upon that he put his pail down and grabbed

309

me. I had him down before he knew it. The girls laughed.
He grabbed me and grabbed me again. I threw him down six
times. Finally he said, "Up we go to milking!" He weighed
over 200 pounds. He had a daughter, we thought a good deal
of one another. We were second cousins on both sides
(Mother and Father).

Out of the $90.00 I saved $70.00. Then I bought turkeys. My brother Anson, fifteen months younger than I, also
worked for Merritt Cook. That summer we agreed to go in
together to buy turkeys. He bought one big gobbler. He
packed him down to our Uncle Stephen Carpenter's place
where I had all my turkeys. He said he would not go in with
me. So I paid him for his gobbler. When I would feed them
Uncle Stephen would get out and gobble with the turkeys, he
and Anson. So I drove them over to Danby to my Father and
Mother's place. I killed them and took them down to Troy
and sold them. I cleared $25.00. Anson and Uncle Stephen
didn't gobble so much after that.

After that there was a good deal of excitement about
California Gold Diggins. So I got gold fever. I saw in the
papers, they were getting up a Company in Boston called
Bunker Hill Mining Association. For three years [sic] voy-
age we had to pay $300.00 and the sailors $150.00 to work
the ship to California and back to Boston. The next town to
Danby was Pawlett. There was eight from that town, and
myself and my second cousin. His name was Amos
E[merson] Rogers. He weighed 240 pounds. He was a clerk
in Senaca Smith's Store at Danby Corners. We all went to
Boston and joined the Mining Co. We bought the Ship
Regulus and we sailed from Boston Wharf March 5th 1849.
All the officers told us not to take any money with us, but
buy clothing instead, so most of us did. After we had been
out about a month, they began to talk about going in to Rio
de Janeiro. I began to think that I would need some money.
I went to the officers of the Ship to tell them I would do their
washing. So I managed to make $3.00 by the time we got
into Rio. We had a fine time there. There was about three
thousand going to California. Like a lot of colts let out of a
stable.

On board we used to wrestle. The best of all the bob-bin' and jumping I ever got was with a Negro waiter. He was about my size. He couldn't get me down, but when my feet did touch the deck I threw him broadside up in the riggins'. It took him some time to get out of it. If we had been in the middle of the Ship he would have gone over-board. We were next to the cabin where the rail is higher. Amos E. Rogers scolded me for wrestling with a Negro. I told him that there was many could throw him!

We had Boxing Gloves and Dances when it was fine weather. And all the racket we used to have at night... roosters crowing, hens cackling, cows bawling, horses whin-nying, pigs squealing, and cats...everything you could think of. When he thought everyone had gone to sleep in his ham-mock, down Amos would come. Then, just to hear him swear, everyone would laugh and holler some more. He could see that he could not do anything about it, so he would just laugh and try to get even. I never enjoyed myself better in my life.

When we came around Cape Horn, we had some very rough weather. They battened the hatches down and would not let anyone out on deck. I was not sick only half a day. There was a blacksmith who was sick every time we had a big blow. We had two closets, one on each side of the ship, near the bows. I was sitting there taking my comfort when here comes the blacksmith. He said "Get out of here!" I just had time to clear the flood from his mouth when he turned his back side loose. I got clear as soon as I could for I did not know what would come next. I tell you I was thankful to God and everybody else that I got clear of both shares! He was like a bear and I did not want any of that!

I managed to get my old three dollars before we went in to Callao [Bay; chief seaport of Peru]. We had a great time. We all got what they call "acquainted." We felt fine... went into a fandango house. There was two Negro wenches, blacker than the Ace of Spades. They were playing a lively tune. The boys wanted to see me dance with the blackest of the wenches. So I told them all right, a break down, when we started. When I put out my hands, she would make a lunge for me. It tickled them. They would holler. The street

311

was full of people. We kept that up until we got tired. Then we all went up to Lima. There we had a good time, to hear the Boys singing out for fat women and their drink. I did not take any of that luxury because my money was getting low. A good many of us came back to our ship. You see a man will make a fool of himself sometimes in life. The idea of dancing with a Negro wench as I did to see the Boys laugh, I feel ashamed of it now.

Well, we were all bound for California. We left Callao for San Francisco and had a fair wind all the way in. The 29th day of September 1849 we arrived. Our Company broke up into small Companies. The Company I was in, there were nine of us, but some of them were twenty-five. After we got here we broke up again. So myself and a young man by the name of Charles Phelps from Pawlett (next town from mine of Danby) joined up. He came ashore on the first boat and I got ashore in the afternoon. He was pretty full of whisky by then. He said to me, "This is the best place out." He showed me about $20.00. He had been playing Chuck Luck. He wanted me to go down and try my luck. I had got my three dollars again so I tried it. My little three dollars soon went; I tell you I felt as though I had lost the world. In a strange Country and no money. Charlie lost the most of his too, so here we are here in California and broke! Misery likes company, so Charlie and I were pretty well fixed.

We got acquainted with a carpenter. He told us to get a saw and a hatchet and go up some of the streets and we would strike a job carpentering. So I got a saw and a hatchet. I was going up Stockton Street and a man came out to me and said, "Chips, want a job?" I said to him, "Well, yes. What kind of job is it?" He says to shingle a small house. I said to him I will look at it. He took me over to look at it. It was 12 x 16 feet. He had the shingles and nails there. I says to him, "How much are you willing to give to have it shingled?" He said, "$40.00." I said, "All right, I will do it." So I went and saw Phelps and asked if he knew anything about shingling. He said, "No, I never shingled anything in my life." I said to him, "Let's go around where they are shingling and watch them." So we went that afternoon and watched. We got the idea of breaking joints and

312

stretching a line to keep the rows straight. Next morning we went up and shingled it and got done by noon. The man came and looked at it. He said, "You got it done I see." We said, "Yes." He said, "I guess you never shingled much did you?" I said to him to tell the truth we never did. I told him we were both broke and a friend of ours told us to get a saw and a hatchet and go up these streets, we would strike a job. So this is the first job we ever did. He laughed and said we had done fine, only we ought to have started with two courses instead of one. "I see you have broke joints alright so it won't leak." He said we would do and paid us the $40.00

After that we got a job in a store packing goods for $10.00 a day each. We were pretty well fixed and worked ten days. Then we got our share in the Company. We came in at $31.00 a piece. We bought a Whale Boat from the Company and some other things and started out for the Mines.

We got up to Stockton. It commenced raining the 1st of November. We met some of our Company of Nine who had been up in the Mines. They gave very bad reports of the Mines and were headed back to San Francisco. So we concluded to sell our Boat and stuff which we did. We got little more than it cost and came back to San Francisco.

After we got back I asked Charlie what he thought we had better do. He didn't know, so I told him what I thought. Up we go and find a house with a good large room and go to washing. They were paying $6.00 a dozen, 50 cents apiece, to wash mostly woolen clothes. We found a house on Stockton Street owned by a Negro for $100.00 a month and rented it. We got a sheet iron stove and a big boiler and soap and provisions and wood.

We started in on our enterprise. I went out gathering up the dirty clothes. I got all I could carry, six dozen pieces. We commenced that night. Filled pretty near all the lines. Charley kept a good fire. I went out again in the morning and filled all the lines. Some of them were dry as fast as we hung them. A lot got dry and ironed. I take them home and get more. We were doing fine.

I was down on Montgomery Street. I went into a gambling house and asked the Gambler there if he had any dirty clothes he wanted washed. He said yes he had a lot and let me have them. There were three or four white shirts among them. So we washed them, but come to ironing, Phelps said he could not iron the white shirts. I told him he must learn, for I gather them up and helped wash them and take them home. So he went to work on them. He would starch and iron them out but they looked awful, great gobs of starch ironed in them. Then he washed them out and tried again. He did that six times. So the last time they looked halfway decent, so I took them home. The Gambler took them and looked at them: "Do you call them washed?" I said, "Yes, I helped wash them." He said to me, "What kind of a woman have you got?" I told him she was an awful good woman and willing, but she was young and you cannot expect a young woman to do quite as well as an older woman. I got him to laughing so he paid me and said he would try me again. So Charlie got acquainted with an Irish woman, right above our place. She showed Charlie how to starch and iron. So I told that Gambler to look and see how my wife had improved. He said, yes, that was fine, and I had no more trouble. I got all the washing from that house, and others by their recommendations.

In the spring almost everyone was going to the Mines on the American River and Yuba and Feather Rivers. So we sold out our washing business and fixed ourselves for the Mines again. We bought another Boat, rocker, grub, and tools, a good outfit, and started up the Sacramento River. We had a good Boatload. We got to Sacramento, where we put our things on an Ox-freight team for Negro Bar on the American River, 23 miles from Sacramento. We had a fine big canvas wall tent, 12 x 14 feet. We pitched at the trail that leads to Negro Bar and the main road that goes to Georgetown just across, quite a good-size creek that empties into the American River. Negro Bar was one mile and a half from our tent.

We prospected about Negro Bar for two days, but didn't find anything. So we went up the Big Creek; the water was high in the creek. We came to a Gulch where three

314

or four Companies were mining. We took up two claims. Below them it was very fine gold. We had a copper washing machine for mining. It paid from the top down to the Bed Rock, pretty near the same. We would wash out about three buckets, then the Hopper off and Apron. There would be a streak of gold above the black sand and the riffle. We would take the iron scraper and take off the rim of gold, put it in the pan and at night take it down to the Big Creek and wash it out. We must of lost nearly half for we didn't know how to pan to save flow gold. For all that we made $16.00 apiece as long as we had water.

The whole Flat Country seemed rich. It is Prairie Country, so the Creek dried up. Then we went up to Salmon Falls on the American River nine miles from our camp. Our Captain Bradford, that was Captain of the *Regulus* that we came to this Country in and some of the others [were nearby]. We did not find anything that would pay. So we left and went up to Georgetown and pitched our tent there. We prospected around there some time and found nothing.

Still there were some very rich diggings there, so we commenced traveling. We crossed the Middle Fork of the American River. Then we came to the North Fork of the American River, over all those high mountains, then we came to the South Fork of the Yuba River. Then the Middle Fork, and to the North Fork up to Downieville. There I took a claim right in front of Downieville along side of the Jersey Claim, between the two Forks of the North Fork of the main River. I was offered ten thousand dollars for it

On the Jersey Claim they flumed the center of the river. There were twenty men in the Company. They were taking out from 15 to 44 pounds each day in gold. I felt sure I had my pile. When I prospected, I sunk a hole 10 feet square. I got down to the bedrock and it was hard flint. I cleaned it up thoroughly, but I could hardly raise a color. So I had to give it up. There was a man there who didn't look like he knew beans. He went up on the side of the mountain, sunk a shaft, and averaged 4 or 5 pounds of gold every day by himself. At the Jersey Claim there was a slide-in that washed down opposite Downieville and my claim. I don't know how it turned out.

I came away the 1st of November. It had commenced to snow and there were six of us who came away. We came down the road by Dobbins Ranch. We camped on a Ravine about a mile and a half from the Ranch. While the boys was fixing up the tent and camp, I took my pan and shovel and pick and went up the creek a little ways from the camp. Some parties had dug right in the middle of the creek a narrow channel. I commenced digging up under the bank which was blue clay and gravel. I took it to a spring there and washed it out. I had to rub the clay in my hands. I got three round pieces of gold, $5.00 worth. I took out that afternoon $44.00 in gold, then it gave out. I couldn't raise a color.

The next morning there was a man in the Company by the name of Captain Beck that I liked. I said to him, "Captain, would you like to go prospecting?" He said yes. So we went up the Creek a little ways above where I [had] prospected yesterday. No water in the creek, and we come to where the water had gouged out a hole about two feet deep. I said to Captain Beck that I was going to take a pan of dirt out of the hole. Oh, he said, I wouldn't find anything, for he said he never found anything in one of those holes during his mining. So I took a pan full and took it down to the spring. In the bottom of the hole it was clay. I washed it out and I had all of $90.00. I put about $75.00 in my left hand, all I could hold in it, and all of $15.00 in the pan. I took it up to the Captain and showed him what I had in the pan. He said, "Did you get that out of that hole?" I said yes, and while he was looking at it, I dumped what I had in my hand. He almost fell down it surprised him so. Then I washed another pan and I got all of $12.00. Then I could hardly get the color of gold. We should have stopped there for it was rich. I heard afterwards another party went in there a little ways from that hole, and struck another pocket and took out several thousand dollars.

We left and came down to Wyendott. We prospected there two or three days but didn't find anything. So we separated. So I, Dewitt, and James Downer went over to Wyman Ravine. I went down in the creek, very little water there then, and I got a pail of gravel and panned it out. I got about 25 cents. I said to the Downer boys I was going to take a

316

claim there. So we all took up claims and worked together. We built us a log cabin and worked there that winter. We averaged $10.00 apiece all winter.

Come on spring the water was getting low, everybody was going to the Mountains where they could shovel it up by the bucket full. So they said. So we started for the Mountains and traveled all summer and prospected. Went up to Big Grass Valley, a fine big valley with grass knee high. We had a horse or mule, a fine animal. We went way up to the head of the valley and prospected in the creeks. We made a little there. There was a band of Indians up there and they were friendly.

We then started for Wyman Ravine. We had cooked a pot of beans and traveling in the sun, it was very warm, and they got a little sour. We were hungry and ate very hearty of them. We all had awful pains that night. Never so sick in my life. We finally got over it. So we started again in the morning and traveled over the mountains and prospected in some of the ravines and gulches, but did not find anything.

We finally got to the Garden Ranch on Wyman Ravine. John Casad kept it and a store. We had traded a good deal before. We were all broke, but he took us all in and treated us all. We got our supper and breakfast and about $40.00 worth of provisions. I told the boys we had better work for ourselves and board together.

So I took up a claim up the Ravine around the bend. I commenced a big hole 12 feet square. I got almost down to the bedrock. Casad sent up word that he had taken a contract to build a road to Bidwells Bar and the Feather River. He wanted us all to come and work for him. He would pay us four dollars a day each. We all went and worked two weeks, paid our bill and had a good deal coming to each of us. So I told the boys I would camp by myself.

I got me provisions and some cloth and made me a tent. Put it up, then I went to work in my hole I had started. I dug a hole in one corner about a foot square. When I got down to the bedrock I dug out a piece. I grabbed it, ran to my tent, and got out my scales. They wouldn't weigh it. I had a box of lead and I made an ounce weight. I found it weighed $41.00. By Saturday night I had $150.00. I was in funds again and it kept paying. I took out about $4000.00.

I got a letter from my mother [Lydia Carpenter Rogers] in San Francisco. I got on the stage in the morning and come to Sacramento, and took the steamer for San Francisco. I found my mother, who was working for a Banker and his wife at $40.00 a month. I let her have $200.00, then I sent my sister a draft for $200.00. I gave the money for the draft to one of the clerks of the American Bank and he gave me a draft for two thousand dollars instead of $200. I said to him, "I guess you have made a mistake." He said, "No, I haven't made any mistakes." If I had known that they were regular swindlers I could of kept that Draft and sent it to my sister in that mail. I don't believe they would of known the difference, for the bank failed soon after and cheated every one they could. I would not have felt right and I am glad I didn't. I told him that he had made a mistake against the bank. I only let him have $200 instead of $2000. Then he was mighty glad to correct the "mistake" but he didn't even thank me!

I don't know what I would do if I had such a chance again. I expect I would do about the same, for I could not feel right about it. I don't want money if I have got to steal it. I would rather have a clear conscience so I can look my God in his face.

I then went back to Wyman Ravine and worked until I could make three dollars a day. So I sold my claim and outfit and came down to San Francisco. When I landed I was walking on Montgomery Street, when I met my second cousin by the name of Hudson Green from Vermont, my town. He said to me, "What are you going to do?" I said to him, "I just landed." He was in the house raising and moving business. There were four in the Company and one of them wanted to sell his interest. He said they were doing well, so I went up to their office, on the corner of Montgomery and Pacific Streets. He introduced me, I bought him out, and went to moving houses and raising houses. I worked just one week at it. I got an idea of bracing and setting the screws. I didn't like the foreman, who was domineering and overbearing. He thought he was better than we were. I told them Saturday night that I was going to take jobs myself. They said, "You take jobs?" "Yes," I said. I would not work under that boss, for he did not know how to treat a white man. I told them what I made I would put it in the Company and divide equal with one another.

So I went above on Pacific Street, where I took a large house to raise ten feet. I commenced it Monday morning. Got men who were good men who understood the business. I paid them good wages. They worked for my interest and I treated them alike and I did not feel above them. I did that job by Saturday night. Cleared $300.00 that week of all expenses. My partners would come around at night. They could see everything was in ship shape. So the next week I took another right next to the first one. Then my partners came around and wanted to sell out to me. I told them what I would give or take. They took me up and I bought them all out. So I was my own boss. I had over 100 screws, lots of tools and blocking, so I commenced contracting. I had at one time six different jobs. I put the men I hired first in as foremen. They worked for my interest. Then I let out screws one dollar a day for each screw. Sometimes I had 60 screws out and had enough for my own work. I was moving a house in between two other houses. I looked up on the street and saw a man there with a Plug hat on that looked as though it had been in a hurricane, all caved in. It kept me pretty busy cutting screws to keep the house from jamming the other houses. I finally got it in place, then this man came up to me. He said, "Why Amos, how does thee do?" He was my brother Anson! Just got off the steamer. So I told one of my men, his name was Hill, to raise the house up and underpin it. So Anson and I went down where I lived. Mother had been through working for the banker. She was living with me, so now we all lived together.

I took Anson in as equal partner and divided equal with him. I took a job to raise six houses sitting on the wharf for $1,000.00. It had been filled in, so we could walk all around on dry ground where the houses were. Sitting on the Wharf was 100 piles. I had bootleg screws, and I could raise them out 12 inches. I cut off every other pile so I could set a screw on it. It took 50 screws. Then I got two more men with Anson and I, and we took two rows each, gave a screw two turns, and passed it on to the next, and so on, until we run the screws out. Then we set a screw on the pile we had raised the timber off of. We raised all of the buildings in one week and underpinned all of them. Cleared $700.00.

I took a contract one time to raise a three-story building on Sutter Street below Montgomery Street for another story in December. Right in the winter, the 1st of January, we had an awful gale. It commenced blowing and I saw we were going to have a big blow. I went to the lumber yards and got the longest timbers I could get, some of them 40 feet long. I put all my men to work bracing the building up. I had raised it six feet that night. Six other Companies had their houses blown down, but mine stood through it all. I didn't have any accidents in all my house moving or raising.

One day I was riding my horse from one job to another and looked up. I saw a large man on the sidewalk. I sung out to him, "Amos." He wheeled and came up to me. He says, "I declare if there isn't another Amos!" He said he hadn't been called Amos since we parted. When we came to California, he went up North and I went to the mines in California. I heard he was killed by the Indians and he heard I was killed by the Indians! [Editor's note: this is Amos Emerson Rogers, Amos Carpenter Rogers' cousin from Vermont].

He had a chunk of Coos Bay [Oregon] coal in his hand. He had a cargo of it, one of the first that had been in the market. I told him, let's go around the corner. I introduced him to Anson and he was surprised to see him. I said let's go up to my boarding house. We went in and I introduced him to my mother, and he was even more surprised. We all had a good long talk. He told us all about Coos Bay. He said he and James and Patrick Flanagan (brothers) had taken up three Coal Claims 160 acres each, and this was the first Cargo that they had shipped. He said it was a place for Lumber besides Coal and good land for farms on the river, and in fact pretty near all the land, for they had plenty of rain. It was all covered with Timber and Brush, and would have to be cleared off. He thought it was bound to be a great place for a poor man to get a house.

320

Mother and Anson and myself talked it over. They thought it would be best for me to go up to Coos Bay with Amos, and take up with me a good stock of goods. Amos would know what kind of goods would sell, for he had been keeping a store there. I talked it over with him and he agreed, so I finished up my jobs and sold out my House Moving Business.

I commenced buying goods. I rented a large room and stored my goods until the Steamer got ready to sail. Name of the Steamer was *The Old McKim*. I asked Amos if there was any girls up there and he said there was one going on 14 years old where he boarded, by the name of Elizabeth Noble. The Steamer got ready to receive my goods, so I shipped them. Just before we got ready to sail, Captain Fisher and the first mate had a row. So the Captain discharged him and got another. After we had sailed, the Mate told someone that would be the last of the *Old McKim*.

So we sailed in fair weather. We were in sight of land until we got below Crescent City. Then it set in foggy, could hardly see a foot ahead of you, and the Captain thought he was thirty miles out to sea. About 10 o'clock we run onto a rock and hung there about an hour. We got a Cage Anchor out at the stern, tide coming, and we finally got off. There was no wind to speak of, and she leaked pretty bad. The stern pumps could almost keep it from gaining on us. Then the Captain kept trying to set out to sea. Every time he pointed her to go there would be a big rock ahead. Then I would run to the Stern and sing out, "Big Rock, bigger than a house!" Then he would go ahead again, and I'd sing out, "Big Rocks!" Finally I went to him and told him, pretty near everything I had was aboard this Steamer, and I would like him to moor her until daylight. So he did. About 12 o'clock a reefer raised her up. She came down and struck a Big Rock right under her, although not very hard. I began to think I would lose all my goods. Well I hurried up and moved her ahead and sounded all around her. We lay there until morning, when we found the place where we could get out to sea. Then the Captain examined the compasses and found a big chunk of iron ore between the two compasses. The cause of our running ashore! I had to raise the goods that the water would hurt twice before we got into Coos Bay, and run the Steamer on the mud flat above the Old Wharf at Empire City, Coos County, Oregon at high tide.

At low tide I got my goods out without any damage and put them in a house owned by Jack Pence. Amos E. [Rogers] had some goods in there. He had had a good store there, but when they began to work the mine it took about all their money. I arrived in Coos Bay June 15th 1855. I opened my store and goods sold fast. After I had been there about two months I could almost double my money. Amos told me what to charge. I boarded right across the street from my store with a man and wife by the name of John L. Henderson, a half-breed Cherokee Indian. They set a good table.

The Indians had broken out and were very bad. They had organized a volunteer Company of Soldiers for the Government in 1854, and in 1855 Jack Pence had joined them. He said to me just before they started in October 1855, "Now Mr. Rogers don't take advantage of me and get Miss Elizabeth Noble away from me." I told him I would not take advantage of him. So they all started for the war. After they had been gone some time I made up my mind to go up the hill to Mr. Noble's boarding house. I went in and Mrs. Noble and Elizabeth had been picking ducks. Elizabeth got a chair and set down not very far from me and kept picking feathers. Her hair was full of feathers and her dress. I liked that better than to see her go and fix up...showed her independence.

I told them all about our trip up the coast. When I got ready to go, I told Mrs. Noble I would like to come there to board. I boarded there some time. The more I saw of Elizabeth, the better I liked her and she seemed to like me every day. So I proposed to her to marry her. She accepted, so we were married the 5th day of December 1855.

The soldiers came back about three weeks after we were married. Jack looked awful downhearted. I had a talk with him. He said, "I don't blame you at all for she is a good girl. I was going to propose to her when we got back." He was a good young man and we were the best of friends. He sold me his house and then he wanted me to go up Coos River with him, and I did. He had put up a notice on a claim.

He said it was a present for me and Elizabeth my wife. He said she was the only girl he had loved. After that he left Coos Bay and went to Portland and married a good woman and made lots of money…so I heard. We parted good friends. So God blessed him.

They had built a fort where we lived in Empire City in 1854. I had sold more of my goods and they went like hot cakes. The Indians was very bad at that time and had killed three men, so the people wanted to take the balance of my goods and put them in the Block House for safekeeping. I knew if they did that I might as well give them away. S. S. Mann was the Government Officer there, so I sold my goods to the government and took government vouchers for them. The balance of my goods came to over $5,000.00, which kept me for about a year.

Then I built a Ten Pin Alleys, two tracks, in the saloon part alongside of the store house. The saloon was two stories, so I deadened the floor over the Saloon, finished off four rooms and closets, and we lived there. I cut an arch from the saloon into the front part of the store. I had billiard tables in the store part, and I had four card tables.

After I had got most everything fixed as I wanted it, there was a liquor drummer from San Francisco. I priced his liquors and ordered two barrels of whiskey at seventy-five cents a gallon, and one barrel at two dollars and fifty cents a gallon, one barrel of brandy, one barrel of gin, one of rum, one of port wine, one hogshead of ale, 100 gallons of coal oil and lamps to hang on the sides of the Alleys and Bar Room and the Billiard Room, and the balls and pins and my Bar fixtures, decanters, and a fine looking glass and a good lot of bitters, and sugar, a barrel of it, and good supplies of cards. I tell him I had a fine bar. The bill amounted to $630.00.

The first two weeks I took in $2,000.00 cash and some on book at twenty-five cents a drink. Everyone played on the alleys and on the billiard table. The card tables, three of them, there was four men at each table playing draw poker. The other table, there was four men playing for the drinks. I tell you it kept me jumping to wait on them. I hired a bartender and found he was making as much as I was, so I let him go and hired another…and he was doing the same, so

I let him go. I tended it myself when the games were out, and they always wanted me to drink with them, so I got a bottle of water and sweetened it and put lots of strong bitters in it and a little whiskey. I kept getting sober while they were getting drunker!

They all liked the seventy-five-cent whiskey the best. The two-and-a-half whiskey, it wouldn't take but a few drinks [to get a man drunk], so I ordered two more barrels of the seventy-five-cent whiskey instead. When any of them got in debt over fifteen dollars, I'd hire him for the month. When his month was up, I'd settle with him and pay him the balance in money. I would send them up to Anson at my farm on the Coos River to cut brush and trees.

I was paying Anson $50.00 a month and board. Our mother was living with Anson, and I furnished the provisions. Mother had sixty hens and four roosters and she made more than Anson did, since eggs were fifty cents a dozen. I used to send her middling and bran, she had all the potatoes she wanted and meat and clam shells and old broken earthen [-ware artifacts?] which she would put up for sale. I got the Indians to get it for me, and when Anson came to Empire he would take the shell and earthen[ware] to Mother.

I kept the Saloon over two years, but it was too much for me. I didn't get more than three or four hours sleep out of twenty-four hours. I had to drink a little to keep awake and lively. I could see the Saloon business was too much for me. So I sold the Saloon and Liquors to James Jordan. We then moved up on Coos River to our farm between the two forks. There I worked some of the whiskey out of me.

The people up there elected me Justice of the Peace and School Director and Road Supervisor. We lived there some time. We sold our farm to Andrew Vasburg and moved to Marshfield, Coos County, Oregon, to the Central House [a hotel]. The people there elected me one of the City Fathers. There was five of us, the first Marshfield ever had. When the City Fathers met, they elected me President of the Board of City Fathers. That is the same as Mayor of the City of Marshfield, and I never voted for myself in my life, and I never asked a man or a woman to vote for me. I am no Lawyer or Minister. That is the way the people treated me and my Dear Wife.

And the Indians liked us. Why did they? It was because we treated every one as we would like to be treated, for all I used to drink with the boys, twenty or thirty of them, all about my age. After I had held Court, I did not ever touch liquor when I had Official business on hand. We all liked one another and everybody else. We did not lie or cheat or steal or rob half-breeds of their father's estates. The Government saw the Indians as nothing more than savages, and did not consider the Indian's customs at all. The Government was fighting the Indians ever since Columbus discovered America.

[Here there is a break in the letter]

Me and my daughter, Lydia A. Rumble, went over the City [of San Francisco] on October 18th 1915 to the Fair [1915 Panama Pacific Exposition]. She got one of them go carts, paid him $1.00 an hour to wheel us all around to the Big Houses. It is wonderful to see what they have got there. Got everything imaginable. I don't know how they could think of everything, and then the nice buildings and electric works and fine streets. It must of taken a man or set of men with bigger heads than I have got or ever had. My daughter and Mr. Rumble, her husband, are awful good to me. I got tired and commenced to have my dizzy spells. She wanted to take me to some wonderful Electric Lights. It was then about 8:00 o'clock. The fog had settled and it was cold. I was afraid I would give out all together. See, I am almost 88 years old. I told her I wanted to get home. She held me by my arm or I would of fell two or three times. We got our supper, a good one too, then we got in one of the steam or electric trains and saw some of the Street Electric works. We got off the cars, we went in where they make chocolate, she bought some and saw the [Merry] Go Around with horses. That was fine. I don't think my head could hold much more. I guess it will last me as long as I live. I am awful glad I have seen it. What galls me most is to think they are a going to take all them fine buildings down. Then to think in 1849 I had been all over this ground. To see such a sight it don't seem possible to see the progress in the whole world. Then to think what wars the world is having for the sake of Kings. I don't see how God allows it. He could stop it in a short time if he wanted to. I guess he wants to let them punish themselves. I think they are doing it all right. I am thankful that the United States is out of it.

Lydia A. and Mr. [George H.] Rumble are going to have a 5-year after-marriage party tonight, October 20th [1915]. They have fine times and lots of company. I am glad to see them enjoying themselves. Me and my wife used to have good times. It was Balls and Parties. My wife was good company and had lots of friends. She has been dead over 12 years. I took care of her five years before she died. She was one of the best women that ever lived. [*Editor's note: Elizabeth Mary Noble Rogers was born February 16, 1842 in Memphis, Tennessee, and died on August 27, 1903 in Berkeley, California.*]

[Another break]

November 27th 1919. Before the world comes to the end, for the Holy Bible says there will be wars and rumors of wars and earthquakes and floods and fires and pestilence. They have been having all of them. It says before the end of this world, we don't know what is going to happen. No one but God and His Son Jesus Christ knows now. So let us all be prepared.

I have had some pleasant dreams. I dreamed that my Dear Wife and [son] John was there. I dreamed we had a good time. I dreamed that God had a tall white hat on his head. When he went away he had two horses and a lumber wagon. He had a long lash, the stock of it was four feet long, about two inches around it, to one inch at the top. It had the bark on it. I see God set as straight with the whip between his legs. He was traveling alongside a river level road. The pastures and meadows, the grass was about one foot high. It was very pleasant country. I could see God and his team all the time. It was the pleasantest dream I ever had.

I dreamed about My Dear Wife and John every night too lately. I believe I am going to see them soon. I am having dizzy spells every day now. My mind is pretty good for an old man almost 92 years old. Who ever thought I would be spared by God to live that long! I don't know of a man or

326

woman as old as I am that are alive in Coos County, Oregon. This day I pray everyday to God and His Son Jesus to take me to them when they want me, as easy as they took my Dear Wife. She did not have a struggle, went right to sleep.

My Dear Wife used to say to me, she would put her hand on my shoulder and say to me, "Father, God will bless me." That was when I was helping her on the chair and off of the chair. She weighed 200 pounds. The way I done it, I got her on the edge of the bed, her feet on the floor, chair alongside of the bed, get her arm around my neck, then I get my shoulder under her arm and raise her up as much as I could, and give a swing onto the chair and the same way back to bed. One time she slid down on the floor. I could not lift her up on the bed. I called Doctor Steel and it was all we both could do to get her in bed. I am so thankful to God that I was able to wait on her to the last. She was a good woman. So now I will close with my Love and best wishes, your poor old Father,

—Amos C. Rogers
(God Bless You)

[*Editor's note: Amos Carpenter Rogers died on May 5, 1920 at his home in Berkeley, California, aged 92 years.*]

INDEX

Note: All city or place names are in California unless otherwise noted.

342

Shanahan, Prof., 251
Sharon, __, 295
Shasta, 151, 199
Shelton, A., 130, 192
Shelton Museum, San Francisco, 129-130, 192
Shorb, Mrs. J. DeBarth (née Wilson), 116
Siberia, Russia, 149, 157, 162, 202
Sicard Bar, 157
Sierra Madre Mountains, (New) México, 76
Sierra Nevada Mountains, 143, 148-149, 169-170, 174, 197, 237
Simpson, __, 304
Simpson, Sir George, 189
Sinaloa, México, 9
Sister of Charity Orphanage, San Francisco, 196
Sisters of Mercy, San Francisco, 195
Sitka, Alaska, 151
Six Months in the Gold Mines (Buffum), 197-199, 205
Skene, William, 99
Slack's Canyon, 268
Slaughter, __, 304
"Slaughter," Washington, 304
slavery and slaves, 115, 121, 133, 220
Sloat, Commodore John, 92
Smart, James, 308
Smartsville, 308
Smith, Cherokee, 308
Smith, Senaca (store owner in Danby, Vermont), 310
Smith, William, 285
Smith—SEE: Kent & Smith
Smith's Bar, 307
Snake River, Idaho, 299
Snyder, __, 302
Société du Lingot d'Or (French lottery), 202
Soberanes family, 21
Soledad, 238
Solís, Joaquín, 14-15
Sonoma, 19, 22, 92, 173, 293
Sonora (mines), California, 145-146, 149, 155
Sonora, México (Sonorans), 18, 23, 29-32, 36-38, 68-69, 94-95
Sotelo, __, 45-46
Sotelo, Ramón, 11
Soulé, Frank, 190-194, 196, 199, 202-203, 206
South Carolina, 209
Spain (Spanish in California), 167
Spanish Alta California (A. Denis), 207
Sprinkulum (British Columbia Indian chief), 302
Standard Oil Company, 245
Stanislous (River & Valley), 152, 163, 165, 199, 226, 231, 254, 293

349

www.ingramcontent.com/pod-product-compliance
Lightning Source LLC
Chambersburg PA
CBHW021215090426
42740CB00006B/229